Keith

Thomas Hodgkin

This portrait, believed to be by Phoebus Levin, hangs in the Gordon Museum of Guy's Hospital Medical School. (Courtesy of the United Medical and Dental Schools of Guy's and St. Thomas's Hospitals.)

Thomas Hodgkin

MORBID ANATOMIST
&
SOCIAL ACTIVIST

Louis Rosenfeld, Ph.D.

MADISON BOOKS
Lanham • New York • London

Published by Madison Books
4720 Boston Way
Lanham, Maryland 20706

Distributed by National Book Network

The paper used in this publication meets the minimum
requirements of American National Standard for
Information Sciences—Permanence of Paper for
Printed Library Materials, ANSI Z39.48–1984. ∞™
Manufactured in the United States of America.

Library of Congress Cataloging-in-Publication Data

Rosenfeld, Louis, 1925–
Thomas Hodgkin : morbid anatomist and social
activist / Louis Rosenfeld.
p.   cm.
Includes bibliographical references.
1. Hodgkin, Thomas, 1798–1866.   2. Physicians—
Great Britain—Biography.   I. Title.
R489.H63R68   1992
610'.92—dc20   92–28528 CIP
[B]

ISBN 0–8191–8633–3 (cloth : alk. paper)

*Dedicated to the Memory of my
Mother and Father
Esther and Joseph Rosenfeld*

Contents

Preface

Few eponyms in medicine have been as long-lasting as that of "Hodgkin's disease." Less well known are Thomas Hodgkin's other medical and nonmedical activities, his commitment to reform of medical education and practice, and his participation in the social reform and humanitarian movements of more than a century-and-a-half ago on behalf of employment, housing, health care, and preventative medicine for the poor. He contributed to geographic explorations, anthropology, ethnology, and even foreign affairs. Hodgkin's opposition to slavery and the slave trade involved him in the development of settlements in Africa for the colonization of freed slaves and disputes with the abolitionists in America. A religious and dedicated Quaker, his strong commitment to social justice and human rights for underdeveloped peoples being oppressed by British foreign policy, especially the North American Indians being exploited by commercial fur interests, contributed to a professional conflict at Guy's Hospital and cut short a promising career in medicine.

The objective of this biography is to widen the appreciative audience for the wide-ranging nonmedical activities of this fascinating and remarkable medical figure beyond that of academicians and scholars. Other groups who will find this biography interesting are physicians, historians, sociologists, and students preparing for these careers, as well as educated general readers interested in history, medicine, or biography.

The story is told in chronological order around the political, social, medical, scientific, and educational changes occurring during Hodgkin's lifetime. His professional work is described without inundating the reader with medical jargon; nor does the book dwell on the Quaker movement. The biography has been prepared with careful documentation, but it is a book intended to be read, not merely consulted. Virtually all references and direct quotations have been consulted in the original to avoid reproducing the errors and misrepresentations that sometimes enter the mainstream of review articles and biographical sketches.

Despite the unrelenting and unsettling assault of social and technological change in the late twentieth century, the social and economic problems of Hodgkin's times are still with us. His integrity and consistency in upholding human rights ran contrary to the conventional wisdom and morality of his times. His active participation on behalf of the underprivileged and oppressed can serve as a moral guide to overcoming today's dilemmas and adversities as we rush pell-mell toward the twenty-first century.

Acknowledgments

The trail of investigation that I have followed in the preparation of this book is even more diverse than the material that has found its way between the covers. In pursuing this research I have benefited from the cooperation and help of a great many institutions and individuals. The unpublished personal papers and letters of Thomas Hodgkin, newspaper accounts, archival records, and government documents have been consulted; also, Hodgkin's books and his many published papers and pamphlets dealing with medicine, science, pathology, and social reform issues; and the diaries of Sir Moses Montefiore.

Reprints of publications, letters, newspapers, and other documents not available through interlibrary loan, and other valuable and useful information, were obtained from the following: Library of Congress (Washington), American Philosophical Society Library (Philadelphia), The Historical Society of Pennsylvania (Philadelphia), Quaker Collection of Haverford College (Haverford), Pennsylvania State University (College Park), Yale University (New Haven), Boston College (Boston), University of California (Berkeley), National Library of Medicine (Bethesda); and (in London) The British Library, Library of the Religious Society of Friends, The Royal Society, Royal Geographical Society, The Royal Society of Medicine, Royal College of Physicians of London, University

College London, Greater London Photograph Library, Royal Anthropological Institute of Great Britain and Ireland, The Wellcome Institute for the History of Medicine; Public Record Office (Richmond); Rhodes House Library (Oxford); and Edinburgh University Library.

I wish to thank J. J. Daws of the Gordon Museum, Guy's Hospital Medical School; A. Baster of the Wills Library, Guy's Hospital Medical School; D.W.C. Stewart of The Royal Society of Medicine; G. Davenport of the Royal College of Physicians; J.T.D. Hall of the Edinburgh University Library; Josef Keith of the Friends House Library; P. J. Bishop of the Cardiothoracic Institute in London; and Christine Kelly of the Royal Geographical Society, for answering my frequent inquiries. I especially wish to express my appreciation to Dr. Edward H. Kass and Amalie M. Kass of Harvard Medical School for allowing me to look through their files of the microfilm collection of the unpublished personal papers and letters of Thomas Hodgkin.

I want to thank the following for reviewing various chapters of the manuscript during the final stages of preparation and for their valuable comments and suggestions: William B. Ober (Hackensack Hospital), John H. Edgcomb (Hoffman-La Roche), Sherwin B. Nuland (Yale University), Charles G. Roland (McMaster University), and Jacques M. Quen (New York Hospital).

Photographs were obtained from Joshua O. Leibowitz (Jerusalem), Royal College of Surgeons of England (London), The Library, University College London, The British Museum (London), Library Committee of the Religious Society of Friends (London), Greater London Photograph Library, National Library of Medicine (Bethesda), and Joel Dana Stern (New York). Credits accompany each photograph.

Throughout the preparation of this biography, I received the help and cooperation of the staff of the NYU Medical Center Library. I am especially grateful to Eleonor E. Pasmik, Associate Librarian, for obtaining numerous books, journals, and reprints of articles through interlibrary services. Other books and journals were obtained at the Brooklyn Public Library, the New York Public Library, the New York Academy of Medicine, the Engineering Society Library (New York), and the National Library of Medicine (Bethesda).

Half of what we have taught you is wrong.
Unfortunately we do not know which half.

C. SIDNEY BURWELL, M.D.
Dean of Harvard Medical School (1935–1949)

The work is not yours to finish, but neither are
you free to take no part in it.

RABBI TARFON
(*Ethics of the Fathers*)

CHAPTER ONE

The Hodgkin Family

The Early Years

It was far from the best of times as the eighteenth century was coming to a close. Great Britain was waging an unsuccessful war with Republican France. Partisans of the Revolution called themselves citizens in imitation of the *citoyens* across the Channel. For many British, the dread of revolution brought panic, suspension of civil liberties, prosecutions of the press, and mutiny in the fleet. Ireland was close to rebellion, and there remained the memories of the long struggle with the American colonies. Disastrous harvests were followed by food riots, and rising taxation by financial hardship and economic depression. In 1795, Prime Minister William Pitt had been hooted and hunted by a mob, and King George III himself had been attacked in his coach. Disaster appeared imminent.

Such were the times into which Thomas Hodgkin was born on August 17, 1798, in Pentonville,[1] a village north of London. He was the third child of John and Elizabeth (Rickman) Hodgkin, who married in 1793. The first two children were also sons. The first, born in 1795, died at four years. The second, born in 1797, died of smallpox by inoculation when only five months old. A fourth son, John, Jr., was born in 1800. Elizabeth Hodgkin (1768–

I

1833) was a frail woman, frequently in poor health and always expressing concern about the health of her two boys.

The Hodgkin family has been traced[2] to the early seventeenth century, the time of George Fox (1624–1691), founder of the Society of Friends. During the generations that followed, the Hodgkin occupations changed from shopkeeper to wool stapler to writing master. Thomas Hodgkin's father, a studious man who preferred learning to the wool business, was encouraged by his uncle (1744–1810), a writing master and teacher at the Ackworth School, and for whom Thomas had been named, to follow a teaching career also. John Hodgkin (1766–1845) became a noted calligrapher and a successful and fashionable private tutor. His pupils were chiefly daughters of wealthy merchants and bankers living near London. Because he gave his lessons at their homes, he rode long distances on horseback, his saddlebags filled with books for his pupils. He taught grammar, the classics, mathematics, and his specialty, the art of handwriting, in which he greatly excelled. To write a good hand was then a very important part of social upbringing. John Hodgkin wrote books on penmanship, grammar, and geography.

The younger Hodgkin boy, John, Jr. (1800–1875), although frequently in poor health, became a successful lawyer, specializing as a conveyancer of titles to property. After a severe illness, John, Jr., retired from professional life at age forty-three and devoted himself entirely to religious and philanthropic work. He traveled widely to different Quaker congregations. In 1847, he was sent by the English Friends to deliver relief supplies to starving Quakers in Ireland during the famine. Visiting America in 1861, at the outbreak of the Civil War, he found that Quaker opposition to war and to slavery tended to draw Quakers in opposite directions.

Prematurely born at seven months, Thomas Hodgkin was a delicate child, requiring close and continuous parental care during his early years. According to his mother, Thomas was a delightful, playful child. His brother John described Thomas as fast afoot, athletic, and more successful than he in childhood games requiring skill or strength. The brothers had quite different temperaments. John was calm and uncritical of the actions of others. Thomas, on the other hand, was "the champion of all sorts of lost causes, who could flame up into very hot wrath when he heard of acts of oppression on his protégés and was not sparing of sharp censure on the transgressors."[3]

Although never robust, frequently ill, and troubled throughout his life by an intestinal disorder, Thomas Hodgkin became a man of unending activity and tireless energy. His walk and movements were like his speech, rapid and full of purpose. He looked upward a little when he spoke, and his face gave an impression of great vigor. A visitor from America characterized him as shrewd, sensible, hard-working, cautious, honest, high-minded, and honorable, and recorded this description:

> In appearance he is very peculiar and striking, being rather below the usual height, remarkably thin, straight as a ramrod, with dark piercing eyes, and such extraordinary convexity of the nose and other lineaments as never to be forgotten when once seen. His disposition appears to be very mild and conciliating, but mixed up with gravity and firmness, in such proportions, as to make him very efficient in any thing he undertakes, and not to be easily turned aside by coaxing or flattery, or any of the other palatable provocatives so readily swallowed, sometimes, by the wisest and best of men.[4]

Quaker Upbringing

Hodgkin wore the distinctive black clothes of the Quaker sect. A "Quaker suit" was made of a plain dark cloth and had no lapels or extra buttons. The coat was shaped like a covert coat and had a stand-up collar. A wide white band was worn about the neck in place of a collar and tie. For street wear, the hat was broad-brimmed rather than the Victorian stovepipe top hat, and it was not removed as a greeting. Quaker dress was originally designed as a rejection of the dictates of fashion and to be simple and unostentatious. But it evolved into a uniform that had nothing to do with the virtue of simplicity.

Hodgkin always adhered to the Quaker style of "plain speech"; it was "thee," "thou," and "thine." "You" and "your" were allowed in addressing two or more individuals. He also used the Quaker terminology for the calendar. The customary names of the days and months were replaced by numbers because the names were considered to be of heathen origin and a form of homage to pagan gods bordering on idolatry.

Hodgkin's parents were strict and observant Quakers, and in both Pentonville and Tottenham they lived in strong Quaker communities. Love of God and devotion to righteousness played an integral part in their religious teaching at home. When the family moved from Pentonville to Tottenham in January 1815, they obtained a certificate from the Meeting in Pentonville to the Tottenham Monthly Meeting of Friends saying that the four Hodgkins were "believed to be of exemplary conduct and leave us in respectable circumstances."[5] Thomas and John, Jr., were brought up "in the repelling, forbidding side of Christianity in the traditional school of Quakerism."[6] This religious training and the teachings of Quaker virtues and beliefs had their impact on Thomas Hodgkin. He was faithful to his upbringing and remained through life a serious and consistent member of the Society of Friends. Except for reasons of illness or absence from home, he rarely missed the religious meetings of the Friends. He served as overseer and as clerk of the Monthly Meeting, but not until about two years before his death was he persuaded to accept the office of elder. He long resisted filling this position because his humility prevented him from assuming any role that was greater than he believed he deserved.[7]

Early Education

Hodgkin, being a Quaker and thus a nonconformist, was debarred from education at Oxford or Cambridge and so was educated privately. Education of Quaker youth was strictly supervised in order to provide a classical education in Greek and Latin that was free of irreligious influences and the "heathen" thought of the surrounding materialistic society. Thomas and John, Jr., were educated by their father in English composition, penmanship, mathematics, and Greek. He was assisted by an émigré French tutor, Peter Vincent Cassanet, who instructed the boys in Latin and French. Thomas also acquired command of Greek and later, during his travels, of Italian and German.

William Allen and Plough Court

After completing his classical and mathematical education, Hodgkin, with the concurrence of his parents, planned to become an apothecary under the tutelage of William Allen (1770–1843). Allen, a prominent Quaker, had been tutored in algebra in 1807 by John Hodgkin, Sr., and the two had become good friends. It was during these visits with his father to Allen's chemical firm at Plough Court that Thomas was impressed by Allen's work as a chemist and his participation in so many philanthropic activities. This was something he would also like to do.[8] Allen's life was one continual round of engagements. He seemed to have time for everything.[9] Hodgkin's father discussed placing Thomas with William Allen to learn pharmaceutical chemistry. Although no specific agreement was made, all indications were that Thomas would be taken in at age eighteen after completing his preliminary education.

Allen lectured in chemistry at Guy's Hospital from 1802 until 1826. Chemistry had been the first subject to be given up to a specialist by the clinicians of Guy's. Plough Court had become one of the centers of scientific research in London, and Allen, a well-known man of science. He collaborated with Humphry Davy (1778–1829) and other prominent scientists and was often referred to for chemical analysis and delicate and difficult experiments.[10] In 1803 Davy asked Allen to give the same course of lectures at the Royal Institution that he was giving at Guy's.[11] Years later, in 1841, William Allen became the first president of the Pharmaceutical Society of Great Britain. This society united for the first time the chemists and druggists of the country into one organization for the protection of their general interests and the improvement and advancement of scientific knowledge.[12]

Allen was a friend of William Wilberforce (1759–1833), leader of the abolitionist movement in Parliament, and of Thomas Clarkson (1760–1846), the outstanding ideological figure in the agitation against slavery and the slave trade. Clarkson stayed at Plough Court whenever he came to London.[13] It was through Clarkson's perseverance that slavery, which had been considered a necessary part of the social economy, came to be regarded as a crime. Although not a member of the Society of Friends but of the Church of England, he was welcome in the homes of many Quaker families and was a friend of the Hodgkin family.

Since the Hodgkins had never considered another career option for Thomas, it came as a major disappointment to them when Allen had to renege on his commitment because there was no opening for an apprentice at Plough Court. As an alternative Allen proposed making Thomas his private secretary. At least this would bring him into the periphery of the apothecary business. When Hodgkin arrived at Plough Court, probably late in 1816, it was a difficult time for the household. Allen's wife had recently died, and he was too distressed to spend much time with Thomas in explaining what were his secretarial duties. However, by the spring of 1817, Hodgkin was attending Allen's lectures at Guy's in chemistry and natural philosophy and assisting him in setting up the classroom experiments. This was Thomas's introduction to medicine and to Guy's Hospital. While at Plough Court Hodgkin also observed how Allen and his associates generated support and money for their philanthropic projects.[14]

Allen called on Thomas Hodgkin when he and Clarkson were visited by delegates from the newly formed American Colonization Society who were looking for information about settlement sites on the west coast of Africa. Hodgkin prepared Clarkson's reply to the Americans.[15] Once roused by these experiences and contacts, Hodgkin's interest in Africa, first kindled by stories of the slave trade overheard at home when he was a child, never waned. He became a steadfast advocate of colonization as a way of promoting civilization in Africa.

Thomas Hodgkin did not stay long at Plough Court. Whatever the reasons, the arrangement did not work out, and by April 1817, after only a few months, Allen decided to end the secretarial association with Thomas Hodgkin. There still was no vacancy for an apprentice, and John Barry, a former assistant and now Allen's partner in the business, who handled the training, objected to taking on Hodgkin as a pupil. Once past this setback, John Hodgkin, Sr., began to question the quality of the training and the attention his son would have received, considering that William Allen was seldom on the premises. Allen had spent a good part of 1816, 1817, and 1818 traveling through Europe on behalf of the Society of Friends, visiting schools, prisons, asylums, and various charitable institutions, as well as Quaker congregations. During his travels then and in later years, he met with political figures and rulers on behalf of reforms and abolition of the slave trade.[16]

Apprenticed to Glaisyer and Kemp

The Hodgkins quickly found a substitute position with Elizabeth's cousin John Glaisyer and his partner Grover Kemp, who operated an apothecary shop in Brighton. By his nineteenth birthday Hodgkin had signed on as an apprentice and moved into the Glaisyer home. Glaisyer, a prominent member of the Society of Friends, had established the firm in 1798. Kemp, who had entered as an apprentice in 1806, became a partner in 1813.[17]

Thomas made an excellent impression. Not only did he work the full twelve-hour shift, 9 A.M. to 9 P.M. six days a week, but he also found time to study chemistry, languages, and mathematics, at times well past midnight. Wishing to remain proficient in Latin, he often wrote to his brother in that language. While at Brighton he attracted attention of a different sort when he rode a veloci-pede—no pedals, no brakes![18]

Pledge to Primitive Peoples

Thomas Hodgkin's concern for the primitive natives of underde-veloped lands began to evolve during the years he was with Glaisyer and Kemp. Around the start of 1819, at age twenty, he completed work on an extensive "Essay on the Promotion of Civilization." In it he urged creation of an organization that would spread Western culture among "uncivilized" people without the deleteri-ous effects that might destroy them. He warned that the North

American Indians faced extermination in the wake of the "civilizing" influence brought by the settlers and traders of Europe: "I shall, I believe, keep quite within the bounds of truth when I say, that in the last five hundred years, those under the name of Christians, have done far more to degrade, corrupt and exterminate their uncivilized fellow creatures than all the heathen world, since the creation of man. Wherever they have gone they have introduced new vices, and new diseases."[19]

In this 100-page document the young Hodgkin declared as his life's main concern the protection of the primitive aboriginal peoples of all continents. He pledged to safeguard their rights, to improve their state of affairs, to support their cultures, and to educate them in the skills that were important for the progress of the white man. Hodgkin believed that civilized nations had an obligation to help the primitive peoples that they encountered. Instead, these people more often became the victims of the ruthless self-interest of the more advanced civilization.

Hodgkin understood only too well that the Indians would be destroyed by the civilizing forces that set out to rescue them from spiritual poverty and technical ignorance. Those that accepted European standards and were able to learn the Europeans' superior skills and customs had the best chance for survival in a different society, but in the process they would lose their identity and their independence. If they resisted, they faced certain death.[20]

The essay was circulated among friends of the Hodgkin family. Readers of the manuscript, especially Thomas Clarkson, whose favorable opinion Hodgkin very much desired, were critical of the secular basis of his civilization proposals and the apparent lack of emphasis on religious instruction and spiritual salvation as a first step. Hodgkin believed that improvement in the wretched living conditions of the Indians should come before attempts at religious conversion. It was a view not shared by most Englishmen of his time. He also disapproved of the missionaries—a view he expressed again later (see chapter 11, note 31). On top of everything, his writing was convoluted, wordy, difficult to follow, and much too long.[21] This was a quality that characterized much of his later writing.

Geological Assistant

It was during his apprenticeship in Brighton that Hodgkin earned his first mention in the scientific literature. After Sunday Meeting he often explored the chalk cliffs in the vicinity, and he was asked by William Phillips (1773–1828), a pioneer geologist and a founder of the Geological Society of London (1807), to examine the layers of rock along the cliffs. Phillips, who was also a London printer and bookseller, and a Quaker and friend of the family, acknowledged Hodgkin's observations and comments in a long footnote in his classic book on geology.[22]

Geology was a challenging and exciting new science. It attracted young intellectuals as well as men of culture and wide interests who were interested in natural history. Contemporary enthusiasm for geology and natural history was depicted in the early Victorian novel wherein leading characters are shown spending leisure hours in the accumulation and contemplation of a cabinet of fossils. Geology was popular because the material was easily understood while its interpretation was highly controversial, and one need not be an expert to have a reasonable chance of making important discoveries.[23]

Hodgkin completed his apprenticeship in the retail apothecary shop in 1819 and took stock of his future prospects. His experiences at Plough Court and Brighton showed him the limitations of a career as an apothecary and convinced him that he wasn't cut out to be a businessman. He knew that he could go on to practice as an apothecary-surgeon, but this would require additional apprenticeship with a surgeon. After much thought and consultation with family and friends—a course he often followed before making an important decision—Thomas Hodgkin decided on a career as a physician. (See chapter 8 for the legal and professional distinctions of the three levels of medical practice.) To practice as a physician he needed a university education and an M.D. degree. This requirement would take him to Scotland and the University of Edinburgh. The city of Edinburgh would be a hospitable place for Thomas. There was a small group of Quakers living there who were related to the Hodgkin family or known to them through mutual acquaintances.

Science and medicine were accepted by Quakers as useful and were among the few professions available to them until well into the nineteenth century. Hodgkin had an interest in medicine, both for its own sake and as the best passport for a traveler in a foreign land and among all races of man.[24] He had been advised on his career change by Joseph John Gurney (1788–1847), a revered Quaker leader. Gurney was the prime mover in the Evangelical movement that redirected Quaker principles into political and philanthropic channels and away from the anti-intellectual Quietist tradition that sought the peace and joy of unquestioned faith.[25] Gurney also advised Hodgkin's brother, John, Jr., to enter the profession of law. Hodgkin's mother had been a governess to the Gurney family of Norwich before her marriage and the families remained good friends.

But first, Thomas had to finish his training as an apothecary by enrolling for at least six months of hospital experience and instruction in medical subjects, a requirement of the Apothecaries' Act of 1815. He would attend lectures in anatomy and surgery, witness operations, and observe dissections and inspections (postmortem examinations).

Guy's Hospital

The register of the pupils of Guy's Hospital shows that he entered Guy's as a physicians' pupil on September 30, 1819. In the column headed "whence they came" is the name of Mr. J. Glaisyer of Brighton. This is the earliest record of Hodgkin's attendance at any institution of formal education. He paid a fee of £10 10s. od. and was enrolled as a Twelvemonth Pupil. On January 28, 1820, his registration was converted to Perpetual Pupil by the additional payment of £11 11s. od., for a total of 21 guineas. This gave him the privilege of returning anytime for additional courses. Few students enrolled as physicians' pupils. These were either recent graduates of university medical schools who wanted additional practical experience or, like Thomas Hodgkin, were preparing for university admission. Physicians' pupils were planning to become physicians rather than general practitioners, which was the career goal of those preparing to become apothecaries and surgeons.[26]

Hodgkin took lodgings within walking distance of the hospital. Whatever reservations John and Elizabeth may have had about their son's exposure to the coarse and rowdy life-style of medical students, they were confident that he would not add to this image. They were comforted by his weekend visits home in Tottenham but, like parents everywhere, hoped these would be more often than they were.

In general, the students at Guy's were a boisterous, riotous bunch fighting one another in nearby taverns, in the operating theater, the dissecting room, and on the grounds of the hospital. Other disturbances included noisy all-night parties, midnight forays for stray cats, disruption of the patients' Christmas party, drunkenness, offensive scribbling on walls, and damage to property.[27] Nurses behaved similarly and were often discharged for drunkenness, insubordination, and theft. At lectures the surgical students resembled a crowd at a sporting event—noisy, gossiping, throwing things, hooting, making catcalls, and generally amusing themselves. It is highly unlikely that the dedicated Quaker and serious physicians' student Thomas Hodgkin participated in such activities.

For more than half of the nineteenth century, medical students were regarded as rude, ill-bred fellows. The resurrectionist (grave-robbing) activities of teachers and students prior to the Anatomy Act of 1832 (see later in this chapter) contributed to the popular mistrust of these brash, brawling, cigar-smoking, cold-hearted young men. Smoking in the anatomical theater was done partly to camouflage the offensive odors.[28] It was not until the 1880s that a new and improved image evolved of the medical student deeply immersed in his studies.[29]

Although physicians had been permitted to bring in two apprentices who could follow them around, there were no formal or organized lectures, classes, or demonstrations for these students. As a result, the numbers enrolled in hospitals for medical teaching were small. In 1814, a survey of hospitals showed sixteen students at Guy's, fourteen at St. George's, six at St. Bartholomew's, one each at St. Thomas's and Middlesex, and none at London and

Westminster.[30] The surgeons, on the other hand, were attended by apprentices, dressers, and pupils who followed them about in droves. They never stopped at the bed of a medical patient. If a student picked up any medical information, it was incidental to medical treatment of surgical cases or by overhearing treatment prescribed by physicians. Patients were not then distributed into separate locations designated medical or surgical.

The physicians were a polite and gentle group. They took off their hats and left them on a table near the door. They were discreet and quiet as they moved about the wards with their small classes. The surgeons kept their hats on their heads, were noisy, and were trailed by their crowds of chattering pupils. It was the style then for a surgeon to be rough and foul-mouthed.[31]

From 1768 to 1815, of all the schools in London, only Guy's had provided a coordinated teaching program of medicine and its supporting sciences. It was the only teaching facility immediately able to comply with the educational requirements of the Apothecaries' Act of 1815. The required courses were in anatomy and physiology, theory and practice of medicine, chemistry, materia medica (medical botany), and attendance at the medical practice of a hospital, infirmary, or dispensary for six months.

The teaching affiliation between Guy's Hospital and St. Thomas's Hospital across the street limited Guy's teaching to medicine, and before the new legislation, the demand was very small. The students were apprentices of apothecaries and had been instructed by them in the art of medicine and therapeutics. They entered the United Hospitals' Medical School for six to twelve months to dissect and to see operations. St. Thomas's contributed the lectures and classes in anatomy and surgery. These were the lectures then in great demand, mainly because of the need for surgeons for the wars with France. What at first had seemed a hardship for Guy's now turned into an advantage.

With the passage of the Apothecaries' Act of 1815, there was an increased demand for medical as distinct from surgical teaching. This brought about a reorganization of the teaching programs of the medical schools of London. The physicians now had to provide clinical teaching at the bedside, as well as organized lectures in the medical sciences, with the same attention that surgeons gave to teaching anatomy and surgery.[32]

The teaching program at Guy's was far from improved by 1819–20, when Hodgkin was in attendance. Bedside or clinical teaching[33] was slow in developing in the other London hospitals, and the students often complained to the editor of the medical weekly *The Lancet*. One student urged the editor "to stimulate the physicians and surgeons to be a little more communicative" and that "in surgical cases in particular, all the pupils may have a proper view of the patients; and that, with respect to physicians' patients, they be informed what the diseases really are." This student had "to hurry through the wards at the heels of a physician or surgeon, without culling any information, and to walk out again just as wise as he walked in."[34] This was the "*silent* visiting" mentioned as the procedure too often followed in England.[35]

As late as 1834, clinical lectures were described as "*quite a new thing*,"[36] and in November 1841, a student from an unnamed London hospital complained that after six weeks of attendance, "I have not heard one clinical lecture, or ten explanatory remarks offered at the bedside, and not one case is written in a book for the information of the students."[37] He had been cautioned, he added, by the other students, not to complain, lest he be singled out for harsh treatment and risk a less favorable wording on his qualification certificates as surgeon-apothecary, i.e., general practitioner. In contrast, a Clinical Report Society—something original—was organized at Guy's, where the students reviewed the lessons learned in the close and practical investigation of disease at the bedside.[38] Guy's fame and leadership in education developed from the then novel concept that patient care and teaching were inseparable.

University of Edinburgh

Armed with letters of introduction and recommendation, including one from Astley Cooper, London's leading surgeon, Thomas Hodgkin entered Edinburgh University as a medical student on October 25, 1820, the year in which George III died. It was a four-day journey to Scotland by ship, and although he was never out of sight of land, Thomas experienced motion sickness.[39]

From the mid-eighteenth to the early nineteenth century the medical education available in Edinburgh was the best in Great Britain.[40] The faculty at the university and at the Royal Colleges of Physicians and of Surgeons in Edinburgh consisted of highly reputable teachers who developed new teaching techniques based on observation, experimentation, and practice. By 1790, Edinburgh had an international reputation for its medical school. From Edinburgh, the concept of affiliating a medical school to a hospital and providing clinical lectures in specialized fields was introduced by its graduates to other centers in Great Britain and abroad.

This style of medical education was introduced to Edinburgh from the University of Leyden in the Netherlands, where clinical teaching by Hermann Boerhaave (1668–1738) had become a permanent part of medical education at the beginning of the eighteenth century. At Edinburgh the integration of clinical instruction at the bedside and the teaching of the basic sciences of anatomy, chemistry, botany, pathology, and physiology in adjoining buildings was comparatively easy. This was not the case in the universities at Oxford and Cambridge, where the highly developed system of colleges made it impossible to adapt to this innovation. For centuries these English universities were concerned with teaching general knowledge for the benefit of the mind rather than an applied skill. Medical lecturing was virtually passive and consisted of philosophical discourses on the ancient Greek and Latin texts. Clinical teaching was nonexistent, and the practice of medicine and surgery had to be learned by apprenticeship. As a result, English students sought their medical education at the Scottish universities or at Leyden, Padua, Montpellier, Bologna, and other foreign universities. The central position of medicine at the University of Edinburgh was sustained by the unprecedented demand for physicians and surgeons for service in the wars and by the government sponsorship of three regius chairs—clinical surgery (1803), military surgery (1806), and medical jurisprudence (1807).

According to student records,[41] Thomas Hodgkin was enrolled as a medical student at Edinburgh for two sessions, 1820–21 and 1822–23. In the first session he took classes in chemistry (T. C.

Hope), practice of medicine (J. Gregory), materia medica (J. Home), botany (R. Graham), medical jurisprudence (W. P. Alison), and clinical medicine. In session 1822–23, his classes were institutes of medicine, also known as theory of medicine, with W. P. Alison, and clinical medicine again, the lectures apparently given in turn by certain professors in the medical faculty. One of these clinical lecturers was Andrew Duncan, Jr. (1773–1832), one of the three to whom Hodgkin later dedicated his graduation dissertation. Duncan had earlier held the chair of medical jurisprudence and later gave the lectures in materia medica. He was editor of the *Edinburgh Medical and Surgical Journal*, which published Hodgkin's first medical paper, "On the Uses of the Spleen,"[42] written for Duncan's clinical course.

Surgery was taught by the physicians—three generations of Monros—a dynasty of father, son, and grandson, extending for 126 consecutive years, from 1720 to 1846. Each was named Alexander Monro, and they were known, respectively, as *primus* (1697–1767), *secundus* (1733–1817), and *tertius* (1773–1859). It was widely known that as good as Edinburgh's science-based medical education was, it could not match the London schools in the teaching of surgical anatomy. Not only were cadavers for dissection in short supply, but Monro *secundus* was not an operating surgeon but a physician. Believing that future surgeons needed to see operations on live patients, the Edinburgh College of Surgeons lobbied hard for a separate chair of surgery following the inauguration of clinical lectures in surgery at the Royal Infirmary. This was bitterly opposed by Monro *secundus*, who insisted that this subject was included in his commission as professor of anatomy and that any change was an infringement of his rights. The Town Council sided with the medical professors, most of whom felt that Monro *secundus* was capable of teaching both anatomy and surgery, and gave him a new commission in 1777 as professor of medicine and "particularly of anatomy and surgery." His proven ability to attract large classes enabled him to keep his monopoly and pass it on to his son, Monro *tertius*. Not until 1831 was the university able to separate surgery from the chair of anatomy, when the Crown intervened to establish two new chairs, in surgery and pathology, respectively. The vigorous protests of Monro *tertius* were unavailing.[43]

The standard of teaching deteriorated at the hands of Monro *tertius*, who lectured in an apathetic manner. The fame of his father and grandfather must have weighed heavily on him as their successor; he is said to have read his grandfather's lectures, written almost a century before, verbatim. He lost control of his classes, and in his later years, they were the frequent scenes of disturbances.[44]

With the developing art of surgery, the prevailing attitude toward anatomy changed. No longer was the academic systematic approach of the Monros wanted. What was needed now was information for the practicing surgeon.[45] *Tertius*'s students usually paid the required fee for the course but received their instruction in surgical anatomy in other classes offered from about 1790 onward by private teachers under the auspices of the Royal College of Surgeons of Edinburgh.[46] The extramural anatomist the students visited during Hodgkin's stay was the popular John Barclay (1758–1826), whose classes accommodated hundreds of students at a time. His superior instruction in practical anatomy and demonstrations of various surgical operations made him the most stimulating teacher of his time. Hodgkin skipped attendance at the anatomy course by *tertius* and spent the time studying with two friends from Guy's.[47]

Medical Faculty

Teaching at Edinburgh University was a very good enterprise. Some classes, such as practice of medicine, chemistry, and anatomy, drew large enrollments that generated large incomes from class fees, which were paid directly to the lecturer. Professors of less popular subjects, such as botany and materia medica, received considerably less. Another lucrative source of income was the writing of textbooks for the large classes. Disparities in remuneration from class fees created jealousy and an atmosphere of professional quarrelsomeness. Ambitious professors transferred to what they hoped would be more profitable chairs.

The class fee system encouraged a proprietary hold on one's chair and the transfer of this source of income to a son or nephew. This nepotism reached its peak between 1786 and 1807. Of ten appointments to medical chairs, eight went to sons of former medical professors.[48] One remarkable example of this practice concerned the appointment to the chair of institutes of medicine. The position was kept vacant for five years after the death of John Gregory (1724–1773), until his son James finished medical school and additional study at Leyden. The Town Council apparently wanted James Gregory (1753–1821) for this chair,[49] which he subsequently held from 1778 to 1790. He was the fifth member of his family to occupy a professorial chair in the University of Edinburgh. In 1790 he succeeded to the chair of practice of medicine, which he filled until his death in 1821. Gregory was a celebrated professor and very popular with the students. He was unrivaled as a lecturer, dignified and eloquent. His great reputation as a clinical teacher contributed much to the reputation of the university.

Hodgkin was enrolled in Gregory's lectures near the end of the famed teacher's life. He described him as tall and thin, suffering from asthma and having to rest for a while after taking his place on the platform, before beginning his lecture in a thin, low, and not always distinct voice. According to Hodgkin's initial impressions, Gregory's lectures were delivered in a conversational rather than didactic style and contained much relatively unimportant information. But he wanted to reserve judgment, since the course had barely begun. Hodgkin was initially disappointed in all the lecturers because they did not start on time and used up several lectures with unimportant introductory matter.[50]

Gregory's treatments for the cure of disease were quite specific and clear. According to "Gregorian Physic," disease was to be attacked vigorously by bloodletting, cold affusion, brisk purging, frequent blisters, and vomiting by the action of tartar emetic. It was the humoral theory of body fluids put into practice. Since Edinburgh's students came from all parts of the British Isles and the colonies, and since Gregory taught theory of physic and practice of physic for a total of forty-three years, this therapeutic regimen dominated medical practice for many years.[51]

The medical professors were all free to pursue private practice, and they regularly put the needs of their patients ahead of their students. James Gregory, for example, was often called to patients at a great distance from Edinburgh. As a result, his lectures were interrupted for days or weeks at a time. He tried to make up lost time by lecturing six days a week but acknowledged that this was not a satisfactory arrangement.[52]

Treatment of patients was largely a hit-or-miss affair with physicians and apothecaries depending on a rather limited number of drugs (e.g., opium, calomel, digitalis, bark (quinine), mercury, antimony tartrate, magnesium sulfate, and linseed oil). These were used singly and in combination for all diseases—venereal, malignant, infectious, mental, paralytic, edematous conditions, tetanus, and epilepsy.[53] Extravagant claims were frequently made regarding their beneficial and curative effects. Rational treatment was impossible without knowledge of the disease process itself, for which an understanding of basic physiology, chemistry, and cellular pathology was needed. The great advances made by Claude Bernard (1813–1878), Robert Koch (1843–1910), Paul Ehrlich (1854–1915), Louis Pasteur (1822–1895), Rudolf Virchow (1821–1902), and Joseph Lister (1827–1912) took place in the second half of the century.

Another of Hodgkin's teachers was William Pulteney Alison (1790–1859), who briefly held the chair of forensic medicine, and whom Hodgkin may have remembered when, some years later, he recommended legal medicine as part of medical education because of the unfavorable impact poorly presented testimony can have on life and reputation.[54]

Chemistry at the beginning of the nineteenth century had developed into a very important subject. Thomas Charles Hope (1766–1844) was the most popular lecturer of science Britain had yet known, with class enrollments of over 500 students. He was the first chemist in Great Britain to teach the new chemical ideas of Lavoisier, whom he had met and befriended while spending a summer in Paris. Hope's lectures, which Hodgkin thought were preached pompously, were uncommonly clear and audible and were illustrated by splendid and consistently successful experimental demonstrations.[55] Charles Darwin (1809–1882), the naturalist, studied medicine at Edinburgh from 1825 to 1827 and preferred reading to the intolerably dull lectures. However, he made an exception when it came to Hope's lectures on chemistry. Darwin described the lectures by Andrew Duncan, Jr., on materia medica on a winter's morning as "something fearful to remember."[56]

At Edinburgh, university officials were often preoccupied with the maintenance of discipline. If the lecturer was poor, the students who did show up in class spent their time talking, fidgeting, and fighting, and in the anatomy classes of Monro *tertius*, they stamped their feet and hissed the speaker. Keeping order among students remained a problem as late as 1854.[57]

Collegiate Life

Student societies and clubs, formed from time to time, served common interests and helped bring individuals out of the isolation of their lodgings. Few of these organizations survived for long. The oldest and most important is the Royal Medical Society, founded in 1737, eleven years after the establishment of the medical faculty. Hodgkin was a member. This society had sufficient resources to obtain a charter from George III in 1778 and to build its own hall and library. It met weekly to discuss papers on medical subjects. Other groups were primarily dining or social clubs, which usually met in taverns. Not until 1876 was a Student's Club established, offering an inexpensive place for dinner or lunch and facilities for reading newspapers and for socializing with other students.[58]

There was no collegiate life at the University of Edinburgh during Hodgkin's stay and for many years afterward. There were literary and scientific societies in the city, not connected with the university, and Hodgkin attended their meetings. He even went to a political meeting to hear a leading Whig, although he wasn't interested in politics. Hodgkin avoided common celebrations, such as the New Year's Eve revelry and public dinners. His rigid manners probably kept him from winning election as co-president in the Royal Medical Society.[59]

In town, private tutors were available for study of modern foreign languages, music, and drawing. Tennis, handball, racket ball, and billiards were played, but at one time or another these activities were either prohibited, discouraged, criticized, or condemned as immoral by university officials. There were golf and bowling. Skating and the theater were winter pastimes; football, archery, riding, and attendance at horse races were summer activities. Dances and concerts were regularly sponsored under respectable auspices.[60]

The absence of scholastic and moral supervision was a recurring complaint by English parents about Scottish university life. Another dissatisfaction involved unscrupulous Scottish landladies who failed to air beds and provide adequate meals. Parents who could afford it boarded their sons in the homes of professors. Hodgkin rented lodgings in a stone building that housed about twelve apartments.[61]

Student magazines—usually short-lived—appeared in the first half of the nineteenth century, inevitably critical of the university or student body and offering suggestions—often contradictory— for improvement. Some contributors denounced professors who prescribed their own expensive textbooks for their classes. According to these articles, the undergraduate activities of a typical Edinburgh student were mainly directed to finding as many different ways as possible of avoiding classes: wandering about, tennis, eating, gambling, riding, reading a novel. When tired of the theater, he turned to billiards or the tavern. There were repeated cases of intoxication by medical students, some of whom spent time in jail for disorderly conduct. Since there was no provision for meals in the university, it was difficult to punish students who claimed that they visited taverns to obtain a meal.[62]

Aside from the disciplinary problems caused by excessive drinking, major causes of disturbances were persistent bullying, striking another student during an examination, discharging pistols in the anatomy classroom, challenging a fellow student to a duel, and snowball fights, which on several occasions degenerated into riots requiring police intervention. In 1818 one student assaulted another on the steps of the anatomy classroom and landed in police court. Following careful investigation of disturbances, appropriate penalties, ranging from reprimand to explusion, were promptly dispensed.[63]

According to Quaker teaching, music (instrumental or vocal), dancing (even within the family circle), theater, gambling, and reading novels were considered detrimental to morals, as were the diversions of the field (hunting, hawking, and shooting for sport).[64] Not much was left for Hodgkin to do with friends. He had some skill at drawing, and it is possible that he developed this ability at Edinburgh. Cross-country hiking to observe the geological formations was another permitted pastime to his liking. And he visited and worshiped with other Edinburgh Quakers and relatives.

While at Edinburgh, Hodgkin had an opportunity in May 1821 to visit New Lanark (near Glasgow), the renowned "cooperative" manufacturing settlement founded by Robert Owen (1771–1858), an early socialist. This model factory town of cotton mills was a social experiment to show that pleasant living and working conditions were advantageous for both labor and management. Hodgkin knew about the community because William Allen was one of the partners. However, Allen was unhappy with certain activities that were contrary to Quaker beliefs and practices. Hodgkin was pleased with the good aspects of the colony but did not approve of the music and dancing, no doubt the result of his Quaker upbringing. He thought there was too much of both, especially the dancing, and he was very critical of Owen's educational use of music and dance. Yet he realized that dancing was better for this class of people than the other kinds of entertainment they might seek out. His dislike of music persisted into his adult years. Hodgkin's nephew later recalled his uncle's "utter detestation of the musical performances with which we used to be regaled during the long and weary *tables d'hôte* at the hotels on the Rhine."[65]

Cousin Sarah

In the early part of the summer of 1821, Thomas Hodgkin rekindled a long-standing romance with his cousin Sarah Godlee (1798–1866), who was visiting relatives in Edinburgh. She was the daughter of his mother's sister, Mary Rickman Godlee, and lived in Lewes, Sussex. Sarah, the same age as Thomas, was a close childhood friend, and as a result of frequent visiting they eventually formed a romantic attachment. This gave the family cause for concern. Not only was marriage between first cousins forbidden by the Society of Friends under penalty of expulsion, but the Hodgkins feared that a strain of emotional imbalance in the Rickman clan might be enhanced in the offspring of such a marriage. Thomas's father, concerned about their developing relationship, wrote to him to caution against becoming too emotionally involved with her. Obviously intending to minimize their personal contact, his father urged Thomas not to escort his first cousin around town and suggested that someone else show her the sights of the city.[66]

It appears that their relationship did become serious. Hodgkin sought permission for the marriage but failed to convince his relatives or the elders of the Society of Friends that marriages between first cousins were not prohibited by scripture or science. Hodgkin's nephew believed that Sarah was not put off by the prohibition.[67] But Thomas, being a dedicated Quaker, yielded to the rule of the society. Eventually, in June 1828, Sarah Godlee married her second cousin, John Rickman (1780–1835) (no prohibition there), and went to live in Edinburgh. He was eighteen years older than she, an accountant, and a widower with two small children.

Study in Paris

Hodgkin was in Paris for additional experience, study, and instruction from October 1821 to September 1822. It was his first trip out of the country. He may have been influenced to make this move by Andrew Duncan, Jr., who had a poor opinion of English and Scottish basic sciences and admired French anatomy teaching.

It was the lure of superior instruction in anatomy in Paris that first drew the English students, nearly all of whom had medical degrees or surgical diplomas. The advantages of the French system very likely came to the notice of British medical men by way of Edinburgh. The Scots' affinities for ideas and things French attracted Scottish medical educators to medicine as it was being taught in France. The exodus of English students began slowly after the end of hostilities between England and France and increased during the 1820s. Hundreds of students and physicians were drawn by the new teaching of pathological anatomy and the translations of French works that had reached England earlier despite the revolution and the war. Pathology, at the time, was still a part of clinical medicine. Texts of pathology were written by clinicians, and clinical instruction was combined with anatomical pathology based on postmortem examinations.[68]

The French Revolution of 1789 that overthrew the monarchy also produced a medical revolution that swept away the "systems" that had ruled medicine during the seventeenth and eighteenth centuries. The old regime's academies and institutions of medicine and education, anchored in medieval traditions, were abolished. In the reorganization that followed, there developed a very new kind of medical teaching that was centered in the clinic and the hospital and made the theoretical and speculative discourses of the past obsolete. The Paris doctor of the 1820s no longer merely "observed" the patient, he "examined" him. The new medicine was based on physical examination by hand (percussion) and ear (auscultation), pathological anatomy, and statistics. Students followed physicians and surgeons from ward to lecture room to dissecting theater and attempted to correlate before-death external symptoms and patient's complaints and appearances with the postmortem pathologic appearances of tissues and organs. Students and doctors came to Paris from all over the world, no longer to read but to see and to do.[69]

The teaching of bedside medicine in the Paris clinic contrasted sharply with the situation in England, where instruction was mainly by lectures illustrated by models and colored drawings. Students of anatomy and surgery in England, Scotland, and Ireland faced a shortage of legally obtained cadavers for dissection or demonstration. There was no such problem in Paris, where a large percentage of hospitalized patients died and were legally available for a small fee for dissection and research if not claimed for burial by friends or relatives within twenty-four hours.[70]

Lawful Dissection in France

In Great Britain, the law, dating back to 1540, allowed a limited number of dissections of executed criminals. In 1752, an act of George II required dissection or hanging in chains of the bodies of all executed murderers in order that "some further Terror and peculiar mark of Infamy might be added to the Punishment of Death."[71] This produced a deep-seated identification of dissection with the commission of serious crimes during life and strengthened the public feeling against dissection even of unclaimed bodies of paupers who died in workhouses, prisons, and hospitals. The general public, quite naturally, was reluctant to submit the bodies of friends and relatives to suffer the fate of an executed murderer.[72] Although legal medical postmortems were tolerated—these were perceived as distinct from *dissection*—they were viewed uneasily and were infrequently requested.[73] The public opposition to legalized dissection was finally overcome by the Warburton Anatomy Act of 1832, after Parliament first repealed the law mandating the dissection of all executed murderers. This removed the connection in the public's mind between dissection and executed criminals and with it, presumably, the stigma and ignominy of being dissected.

Laennec, Stethoscope, and the New Doctor–Patient Relationship

With the publication in 1821 of John Forbes' (1787–1861) English translation of parts of Laennec's *Traité de l'Auscultation Médiate*, the new technique of listening with the stethoscope became an additional attraction to those with clinical interests. The stethoscope was the first major diagnostic tool available to clinical medicine. However, Forbes criticized the new technique as "ludicrous" and doubted it would ever come into general use.[74] He had a complete change of attitude by the time of Laennec's second edition in 1826 and called it a "most valuable" work.

René-Théophile-Hyacinthe Laennec (1781–1826) rapidly acquired many disciples in France, but his reputation spread more quickly in foreign countries, especially in England, where bright young medical men took up the new art with enthusiasm after learning it first-hand in Paris from its inventor. Laennec compiled a list of some 300 students and foreign visitors who had attended his ward rounds and lectures. Some, like Thomas Hodgkin, were mentioned by name in the preface to Laennec's second edition as having been particularly noteworthy in following his teachings and in the study of the stethoscope. Partly on account of his many foreign students who did not understand French, as well as not to alarm his patients, Laennec spoke Latin in his clinical teaching. Hodgkin wrote home that he had made rounds, almost alone with Laennec, and that Laennec spoke to him in Latin with ease and fluency.[75] Although Hodgkin was conversant in French, he took lessons to improve his fluency.

The French students were not very hospitable to the English visitors, who sometimes complained about their hostile attitudes. For Hodgkin the unfriendly atmosphere was relieved by the presence of some of his Edinburgh friends. One of these was Robert Knox (1793–1862), an 1814 Edinburgh graduate who had come to Paris for additional study after army service in South Africa. Knox rented a private dissecting room at the Pitié and invited Hodgkin to join him in dissection and study of pathologic anatomy. This was a common French practice, and groups of English students followed suit and organized their own study courses in normal and pathological anatomy. After returning to Edinburgh, Knox became a leading extramural teacher of anatomy. His career was destroyed by his involvement with the murderous body-snatchers Burke and Hare, from whom he bought cadavers for his classes. Although cleared of complicity, he was shunned by the profession, and he turned to medical journalism and public lecturing, often on topics of race (see chapter 11).[76]

Hodgkin's year in Paris was accompanied by growing political unrest centering in the medical school. France enjoyed little respite from the social upheaval and political turmoil of the Napoleonic era. By 1820, after only a few years of constitutional liberties under Louis XVIII, the counterrevolution was in the ascendancy. The years were marked by increasing conflict between radical students and conservative government as the Bourbon monarchy became more repressive and the Church tried to regain its former authority over the university. The political situation deteriorated in June 1822. Student demonstrations and battles with the police that spilled into the classroom (Hodgkin slipped out in time) led to a temporary shutdown of the medical school. When it reopened in March 1823, its new pro-royalist administration replaced Bonapartist professors with royalist sympathizers. Laennec finally became a professor, not because of his recognition abroad, but because of his royalist-Jesuit connections at home. The failure of the monarchy to reconcile its tradition of divine right with the democratic spirit born in the Revolution of 1789 precipitated the Revolution of 1830. The royalist professors were discharged and replaced by the faculty dismissed in 1823—to the extent that members of both groups were still alive.[77]

On his return to England from Paris, Hodgkin read a paper to the Guy's Physical Society on Saturday, October 5, 1822, on the use of the stethoscope, which he had brought back with him. Unfortunately, his presentation was torn out from the records of the society, but a copy of his talk is preserved among his collected papers.[78] Hodgkin has been credited with introduction of the stethoscope to London and the rest of Great Britain,[79] but there is no evidence for this.

Laennec's work and the stethoscope were well known in Britain before Hodgkin's presentation. In fact, stethoscopes were imported as early as November 1819 and were sold with Laennec's book for an extra two francs. In January 1820, copies made in Piccadilly sold for four shillings. Reviews of Laennec's two-volume treatise and descriptions of the stethoscope and its use appeared in London publications at the same time.[80] However, Hodgkin's report surely stimulated an interest in this instrument and probably led to its use at Guy's.[81]

The unitubular, or monaural, instrument designed by Laennec underwent repeated adaptations and modifications to improve its efficiency and minimize the inconveniences in its use. Its short length and rigidity required doctor and patient to change position repeatedly. Hodgkin's friend Dr. William Stroud (see chapter 4, note 32) adapted the flexible speaking tube commonly used by deaf persons into a flexible stethoscope.[82] These early instruments were a personal tool dependent on the user's experience and expertise. Many physicians believed that the skill and perception of the physician were more important than the instrument and continued to listen with the unaided ear applied directly against the chest.[83]

The use of the stethoscope began the transformation of the practice of medicine and the doctor-patient relationship. The physician no longer merely observed his patients and listened to their complaints. Now he examined them and formed a diagnosis primarily from objective findings. The heart and lung sounds were independent evidence that the patient could not simulate, conceal, exaggerate, or minimize. The physician had entered into a new universe of physical changes concealed from the patient. With less and less dependence on the patient's subjective signs of illness, the physician's medical knowledge and skills assumed a greater importance than his social and family connections. As for the physician's dislike of close physical contact and use of the hands, because it might damage his professional and social status and put him in a class with the surgeon as a mere craftsman, this was lessened by placing an instrument between himself and the patient.[84]

CHAPTER TWO

Nepotism and the Upward Climb

Graduate in Medicine

The course of medical study required for graduation from the University of Edinburgh was three years, of which at least one year had to be spent at the university.[1] Thomas Hodgkin, having studied medicine for three years, and having paid a 13-guinea graduation fee and a £10 Scottish stamp duty on his diploma,[2] was graduated as M.D. in 1823. His thesis was a *Dissertatio Physiologica Inauguralis* of seventy-eight pages titled *De Absorbendi Functione,* which contained some original observations on the mechanisms of the absorbing function of blood and lymph. The thesis, dated Day 1 Month 8 (KAL. Aug.) 1823, contains lengthy and separate dedications in Latin to Alexander Humboldt (1769–1859), German scientist, naturalist, and explorer; to Professor Andrew Duncan, Jr.; and to his father, John Hodgkin. Humboldt had been kind to Thomas Hodgkin in Paris. Andrew Duncan, Jr., was his clinical teacher at the Royal Infirmary in Edinburgh and cared for him with paternal solicitude while he was suffering from scarlatina.

Although lectures were given in English, medical degree examinations were conducted in Latin, and M.D. theses were written in Latin. The thesis was submitted two months before graduation,

and if it was approved, an oral final examination by two professors, designed to test the candidate's proficiency in medical knowledge, followed.[3] Final examinations were held at the home of one
of the examiners. The host for the evening provided most of the
questions. Question and answers were in Latin. The candidate also
was required to make a written commentary on an aphorism of
Hippocrates, a written consultation on a case presented by a
professor, and a written defense of the thesis. These were done at
home in Latin, many for a fee by the candidate's professional
crammer, or *grinder*.[4] These medical coaches taught the Latin
jargon required for degree examinations.

Hodgkin's dissertation was complimented for the quality of its
scientific content and praised for the excellence of its Latin composition. However, he had gotten help. The prose progressively
improved as the manuscript traveled back and forth between
university and home. Revisions and corrections were made by his
father and brother and other talented Latinists among their friends,
including Hodgkin's former tutor, Mr. Cassanet.[5]

During the 1820s there were about 2,200 students at the university studying arts, law, divinity, and medicine—two out of five
were in medicine. In the early years of the century the University
of Edinburgh granted more than a hundred medical doctorates
annually, although Hodgkin's graduating class of 1823 listed only
ninety-three members.[6] The numbers are misleading and conceal
the actual significance of Edinburgh in the medical education of
the eighteenth and nineteenth centuries. The great majority of the
medical graduates, whether from England, Ireland, or the colonies,
had previously studied at other universities before coming to
Edinburgh for a final year and that coveted diploma. However, not
all of the 400 to 500 who attended the anatomy class each year
planned to practice medicine. Many were army or navy surgeons
who, having left the service on half-pay after the French wars,
wished to complete their training.[7]

Attendant to Abraham Montefiore

After graduating in August 1823, Hodgkin set out on one last
walking tour of the highlands before returning to his home in

Tottenham. While still in Scotland, uncertain plans were unexpectedly given direction by an offer from Paris to serve as traveling physician to Abraham Montefiore (1788–1824), younger brother of Moses Montefiore (1784–1885).[8] Abraham had tuberculosis and, planning a trip to southern France and Italy in hope of restoring his failing health, wanted a physician to travel with him. The Montefiore brothers acted for Nathan Mayer Rothschild (1777–1836) on the London Stock Exchange and were related to Rothschild by marriage. Moses was married to Judith Cohen (1784–1862), sister of Rothschild's wife Hannah (1783–1850), and Abraham was married to Rothschild's sister Henrietta (1791–1866).

How did this newly qualified and inexperienced young physician come to be considered and eventually engaged for such a responsible position? It wasn't that unusual. Senior practitioners often recommended young colleagues, upon completion of their training, for temporary private engagements as medical attendants to traveling aristocratic families. A well-established practitioner could not afford to neglect his regular practice, but for a beginner it was an excellent opportunity. Pay was good and the travel provided an introduction to good society and valuable connections.[9]

In Hodgkin's case the recommendation came from Benjamin Thorpe (1782–1870), a clerk at the Rothschild bank in Paris. Hodgkin first met Thorpe when the elder Hodgkin transferred funds to the bank for his son's use. They became friends, and Hodgkin treated him for a serious pulmonary disorder, probably tuberculosis. Hodgkin later accompanied a very sick Thorpe to England in September 1822 before returning to Edinburgh for the final year of medical school. Thorpe's health improved and he attributed his recovery to Hodgkin's care. When he returned to Paris and learned of Abraham Montefiore's traveling plans, he suggested Thomas Hodgkin as a "compagnon de voyage." Hodgkin was reluctant to undertake this type of employment because of the loss of independence such a relationship entailed, but recognized this opportunity to travel, to see foreign lands, and to experience new cultures—and to be paid at the same time. Hodgkin's parents had their own concerns about the job offer. They feared exposure to the patient's illness and the distractions of Italy.

Furthermore, Henrietta Montefiore had a reputation as difficult, but they were reassured when they met her during a brief visit to London.[10]

On September 16, 1823, they left Paris. The patient and his wife rode in one carriage, their children and a governess in another, and Hodgkin with the latter or on horseback. When Abraham suffered a serious relapse in Rome, Hodgkin decided to keep him comfortable and to rely on a strict and regular diet, but to take no aggressive measures. Not pleased with the cautious treatment, Abraham and his wife called in Italian consultants, who recommended blistering and bleeding.[11] According to Hodgkin, they tried to transfer the tubercle from the lungs to the leg.[12]

Henrietta Montefiore was especially disagreeable, but growing tension was relieved when Moses and Judith arrived. "I am very sorry [to] say that Abm Montefiore continues declining—It is a great satisfaction to me that his brother Moses is here. I have mentioned meeting him at Paris where I was much pleased with him & I am certainly not less so now that I have a fuller opportunity of becoming acquainted with him."[13]

In another letter Hodgkin wrote: "The diametrically opposite character of MM often makes the days pass by no means unpleasantly."[14] However, the relationship between doctor and patient continued to deteriorate and Hodgkin was barred from the sickroom. On January 8, 1824, he was fired and paid 125 guineas to cover traveling expenses. Hodgkin was certain that Henrietta was responsible. "I think she has got a most unfortunate and accursed power of causing trouble for other people." Despite his unsuccessful relationship with Abraham Montefiore and concern over the potential damage to his reputation, Hodgkin believed that he remained on good terms with Moses Montefiore. "While I shall not have any error of commission on my part to regret, I may flatter myself that I retain on the separation so much of the good will & good opinion of Moses Montefiore & other members of the family who are here, as will counteract any unfavourable report which may have passed respecting me to any of A. M.s friends in England, though I have some reasons for believing that nothing of the kind has taken place."[15]

Hodgkin's experience with Abraham and Henrietta Montefiore

had no negative repercussions in London. When Moses and Judith returned to England, they had only favorable comments about Thomas's medical skills. Now that he was on his own, Hodgkin was free to travel and see the country. Despite letters from home warning of the dangers of travel in Italy—they included everything from bandits, unhealthy summer climate, unstable politics, difficult terrain, and the women—he set out for Naples and Sicily. He climbed Mt. Vesuvius and visited the ruins of Pompeii. In Sicily he saw the Greek and Roman antiquities, Saracen ruins, medieval castles, the geology, and the local plant and animal life. He returned to Naples and Rome, and continued to Venice and eventually via Milan to Geneva. Wherever he went he sought out interesting local men of science and made friends with other touring young Englishmen who, like himself, were eager to explore new lands and cultures.[16]

Hodgkin returned to Paris early in September and learned that Abraham Montefiore had died in Lyon on August 24. Thorpe had apologized to Thomas for the introduction, but Hodgkin replied, "I owe to this introduction the gratifying and valuable friendship of M. Montefiore & of some other members of his family."[17] Thorpe later changed careers and became a leading scholar of Anglo-Saxon languages.[18]

Letter to a Mohawk Chief

In Paris, Hodgkin took courses in mathematics, spent time at the hospitals, and still found time for a continuing commitment in his life, namely, the relief of problems brought by European settlers and the improvement of the status of the natives of the overseas British colonies. He decided that much progress could be made toward these ends by sending intelligent adolescent sons of tribal chiefs to England for education, training, and acquaintance with the ways of the white man. These future leaders could facilitate the transfer of European knowledge and values to their people. It was a theme that appeared many times in his private and public writing. In his letter[19] to John Norton, a Mohawk chief from Canada, dated December 17, 1824, Hodgkin explains the origins of his interest in the problems faced by the Indians and outlines his own plans for direct action.

> Though I recollect with pleasure having been in thy company during thy visit to England in 1807, both at our Friend William Allen's & at my Father's house at Pentonville, yet as I have no idea that thou canst have any recollection of one who at that time was too young to attract thy attention, I must introduce myself as a friend of William Allen & Luke Howard, & indeed of most of those members of the Society of Friends with whom thou becamest acquainted during thy stay in England.
>
> From the time that I was first capable of reflecting on the subject down to the present hour, few circumstances have excited my interest in so lively a manner as the signal injustice & cruelty which the natives of your Continent have too generally received from Europeans & their descendants. I was grieved to understand that even that intercourse which was kept up under a friendly appearance, frequently had a tendency to corrupt & degrade the character & accelerate the extermination of your noble Race. I longed to exert myself in a counteracting direction, & was anxious to devote my abilities to your cause.

Hodgkin was not satisfied with the work of the missionaries, who, though well-intentioned, managed to abuse their trust or introduce divisions in the tribes. He decided that what he could do "would be to educate one or two young Indians of promising abilities & who as the sons of Chiefs, or eminent individuals, might be reasonably expected to have influence with their Brethren." Hodgkin learned of John Norton in Edinburgh, obtained the address from a relative, and decided to write to him to ask his opinion of this plan. And, continued Hodgkin, "if the youths' abilities, zeal & progress should fairly realize my hopes, it is probable that I may repeat some of these excursions & finally accompany them to their Native Land." Hodgkin wanted young men about seventeen to twenty-two years old, with the best natural abilities and some cultivation so that less time would be needed for elementary instruction.

> It is of course desirable that the Individuals, of whatever age they may be, should already understand a little of some European Lan-

guage, but it is immaterial whether it be English or French. It is also of comparatively little moment to me whether they are attached to the interest of England or the United States, as I have no wish to disturb the alliances of either.—My only wish is that they may be such characters as may be a credit to their countrymen whilst they remain in Europe & be most likely to be of essential benefit to them on their return. . . . If you can forward the young men to New York I will bear half the expense of the voyage and relieve them from every other expense till their return to their friends, which would probably be in a little more than two years. I should prefer two persons to one, as I am anxious that so important an object should not depend on a single chance. Thou wilt of course take care that they be persons of good constitution, & that they have had the cow or small pox.

Nothing came of this request.

Years later, in 1845, Hodgkin did get the opportunity—at the request of the government and independent of his own efforts—to guide the education and development of a young aboriginal Australian boy named Edward Warrulan. The youth (and one other, who was sent back because of a vicious temper) had been brought to England by John Eyre (1815–1901), explorer and resident magistrate in Australia, and later renowned as "the Butcher of Jamaica" for his suppression of an uprising on that island. The children were quite a novelty and were presented at Buckingham Palace. Young Edward went to school, learned to read and write, and was taught the trade of glover and saddler. Afterward, while learning harvesting procedures, he caught cold and died of pneumonia in October 1855, at about seventeen years of age.[20]

Up until then, the aboriginal races of Australia had been greatly misrepresented and very often unjustly described "as the lowest and most degraded of mankind; forming . . . only a connecting link between the human family and the lower orders of the creation." The two boys were examined by eminent phrenologists, who found "their developments . . . very good, and far superior to those of the negro race generally."[21] It was hoped that the notice taken of them by Queen Victoria would help dispel the unfavorable impressions generally held of the aboriginals and lessen the evils that the occupation of their country had brought to them.

Sojourn in Paris and a New Romance

Hodgkin was in Paris from September 1824 until June 1825. One of the attractions of Parisian intellectual circles was Mrs. Sarah (Wallis) Bowdich (1791–1856), a worldly, talented, and educated woman, whom Hodgkin had probably met at one of the Saturday soirees of Baron Georges Cuvier (1769–1832), French naturalist and paleontologist. His salon attracted the scientific and literary intelligentsia of Paris, and Hodgkin, armed with a letter of introduction from William Allen, had been a frequent visitor during his student year of 1821–22.[22] Mrs. Bowdich's husband, Thomas Edward Bowdich (1791–1824), a traveler and writer on Africa, had recently died of fever while on a surveying trip to the Gambia River, leaving her a widow.

Hodgkin was strongly attracted to Mrs. Bowdich. The impression soon developed among their Parisian friends that he was about to propose marriage, and several of them tried to help things along by matchmaking.[23] However, she was not a Quaker, she had children to support and very little property, and she was seven years older than Thomas. On the positive side, she was knowledgeable in mathematics, languages, and natural history. Characterizing his acquaintance with her as extremely slight, he wrote to his father for advice, stating that "the decision will finally be subservient to the filial obedience of Thy dutiful son."[24] There is no record of his father's answer, but nothing developed between Hodgkin and Sarah Bowdich. She married a Mr. Robert Lee in 1829, and under her new married name became a popular writer of books about nature, travel, and adventure, many for children, and many attractively illustrated by herself.[25]

Sir Astley Cooper

By June 1825, after some prompting by his family, Hodgkin realized it was time to return home and begin the practice of medicine. Before the end of July he was in London. During the next few months, while his private practice was developing, he became associated with his alma mater, Guy's Hospital, as an unpaid clinical clerk. His voluntary service was rewarded early in 1826 by an appointment to the dual position of Inspector of the Dead and Curator of the Museum of Morbid Anatomy. Hodgkin had come to the notice of Sir Astley Paston Cooper (1768–1841),[26] a force of great influence in the medical world of London. Cooper and a small handful of others were the dispensers of patronage and makers of careers.

Astley Cooper, a great clinician and the leading British surgeon of the day, drew hundreds of students to his clinics and lectures. His bold and daring vascular surgery was all the more remarkable because there was no anesthesia, no aseptic technique, no blood transfusion, and no antibiotics. His manual dexterity and knowledge of anatomy enabled him to make his incisions and manipulations with great certainty and speed. Cooper knew the importance of morbid anatomy and urged his younger colleagues to spend as much time as possible in the postmortem room.

Astley Cooper, who lectured at St. Thomas's Hospital but worked at Guy's, was anxious to replace the large pathological collection he left behind at St. Thomas's following his retirement. In Hodgkin he recognized someone whose interest and skill in morbid anatomy and experience with the French School was admirably suited for this project. Hodgkin, aged twenty-seven, had returned to London and come to the attention of Astley Cooper at a most opportune time.

Nepotism and the Upward Climb

Guy's Hospital Medical School came into being in 1825 as a result of a dispute between St. Thomas's and Guy's hospitals over an appointment to the staff of St. Thomas's Hospital. Appointment and promotion in the London hospitals were virtually the property and inheritance of a small irresponsible oligarchy that thwarted the ambitions of young and talented outsiders. Appointments were made on social criteria. Letters of reference dealt with personality, style, moral conduct, and character. There was little notice of medical or surgical skills or scientific expertise. Appointments often went to relatives, apprentices, or assistants of those in office or to past students of the hospital's staff. Astley Cooper was one of the most successful practitioners of nepotism. In 1840, every full surgeon at Guy's was one of his former apprentices: John Morgan, Charles Aston Key, Bransby Cooper, Edward Cock, and Thomas Callaway. Three of them were nephews by blood or marriage.[27]

Practitioners ignorant of the system of patronage or without connections, influence, or ambition could not establish themselves in private practice and were pushed aside. Those who did not cultivate "the mean arts of subserviency and intrigue" were "doomed to chafe and fret under the rule of ignoble mediocrity."[28] The price of failure was obscure practice at the margins of the medical profession—the colonial service, the military, or as a grossly underpaid Poor Law medical officer.[29]

When Sir Astley Cooper decided to retire, he proposed his young nephew Bransby Cooper (1792–1853) to succeed him as lecturer in anatomy at St. Thomas's, in keeping with the established practice of nepotism at this and other hospitals. To the surprise of all, the governors of St. Thomas's, who never had failed to confirm a recommendation of succession, refused to accept his selection and appointed another surgeon, J. F. South, without prior consultation with the governors of Guy's, as had originally been agreed to. Sir Astley tried to withdraw his resignation but was told it was too late. What probably annoyed the St. Thomas's staff was that all but one of the lectureships of the United Hospitals were held by Guy's men. If the succession to posts were controlled by the holders, there was little chance of the St. Thomas's staff getting a fair share of these income-producing teaching appointments.[30]

The New Guy's Hospital Medical School

Because of the rebuff to his selection of a successor, Sir Astley decided to move his anatomical specimens (about half of St. Thomas's collection) to Guy's Hospital, where they would form the nucleus of a new museum. However, St. Thomas's refused to part with any of it and offered instead to return the £1,000 that

Astley Cooper had contributed to the building of their museum in 1814.[31]

What followed was a complete break with St. Thomas's and the establishment of a new and independent school at Guy's for the teaching of anatomy and surgery, in addition to the existent teaching of medicine and midwifery. The money was accepted from St. Thomas's and, with the approval of Sir Astley, was put toward the cost of the new buildings, which were ready enough for the fall session opening October 1, 1825.[32] It was generally believed that Astley Cooper encouraged the break in order that the new Guy's medical school could provide lectureships in surgery and anatomy for his nephews Aston Key (1793–1849) and Bransby Cooper, respectively.[33]

Founding the new school was not a difficult matter. Medical education in England at that time barely went beyond attendance at lectures in medicine and surgery. When the union of the two schools was ended in 1825, Guy's found itself well staffed with lecturers actively interested in fields that were destined for the most rapid advances during the coming years. The new school was an immediate success. Its rise was accompanied by a concurrent decline in enrollment of students at St. Thomas's.

Licentiate of the College of Physicians

This was the London world of hospital nepotism and politics that Thomas Hodgkin was about to enter. Little did he suspect, on October 31, 1825, as he applied for the Licentiate of the College of Physicians, that he would one day fall victim to the system. He took his first examination, "in parte Physiologicâ," on November 4, "when he produced a diploma from the University of Edinburgh by which he was created Doctor of Physic 1st August 1823." His second examination, "in parte Pathologicâ," was on December 2, and the third, "in parte Therapeuticâ," was on December 22, when he was approved by the examiners. Later the same day he was admitted a licentiate by the full Comitia and given his diploma.[34]

Physician to the London Dispensary and Jewish Friendly Societies

Shortly after becoming a Licentiate of the College of Physicians, Hodgkin was appointed to a post as physician to the London Dispensary (established in 1777), which served the poor of Spital-fields. His application was supported by Sir Astley Cooper, William Babington, James Cholmeley, and William Allen from Guy's Hospital and by Thomas Young (1773–1829), a friend of Hodgkin's father and physician at St. George's Hospital, and known for reviving the wave theory of light. At about the same time, Hodgkin also served as physician to two Jewish friendly societies, probably as a favor to Moses Montefiore, who was involved in relief efforts for the Jewish poor.

As physician to the London Dispensary he saw the squalor and misery of the poor as he made house calls in the crowded tenements. He knew that much had to be done and how little he could actually do and how temporary the relief would be. Near the end of 1827, Hodgkin had a falling-out with the officials at the London Dispensary and resigned his position. It appears he acted in anger because of critical comments about his absence from work due to a brief illness. His letter of resignation clearly expressed his irritation and chagrin.

> That the reasons for my resignation may not be unknown to you, I cannot forbear remarking that my feelings have been severely wounded by the fact that, though absolute and total indifference attended my gratuitous, continued and zealous exertions in the service of the institution, a service which has occupied ten or twelve hours in every week, and often considerably more, and in the performance of which, almost every hour in the day, nay every meal has been liable to be broken in upon, my attendance was no sooner suspended most unavoidably by a sudden, severe attack of illness, which wholly confines me to my bed, than with unjust and unfeeling promptitude you proved your readiness to censure.[35]

The governors of the London Dispensary expressed the highest esteem for Hodgkin and were dismayed at his annoyance. The members couldn't understand why he resigned and chose such "hasty and uncalled for" language in doing so. They denied any action of censure and regretted that Hodgkin distributed copies of his letter of resignation with additional comments that were "more uncourteous" than before. Hodgkin subsequently made a qualified retraction of his criticisms.[36] Although the governors appeared willing to make amends, Hodgkin did not resume his attendance at the dispensary.[37]

CHAPTER THREE

Hodgkin in Caricature

The Improved Compound Microscope

One of Hodgkin's friends was the Quaker Joseph Jackson Lister (1786–1869), father of Joseph Lister, who introduced antisepsis in surgery. The elder Lister was a prosperous London wine merchant and amateur scientist who spent his leisure hours on problems of optics. Distortions in the field of vision caused by technical imperfections of early microscopes led to speculations based on optical illusions and to false conclusions about what was seen through the lens. Blurring of the image, especially chromatic aberration in the compound microscope, led many users to prefer the better-resolving lower-power single-lens instrument.[1]

During the 1820s, practical compound microscopes with increased power of magnification and corrected chromatic aberration were being built, but the resulting spherical aberration could be kept to a minimum only by selecting and positioning the lens components by trial and error. The problem of accumulated spherical errors in achromatic lenses for the compound microscope was finally solved by J. J. Lister. By experimentation, he developed a theoretical basis for selecting fully corrected achromatic lens combinations and carefully placing them at the aplanatic foci so

43

that no additional spherical error was introduced.[2] For his work he was elected a Fellow of The Royal Society in 1832.

Lister's innovative correction of spherical aberration removed the fuzziness of the image and helped make the compound microscope a reliable instrument for scientific investigation. It now became possible to study the minute structure of plants and animals and to discover that both consisted of cells with nuclei.

Working together, Hodgkin and Lister made some notable discoveries with the improved microscope. Lister's observations were at first directed to vegetable structures, but at Hodgkin's suggestion he investigated animal fluids and solids. One of their initial findings resulted in a correct view of the structure of human red blood cells, which had been described by Anton Leeuwenhoek (1632–1723) and other microscopists as having a globular shape. Hodgkin and Lister provided a new description of human red blood cells, which for the first time were described as biconcave discs: "To us the particles of human blood appear to consist of circular flattened transparent cakes which, when seen singly, appear to be nearly or quite colourless. Their edges are rounded, and being the thickest part, occasion a depression in the middle, which exists on both surfaces."[3] They described crenation, osmotic swelling in water, and rouleaux formation, and made the most accurate measurement of the red cell's diameter yet recorded.

They commented briefly on the microscopic appearances of milk, pus, nerves, arteries, cellular membranes, and brain. They discovered the fine fibrillar structures and striations of voluntary and cardic muscle and the absence of striations from involuntary muscle (arteries). However, the technology for successful use of microscopes in pathology for distinguishing abnormal from normal tissues on the cellular level by differential staining of ultrathin sections of tissue was still in the future. As of 1827, study of organs and tissues was limited to their gross examination as part of the postmortem.

Prior to the start-up of the new Guy's Medical School, postmortems were infrequent. The schedule of instruction of the school stated, "*Post-mortem* examinations are not conducted with regularity, but they are tolerably frequent, and free to all the pupils."[4] A physician or surgeon wishing a body to be inspected because it was an interesting case from which the profession might learn much valuable information would deliver a written request to the hospital steward.[5] However, requests were usually made only in special cases. To a pragmatic practitioner they were of no use, since therapy was not guided by knowledge of the cause of death. Anatomical lesions were considered to be the effects, not the causes, of disease. The prevailing attitude of the physicians and surgeons during the early part of the nineteenth century was that the cause of death was too obvious to need confirmation and that inspection need be done only if the diagnosis was in doubt. They did not understand that the knowledge gained from postmortems would improve their ability to diagnose and to avoid therapies that might add to suffering or hasten death.

The hospital during Hodgkin's time contained 421 beds, and there were nearly three hundred deaths each year.[6] During the years 1826 to 1836, Hodgkin made about one hundred autopsies annually. By 1854, the number had risen to 250.

Curator of the Museum

When Hodgkin began his study of medicine, he developed a strong interest in pathological anatomy. This made him especially receptive to the instructions and demonstrations of Laennec at the Hôpital Necker and of Léon Rostan (1790–1866) at the Salpêtrière, as well as the numerous inspections made by Gabriel Andral (1797–1876) at the Hôpital de la Charité. These contacts and others in Italy and elsewhere on the Continent shaped his understanding that the next major advances in medical science would come from correlations of morbid anatomy with clinical disturbances during life. It led him to accept the position of Inspector of the Dead at Guy's Hospital, together with responsibility for the small museum of anatomical specimens.[7]

The museum was not totally bare. Benjamin Harrision, Jr., the treasurer of Guy's, impressed with the importance of obtaining a more permanent benefit from the remarkable cases that periodically were seen at the hospital, had directed that drawings, models, and casts be made. In 1802, and possibly even earlier, there were facilities for anatomical demonstration and dissection and for postmortem inspections. As a result, a small collection of anatomical preparations dating from around this period became available to illustrate the medical lectures at Guy's Hospital. In 1806, Harrison directed that all specimens of morbid structure, either dissected by the pupils or inspected at the request of the medical officers at the hospital, should be added to the collection. However, since no one was specifically assigned the task of preparation and preservation of the removed parts, the additions were few and the total amounted to fewer than five hundred specimens at the time of Hodgkin's arrival in 1826. With the founding of the school, the museum took on an increased importance and received specimens not only from internal sources but also from numerous outside contributors.[8]

Thomas Hodgkin was the third of a trio of graduates of the University of Edinburgh who, in the early 1820s, joined the staff of the Guy's Hospital and Medical School. Richard Bright (1789–1858) and Thomas Addison (1793–1860) were the other two. These three remarkable men were the first at Guy's to approach the study of disease from the modern point of view. It was from their time that the school took on a dual function as a place of medical education and an institution for research.

Bright and Addison were both excellent clinical observers and in Hodgkin they had an outstanding morbid anatomist. These contemporaries shared in the important new scientific approach to medicine: the careful and detailed correlation of postmortem findings to the clinical disease seen in the wards. They represented the clinico-pathological trend in the medicine of their time, which preceded the later emphasis on laboratory investigations.

Morbid Anatomy

The Theatre of Morbid Anatomy of Guy's Hospital was opened in January 1828. Hodgkin's remarks to the pupils on this occasion not only demonstrate the new importance on autopsies, but they also revealed the state of the art in pathology that had evolved since the middle of the previous century. He discussed the kinds of changes and diagnostic clues observed in the body on postmortem examination and how they explained the mechanisms of disease. Differentiation, he noted, should be made between changes resulting from cadaveric phenomena and those relating to the death and last illness of the subject, and those resulting from chronic diseases not immediately connected with the cause of death, as well as the permanent marks left by past diseases. Much practical usefulness would be lost if there was no way of correlating the morbid changes observed at postmortem with the symptoms that they might have caused during life.[9]

In concluding remarks he assured his listeners that "it will be my constant aim, whether I may be fortunate enough to reach the mark or not, to co-operate with those who are strenuously endeavouring to render the school of Guy's Hospital the first medical school in the kingdom." There is no doubt that Hodgkin was a team player and strongly identified with his institution.

Medical Education Reform

Hodgkin's concern for the quality of medical education in London led him to offer his own plans for reform in 1827 at a meeting of the Physical Society of Guy's Hospital: "If, from the circumstance of my bringing forward this question, it be inferred that I consider our present system of Medical Education liable to objection, I must admit this to be the case, and confess that I regard it, more especially with respect to the general practitioner, as objectionable in nearly all its stages."[10] By criticizing medical education, he was intruding into an area tacitly reserved for senior physicians of experience and authority and was risking professional ostracism.

At the start of the nineteenth century, medical education was loosely regulated and hardly guided by standards. The few who intended to become physicians attended Oxford or Cambridge university, or one of the Scottish or Irish universities, or one of the foreign universities on the Continent. As for the mass of medical students, the core of their "medical" education during this period was the one-to-one relationship as an apprentice to a surgeon or an apothecary for five years or more. This private education was often supplemented by a course at a private anatomy school and subsequent enrollment in a hospital "walking the wards" and observing the physicians and surgeons.

This arrangement did not allow the young student to obtain a good general education and often prevented it altogether. The inherent obstacle was the Apothecaries' Act of 1815.[11] Intended to regulate the practice of apothecaries, the act specified new educational requirements and reduced to five years the traditional seven-year apprenticeship as qualification for membership and the diploma of the Society of Apothecaries, a trade or craft guild. The negotiated conditions and cost of an apprenticeship often made the student little more than a menial servant acquired on highly favorable terms. Training could be haphazard and unsystematic, with undue emphasis on the empirical at the expense of the theoretical.

Critics of the apprenticeship requirement knew that these valuable early years could be better spent in secondary education to develop the mind with classical, scientific, and general knowledge. However, a liberal and classical education, the mark of the Victorian gentleman, was acquired by only a few in medicine. The patchy preliminary education of ordinary general practitioners provided little basis for claiming that medical men belonged to a "learned profession."

Although in the past, said Hodgkin, "when the business of the Apothecary resembled more closely than at present that of the Confectioner, to which it was once united, five, six, or even seven years, might not be an unreasonable time to be spent in instructing the apprentice, by the purely routine and practical method, in the mystery of preparing the numerous and complicated farragoes, which it was the business of the Apothecary to administer, under the direction of the Physician." But, continued Hodgkin, the situation had changed markedly. Apothecaries' shops had fewer articles, and most of these were supplied already prepared by the wholesale druggist. Learning to distinguish, measure, and mix the various articles of the materia medica did not require standing behind a counter for five years. A very few months, or a year at the most, would be enough.[12]

If more time be allotted to this branch, it must be abstracted, either from that which should be spent in the pursuit of a liberal preliminary education, or from that which ought to be devoted to other departments of professional knowledge. It is more than probable that the years thus consumed, are not merely lost, but that they materially tend to undo what may have been done for the attainment of the first object, as well as to unfit the mind for the vigorous pursuit of the latter.[13]

For many centuries the teaching of medicine had been almost confined to the teaching of therapeutics. As an apprentice to an apothecary the student learned the nature of the plants and herbs which he must use, their preparation and mixture, their dispensing and administration, and the diseases for which they were used. He also learned the treatments then in style—poulticing, cupping, blistering, application of leeches, etc. Even in the hospital setting the lectures were largely devoted to pharmaceutical chemistry, medical botany, and materia medica. If there was any study of diagnosis, it was limited to the interpretation of symptoms.

Citing the practices in France and Germany, where a liberal education was required as a prelude to medical study, Hodgkin urged more clinical medical instruction, the study of more anatomy, physiology, and internal pathology (morbid anatomy). Regretting the nearly total neglect of clinical medical instruction in the hospitals of London, Hodgkin briefly described the procedures followed in some of the continental schools. At the Salpêtrière in Paris, Rostan taught diagnosis by lecturing at the patient's bedside. Pupils prepared case histories and followed the progress of the disease. Their reports were read in open class and were reviewed by the teacher.[14] Referring to the practice by many pupils of taking notes as they moved from ward to ward, he said, "Still I could wish that the regulations of our schools did not wholly leave this important point to the discretion of the pupil."[15]

Hodgkin's most interesting suggestion concerned the introduction during the clinical years of clerks into the medical wards to assist physicians. These would be comparable to the dressers who for so long had assisted the surgeons in performance of operations and accompanied them in the surgical wards carrying the boxes with the applications for wounds, i.e., plasters, bandages, and dressings. Hodgkin's plan would allow the student to see all the medical patients, but would have him associate with one of the physicians in particular, in the same manner as the dressers did with respect to the surgeons. The only difference would be the number attached to each physician need not be limited.[16]

Urging greater attention to the study of morbid anatomy because of the opportunity for comparing symptoms with structural derangement, Hodgkin dismissed the insinuations coming "from the highest medical quarter in this country" that investigation of diseased appearances diverted the medical man from the study of disease and its treatment during life. Hodgkin blamed the indifference to pathology, and the small number of morbid anatomists in England, on the premature introduction of the student to medical practice. Consequently, the student became poorly acquainted with the healthy structure and must necessarily be incompetent to judge the endless variations brought on by disease. Hodgkin believed that his plan would do away with this evil. He also urged physicians to adopt the plan followed on the Continent, of publishing reports of case histories and postmortem inspections, so that the medical profession could get this information directly instead of through irregular channels.[17]

These suggested reforms reflect Hodgkin's exposure to the French and other continental systems of medical training. These programs could hardly have been popular in a professional atmosphere not distinguished for the furtherance of revolutionary causes or controversial subjects.

Hodgkin's presentation stimulated an animated debate, and it was decided to continue the discussion on the following Saturday and allow open admission to the meeting. The publicity given to the subject and proceedings of the former evening resulted in a very large turnout for a second reading of the paper. Needless to say, not all were in agreement with Hodgkin's views. Some of the comments are interesting, even amazing. Dr. Whiting said it was a waste of the student's limited time to learn the minute anatomy of vessels and nerves. He thought that general anatomy was sufficient for all practical purposes. Dr. Rees disagreed, although he had contended earlier that too much education makes a boy unfit for an apothecary. He approved of an apprenticeship, as it inculcated habits of regularity, morality, and "*subserviency.*" Mr. Dodd spoke of the "lamentable state of ignorance" shown by most of those entering into the practice of medicine. He regretted that the love of science prevailed so little, that the medical profession in England should be degraded into a mere "money-getting trade."[18]

The reform-minded *Lancet* reminded the reader of "the defect of clinical instruction at the London Hospitals, as contrasted with the foreign schools." It noted that Dr. Hodgkin had shown that the superiority of the French and other nations in pathology was due to the full and complete clinical instruction given to the students. These comments should not be taken as arbitrary or as criticism for its own sake. After 1820, many in England thought that the new French methods were far superior to those available at home.

These beliefs were brought back by the many medical students and doctors who absorbed Parisian ideas and techniques in person. Only a few graduated at Paris, but most stayed from a few months to a year or two. Their influence was amplified by the English medical review journals. The same was happening in other European medical centers.[19]

A Case of Medical Libel

The stir that Hodgkin set off with his recommendations on medical education was nothing compared with the big ruckus at Guy's Hospital that year. The leading character in this new drama was not Hodgkin, but he certainly was a featured player. The provocative event was a report of an operation published in *The Lancet* in March 1828 charging malpractice by Bransby Cooper. The article was written in so venomous and malignant a style, and caused so much comment, that the accused surgeon had no choice but to seek vindication by initiating a legal action. No specific amount was claimed, probably because the primary object of the plaintiff was not the recovery of damages but the clearing of his professional reputation against the false, scandalous, and malicious libel. The published report that brought about the libel suit was based on an account by a surgeon named Lambert, who was a free-lance reporter for *The Lancet*.[20] The two-day trial was held in December 1828.[21]

Thomas Wakley (1795–1862),[22] surgeon, founder, and editor of the medical weekly *The Lancet*, did much to bring about reform of teaching and the practice of medicine by exposing abuses and excesses. He fought for improved teaching facilities for medical students, and he attacked the arbitrary barriers put up against the young London physicians who sought a staff appointment in a teaching hospital. But in the process he often heaped personal abuse on those merely guilty of having differing opinions, often using galling and offensive nicknames while referring to personal infirmities and handicaps. Admitting that "we have no great talent for saying civil things to our enemies,"[23] he freely criticized the prominent physicians and surgeons of his day. His vicious denunciations led to numerous libel suits. When the verdict went against him, his expenses were usually defrayed by contributions from supporters and admirers in and out of the profession.

The main target of Wakley's smear journalism was the system of appointment to the hospital staffs. Although the hospitals had distinguished members on their staffs, selection and promotion were seldom impartial. The dispensers of patronage became the primary targets of Wakley's assaults against the method of staff appointment to the London teaching hospitals. He charged that as a result of the widespread monopoly, conspiracy, and nepotism, incompetent persons were appointed merely because they were relatives of current staff members.

The Lancet was first to publish detailed accounts of the surgical failures of the leading hospital surgeons. This particular time it charged that Bransby Cooper's inept procedure for removing a bladder stone caused the death of the fifty-three-year-old patient, Stephen Pollard. Bransby Cooper was described as an unskilled surgeon who had been appointed to the staff of Guy's Hospital because he was the nephew of Sir Astley Cooper. A picture of utter confusion and ineptitude was drawn of an incompetent and hapless surgeon verbalizing his frustration and helplessness in front of the conscious patient and taking nearly an hour for a surgical procedure that a skillful surgeon could accomplish in about six minutes and that had been done in one minute. When the operation was over, Bransby Cooper was so concerned with his exhibition of ignorance that he attempted to explain the difficulty to the appalled assembly of surgeons and students while the suffering patient was still bound on the table. The report led to a long-running feud between Guy's Hospital and *The Lancet*. Wakley used the pages of his weekly to hurl insult and invective at the hospital, its managers, and staff. Guy's responded by threatening to expel any student who wrote for the publication.

It was quite clear from the testimony of witnesses supporting Wakley's allegation that, owing to Bransby Cooper's violence and lack of skill, the original incision was wrongly made, that he forcefully made an opening between the bladder and the rectum instead of going straight into the bladder, that his difficulty in extracting the stone was because his forceps had not been in the bladder at all, and that this injury had been the cause of the patient's death about twenty-nine hours later.

Thomas Hodgkin performed an autopsy and testified for the plaintiff. He found no opening in the bladder except the one made by the surgeon from the external surface into the bladder. It was brought out by testimony that Lambert was also present at the postmortem and had asked to see the specimen. At this point during the autopsy, Hodgkin left the room for a few minutes, probably to wash his hands. When he returned, Lambert showed him and the pupils an opening in the specimen between the bladder and the rectum that he claimed had been made by the surgeon. At the trial Lambert testified that he had examined the parts after they were removed from the body and that without using the slightest force or breaking any structure, he could easily pass his finger between the bladder and the rectum.[24]

Hodgkin apparently was aware, while writing up the postmortem report, of the imputation that Bransby Cooper had caused this injury, and he took care to record, "In this preparation a passage exists at the side of the bladder. This was not noticed by Dr. Hodgkin till after it had been in the hands of the reporter of *The Lancet*, and from the extremely lacerable state of the parts it might easily have been formed after the removal from the body."[25]

Apparently, Hodgkin believed that Lambert had tampered with the parts after they had been removed from the body and while he was out of the room. Hodgkin testified he had not seen this opening during his examination. "From the appearance of the parts, I was aware of no other wound, except one from the external surface into the bladder. There was none between the bladder and the rectum."[26] He was convinced that it was made after death. Hodgkin accused Lambert of making the hole and is reported to have said: "If there be an opening, friend, it is thyself has made it."[27]

The jury deliberated for two hours and returned with a verdict for the plaintiff of damages at £100. The jury apparently believed *The Lancet*'s main contention that malpractice had occurred, but it decided that *The Lancet* ought to be fined anyway, considering the indecency of the language that it printed. The small sum also may have reflected a greater concern for freedom of the press than for the personal injury done to Bransby Cooper. The amount of the damages, plus the plaintiff's legal costs and sheriff's poundage, came to £408 7s. 9d. and was raised the next day at a public meeting at the Freemasons' Tavern by members of the medical and surgical profession and other gentlemen.[28]

The reader may wonder at the ease of gaining admission as a spectator of the surgery. Admission was not difficult to come by. Former students were entitled to this, and the crowding in the operating theater was such that it was very difficult to keep unauthorized persons, such as reporters and students from other establishments, from pushing their way in.[29] It was frequently so crowded that the patient and surgeon were greatly inconvenienced and hindered by the closeness of the spectators. *The Lancet* knew why the surgeons tolerated the crowding and jostling around the operating table. "Each dresser pays upwards of fifty guineas for these privileges, and the surgeons would rather incur these personal inconveniences, than yield to the sacrifice of so much money."[30]

Early nineteenth-century surgery was a brutal business and was conducted in a chaotic atmosphere. Before railings were placed around operating tables in the 1830s, the students and other spectators crowded around the operator and blocked everyone else's view with their hats, which they wore everywhere. Tension ran high as the patient was tied down and began to squirm in anticipation of the knife. This was accompanied by increasingly louder yells of the students as they released their nervous tension.

Then, as the first incision was made, there was a sudden silence, followed by a resumption of joking and laughter among the students and with the surgeon. Students smoked without stop, filling the operating theater and the wards with their cigar smoke in an effort to blot out the bad smells.[31]

Hodgkin in Caricature

There now followed publication of several of the vulgar and scurrilous type of caricatures that were common in the days of the Regency and for which there was a wide public audience at the time. Hodgkin was featured in one of them.

The caricaturists of this period had no real knowledge of the appearance of their subjects unless they were members of Parliament and could be sketched from the visitors' seats. Ordinarily, the figures in the drawing were identified by puns, props, labels, or by sentences in balloons, vulgarly known as "bladders," in the style of the modern comic strip. Caricaturists performed a function similar to that of the cartoonists of today who satirize newsworthy items of the day. Caricatures were sold as single-sheet prints from printshops.

The most interesting of three lithographs about the trial is called "The Seat of Honor, or Servility Rewarded"[32] (Fig. 1). It satirizes the autocratic rule of Benjamin Harrison, Jr., treasurer of Guy's Hospital, shown seated on the padlocked treasurer's box of Guy's Hospital. To his right stands Sir Astley Cooper, and next to him, Bransby Cooper, who had lost the use of an eye in a childhood accident, is shown (like Polyphemus) with a single eye in the middle of his forehead. On his head is a vase presented as a consolation by his students. To the left is Sir Astley's other nephew, Aston Key. The other figures are patients, students, and doctors.

The insert in the upper left corner of the caricature is inscribed *Dead House* and *Oh! Monsieur de Quaker*. Thomas Hodgkin is represented as a vulture in the postmortem room. He is wearing a broad-brimmed hat that identifies him as a Quaker. Clutching a knife, he emerges from a small trap inscribed *A French Trap for an English Booby* and leans menacingly toward a naked man, dead

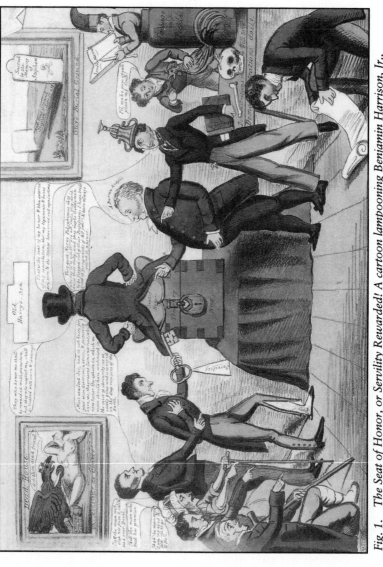

Fig. 1. *The Seat of Honor, or Servility Rewarded! A cartoon lampooning Benjamin Harrison, Jr., probably by Robert Cruikshank. (Reproduced by the courtesy of the Trustees of the British Museum.)*

or moribund, saying, "Art thou dead friend?" Although this colored lithograph (shown here in black and white) is unsigned, the detailed factual treatment and use of inset pictures is characteristic of Robert Cruikshank (1789–1856).

In a review of Wakley's life following his death from pulmonary tuberculosis in 1862, *The Lancet* admitted, "Such a report could not now be published."[33] *The Lancet* still appears weekly and is one of the world's foremost medical news and research periodicals.

As for the stone that was the cause of this famous trial, it was a small, flat, oval-shaped uric acid calculus, specimen number 1864 in the Gordon Museum's catalogue, weighing 120 grains (7.8 grams) with a laminated structure and irregular dark brown surface. It is still on display. The postmortem preparation was in the museum for many years but was lost at some time when the museum was being recatalogued.[34]

The courtroom experience undoubtedly strengthened Hodgkin's awareness of "how materially life or reputation may be affected by the evidence which medical men are continually called upon to give, in our Courts of Justice."[35] This was another example of the influence of his experiences in the French capital. A chair for legal medicine had existed at the Paris medical school (École de Santé) since 1794, and since 1803, students had had to pass an examination in this subject.[36]

Even before the trial, Hodgkin had advocated the inclusion of legal medicine within the medical curriculum. It is a result of the general neglect of the study of pathological anatomy that "so large a portion of the accounts of inspections, whether made for judicial purposes or to gratify curiosity in rare and remarkable cases, are so extremely imperfect, that nearly all we can say of them is, that one is more vague than another."[37]

A few months after the trial, Hodgkin performed a postmortem on another case of lithotomy by Bransby Cooper. At the conclusion of his report, he says, "There was a clean and good cut through it [prostate] into the bladder . . . as the knife had been but once introduced."[38] Could he have been thinking of the Pollard case?

Anonymous Critic

During the brouhaha leading to the Cooper *v.* Wakley trial and
into 1829, Thomas Hodgkin was involved intermittently in his
own private war of words with an anonymous writer. This too
was chronicled in the medical press. Not *The Lancet* in this case,
but the *London Medical Gazette*. It is hard to imagine Thomas
Hodgkin guilty of unethical professional conduct, but that essentially is what the charge amounted to. Hodgkin, the civilized
intellectual, handled it in a civilized manner.

It seems that one of Hodgkin's publications, a lengthy article
dealing with the description and classification of the various kinds
of tumors, such as hydatids, cysts, malignant growths, and ul-
cers—subjects that were not very well understood in the early
nineteenth century—was sharply criticized for his terminology and
the distinctions that he drew.[39] The writer, who signed with a
pseudonym,[40] had registered an earlier complaint[41] in connection
with a report of a tumor dissection by Hodgkin.[42] The charge now
was that Hodgkin was unacquainted with the literature on the
nature and manner of growth of such tumors and that he may have
deliberately withheld appropriate acknowledgment of prior au-
thorship by someone else.[43] Hodgkin, quick to come to the defense
of others, preferred to pay no attention to the letters, but changed
his mind, as he explained in his own letter to the editor:

> I am so averse to enter into controversy, that I have felt strongly
> inclined to allow the letter inserted in the medical Gazette of the
> 25th ult. to pass unnoticed, as I did that which appeared in it in the
> autumn of last year; trusting that when my paper on certain adven-
> titious structures shall have been published entire in the transactions
> of the Medical and Chirurgical Society, the impartial judgment of
> my professional brethren will form my most satisfactory acquittal
> from the charges contained in the letters in question. Yet as months
> may elapse before this publication takes place, I am unwilling that
> my silence in the interim should offer an apparent confirmation to
> imputations as unjust as they are ungenerous.

He goes on to state that his views were derived solely from his
own personal observations and are original, and hence he owes no

acknowledgment for having "borrowed" them. "Trusting that I have already said enough to clear me in the eyes of my professional brethren from the insinuations of an anonymous critic, I hasten to conclude by subscribing myself, very respectfully, Thomas Hodgkin."[44]

Of course, this event was of no importance, but it shows the kind of bickering and sniping that went on within the medical ranks, in print and in public, and helped to fuel the public's distrust and low esteem of medical men (see chapter 12).

CHAPTER FOUR

The New Pathology

Lectures to the Working Class

In 1829, Hodgkin delivered a series of four lectures at the Spitalfields' Mechanics' Institution in London's East End. This institute and many others like it were the result of a widespread movement pioneered by George Birkbeck (1776–1841), a physician and Quaker, to make scientific and technical information available to the working class. The success and rapid growth of the movement, which originated in Glasgow in 1823, was related to the increasing need, owing to new inventions and technological developments of the Industrial Revolution, for skilled workers possessing the elements of scientific knowledge.[1] In addition, a well-trained work force meant more and better jobs, an improvement in living conditions, and less crime.

Hodgkin's lectures were designed to present "in an intelligible form, practical hints calculated to promote the healthful condition of the people."[2] Most of the working-class public were poorly informed about the causes of illness and ways and means of safeguarding their own health. Many physicians, Hodgkin among them, were aroused by the practices of quackery and the ineffectiveness of the great variety of popular nostrums. Hodgkin summarized the knowledge of the physiological functions of the body

and presented a detailed series of recommendations for the preservation of health. These lectures, published later in a book, were
patterned after a series known as the Working Man's Companion,
sponsored by the Society for the Diffusion of Useful Knowledge.
Covering a very wide range of subjects, Hodgkin emphasized
preventive care, the preservation of health, and the avoidance of
illness. He also managed to inject a few lessons in middle-class
morality.

"When I entered on the duties of my office of Physician to the
London Dispensary, I quickly perceived that to cure or to alleviate
actual sickness was not all that was necessary to be done. Whilst I
saw that it was far more important to confirm and preserve health,
I saw that there were many causes constantly operating to disturb,
ruin, and destroy it,"[3] Hodgkin said.

If a letter to his friend Dr. Samuel G. Morton of Philadelphia is
any indication, Hodgkin may have been motivated by the damaging effects of alcoholism. Hodgkin was disappointed in his efforts
and was not optimistic about the response from his working-class
audience.

> We have lately heard much of the extraordinary success which has
> attended your temperance societies. Hast thou taken an active part
> in any of them & what have been the means which you have found
> the most powerfully influential on the lower orders? I have almost
> ever since the time when I first became connected with a Dispensary
> in this city, been forcibly struck with many causes, besides that of
> intemperance in liquor, which act very injuriously on the health of
> the labouring classes & soon formed the design of giving a few very
> popular lectures on the means of promoting public health, in order
> to serve in some degree as a substitute for a medical police. . . . This
> design I have very recently put in execution, but from the combined
> influence of want of the requisite talent in the lecturer, & want of
> interest & zeal in the class for whom the lectures were designed, I
> apprehend that no sensible result will follow the step.[4]

In his first lecture, Hodgkin discussed the importance of fresh
air, light, habits of cleanliness, the virtues of bathing, adequate
clothing, and the influence of these factors on the function of
respiration and general health. He noted the harmful effects of

faulty clothing, especially the tight lacing of corsets. He stressed the harm arising from filth, crowding, bad sanitation, poor housing, and the importance of cleansing of streets.

The second lecture took up food, drink, and digestion. Hodgkin quoted an unidentified but widely-traveled gentleman: "The English cooking is the cooking of the savage, perfected. The French cooking is the cooking of corrupted man."[5] He also discussed the relative values of roasting, broiling, baking, boiling, stewing, and frying, and concluded that frying was the least satisfactory. For those with a tendency to apoplexy (high blood pressure) and those of a highly irritable, irascible, or choleric temperament, he recommended a vegetable diet. He discussed sources of drinking water (rain, snow, spring, river) and warned of the dangers of using stagnant water.

Hodgkin's observations on the pernicious effects of the habitual and excessive use of alcohol were, according to one reviewer of the published book of lectures, extremely interesting and of the greatest usefulness when considered in relation to the class of society to whom the lectures were addressed.[6] It should be noted, however, that Hodgkin was not a teetotaller. A majority of Friends became total abstainers in the course of the century and played an important part in the temperance movement. However, abstention was never compulsory and did not become universal. In the late '30s and '40s, Quakers were sharply divided over this issue. Some owned breweries or were wine merchants.[7]

In his third lecture, on the physiology of muscular motion, Hodgkin dealt with gymnastics and sports. He recommended athletic exercises but made a very important exception "to those which are likely to stir up angry and ferocious dispositions," such as "the barbarous prize-fights which disgrace this country. Their demoralizing effect is by no means confined to the parties actually engaged in these combats. . . . Perhaps, in many instances, the greatest evil is the effect produced upon the spectators."[8]

Hodgkin also provided a detailed account of various occupational hazards and their special relationships to health, including the influence of inactive or sedentary occupations. He argued for improvement of the working conditions and environment in factories, especially those experienced by milliners' and dressmakers' girls, and tailors. He also denounced chimney sweeping by children.[9] This hazardous occupation was associated with cancer of the scrotum in the classic description by Percival Pott (1714–1788), a surgeon, in 1775. It was the first example of a specific neoplasm related to a particular occupation. The House of Commons had passed a bill forbidding the employment of children for chimney sweeping, but the House of Lords rejected it repeatedly. The upper chamber of Parliament remained an impregnable citadel of conservatism, impervious to criticism and therefore unwilling to make concessions. The mildest measure of social reform faced extreme difficulty in the House of Lords if it threatened any vested interest—even one so low as that of a chimney sweep in his climbing boys. Attempts to improve the working conditions of this unpleasant occupation met with no success. These failures were symptomatic of the same difficulties encountered by other reform campaigns during Tory rule before 1832. The upper house always managed to convince itself that doing nothing was the best course of action.[10] Eventually an act was passed in 1840 making it illegal to employ climbing boys for sweeping chimneys and specifying fine or imprisonment for violation of this law.[11]

In the fourth lecture, Hodgkin's advice to the young produced this comment from a reviewer: The author "touches with great art and delicacy on the pernicious effects of disregard to the obligations of personal chastity, so prevalent among the young of all classes, and the manifold examples of incurable disease, irreparable misery, and premature death which may be traced directly or indirectly to this cause."[12]

Hodgkin also discussed the management of the aged and infirm, and the young in the various stages of their growth. He had suggestions for the education of females to enlighten their minds and become useful to themselves. In the Appendix, Hodgkin's "Hints to a Young Man, Coming to London" urged him to be virtuous and industrious, and careful in making friends, choosing companions, and spending money. As an example of the greatness achieved by virtue and industry, Hodgkin named Benjamin Franklin.[13]

Trades' Unions, Elections, and Tobacco

Hodgkin sharply criticized labor unions and denounced the use of tobacco. His comments on unions reveal the prejudices of a member of the upper middle class and a firm believer in free enterprise.

> Those who join themselves to a Union, do so, in all probability, without considering this important feature in its character. . . . They are no longer their own masters, or the servants of those from whom they receive their wages—a service which, be it remembered, is voluntary, and in which they are a party to the adjustment of the terms; but they are in reality the slaves to the heads of the Union, and may be made to suffer by their indiscretion and want of judgment, as well as by their absolute criminality. They are taxed by them, and drained of their past earnings, without having controul over the funds to which they contribute: they are restricted in the arrangements which they may desire to make for the employment of their exertions to support themselves and their families, and may therefore have their earnings suspended. . . . But the tyranny of the Unions is not confined, in its influence, to those who have had the imbecillity to become their voluntary subjects. Those operatives, who may have preferred to retain their independence, become the victims of its attacks.[14]

A reviewer commented on "the familiar and intelligible mode" in which the information was conveyed. He was certain that few would begin the book without finishing it, and that few would be satisfied with a single reading. Although addressed to one particular class in the community, everyone would find it in "their interest to study and apply the principles so ably laid down by the author."[15] Another reviewer, while acknowledging the "great deal of useful popular information," criticized the inclusion of "political hints."[16]

Politics and politicians being what they have always been, it was inevitable that Hodgkin would have something to say on that account. And so he stressed the importance of voting in elections and being an informed voter. "When the time of election arrives, commit yourselves to no party; but deliberately weigh the character and pretensions of the candidates, and form your opinion on the ground of past actions, rather than be influenced by fine speeches, fair promises, or any flattering offers for the advantage of your private or local interests."[17] Although there was no substitute for moral worth and integrity, that alone, cautioned Hodgkin, was not enough if the candidate was weak in judgment or lacked knowledge or other qualifications for the office. These must have been the "political hints" to which the *Medical Gazette*, in its very brief review, objected.

As for tobacco, which Hodgkin detested, his concerns for personal hygiene and public health led him to active participation in the British Anti-Tobacco Society. According to his niece, he had a very sensitive sense of smell, and she believed this may have been responsible for his attitude toward tobacco,[18] although Quakers generally opposed its use.

During the sixteenth and early seventeenth centuries, extravagant medicinal properties were attributed to tobacco, and it was taken internally or applied externally for numerous ailments. But it was more often used for pleasure than for health. Following the isolation of nicotine in 1828 and the demonstration of its poisonous qualities, tobacco gradually lost the favor of the medical profession, but it remained a popular folk medicine.

Hodgkin's denunciation of tobacco includes the following critical (but amusing) observations:

> I have said that smoking tends to encroach on the freedom and comfort of others. Smokers, in general, fall into this evil from culpable indifference, rather than maliciously; and would perhaps be disposed to deny the fact, that theirs is essentially a tyrannical practice. If the smoker kept the smoke to himself, this objection would be done away with; but the fact is, that for his own useless, if not culpable gratification, he inflicts the smoke of his tobacco and his smelling breath on all indiscriminately.[19]

There had long existed a considerable European literature on the rules of daily living. One of the earliest such guides to good health was the *Regimen Sanitatis* from Salerno. Written around 1260, in verse form, it gave advice on healthful living in a series of very sensible dietetic and hygienic maxims. The poem embodied the essential principles of a school that used dietary regulations and simple drugs as the basis of its treatment.

Hodgkin wasn't alone in his prescriptions for healthful living. Another book on the same subject was reviewed at the same time, "as both agree in the object kept in view by their authors, namely, the dissemination, in a popular shape, of that form and degree of medical knowledge which is adequate to the preservation of health."[20] Although not as wide-ranging, the book by Dr. Andrew Combe quickly went into a second edition and was subsequently republished in America with annotations.

During this period there also were numerous French treatises on hygiene dealing with individual and communal prevention of disease. The most widely read for many years was *Élémentaire Course* (1822) by Léon Rostan, whose teaching Hodgkin had attended at the Salpêtrière. Hygiene was a topic of public awareness. The distrust of and disappointment in the therapeutics of the day generated an interest in prevention.[21]

Hodgkin did not publish his lectures titled *The Means of Promoting and Preserving Health*, until 1835, when he was confined by a severe accident (not specified). He made frequent references to his illnesses. In this case he may have been sidelined with a broken leg, an experience he referred to in one of his lectures.[22] The book sold out; a second edition, with new material, appeared in 1841. The book was dedicated to his father and his two nephews, John Eliot Hodgkin and Thomas Hodgkin, Jun. It is recommended reading for anyone interested in the progress of public health and personal hygiene.

The Catalogue

Hodgkin's lectures on preventive health care were a nonhospital activity. His primary responsibility to Guy's Hospital was to organize and improve the Museum of Morbid Anatomy, which at the time of his arrival numbered fewer than five hundred specimens. After only four years of work, he published "A Catalogue of the Preparations. . ." with 3,205 entries of normal and pathological specimens, including over two hundred wax models and casts.

Characterizing his catalogue as an unfinished work in progress and inappropriate for dedication, Hodgkin acknowledged that a tribute was deserved by Benjamin Harrison, the founder of the museum, and he expressed "his respectful and grateful acknowledgments to that zealous and enlightened Gentleman" for his very efficient and liberal support for the museum. Hodgkin continued by noting Harrison's "sincere regard for the Officers of Guy's Hospital, by whom not only the benevolent views of the Founder, but the interests of Medical Science, are ably promoted;—and, likewise, of his cordial good wishes for the honourable advancement and well-earned prosperity of the Pupils attached to the School."[23]

Hodgkin's objective in building the museum's collection was to develop the science of pathology as the basis of scientific medicine. His catalogue was a very important publication. By describing the effects of diseases according to the different tissues of the body, Hodgkin was among the first to follow in the path of Marie François Xavier Bichat (1771–1802).

Anatomical teaching in Edinburgh and London during the first quarter of the nineteenth century was very rudimentary and included almost nothing of the detailed structure of the nerves and viscera. It "was a hap-hazard sort of study, fragmentary, at times minute and complex, at times coarse and contemptible. . . . Nobody seemed rightly to understand what descriptive anatomy meant; the general anatomy of man was unknown."[24] Only the effects of disease on the body's organs were considered. Bichat shifted attention from the organs to tissues. Tissues, not organs, were the important structural units of the body. Bichat did not use the microscope (neither did Laennec). Dissecting by hand with fine tools and physical and chemical reagents, Bichat founded a system of normal and pathological anatomy based on a detailed description of grossly visible structures which he called *tissues*. His painstaking analysis and classification of human tissues just before 1800 added a new dimension to systematic postmortem examinations and made possible a more discriminating examination of disease processes. However, real advances in this new medical specialty of *histology* had to await improvements in the design of the microscope, development of the Schleiden-Schwann cell theory, and tissue preparation and staining techniques.

In addition to his work as morbid anatomist, Hodgkin gave a lecture course on the pathological changes occurring in tissues. It followed his arrangement of specimens in the catalogue with emphasis on correlation of clinical with pathological study of disease. Hodgkin's perception of the importance of postmortem anatomical examination is clearly stated in his introductory lecture.

> We can only become properly initiated into our profession by personal acquaintance with disease, founded on our own patient investigation at the bed-side of the sick, and by a diligent examination of the effects of disease, as brought to light by cadaveric inspection. The practice of examining the dead, for the purpose of ascertaining the seat and effect of disease, is absolutely necessary to complete those ideas which it is impossible for the best verbal descriptions perfectly to convey: and it is also necessary, as the means of detecting that which yet remains to be either wholly discovered or more fully elucidated.[25]

Medical practice as a means to riches was not on Hodgkin's agenda; his fees were small, and he treated his friends and the poor without charge. But he knew that income was important to many students. Early in his career he told the pupils of Guy's that they were being misled by their teachers if they "estimate the value of a study by the extent of pecuniary advantage they may expect to derive from it, rather than its scientific tendency."[26] He repeated this theme in his first lecture when he said that the study of morbid anatomy wouldn't make them rich but would enhance their ability to treat patients successfully.

> To those who may place the *summum bonum* of medical practice in converting the largest quantity of physic into gold, morbid anatomy must, I am aware, be an object of disgust, rather than of attraction; but those who are aspiring to become the worthy members of a profession which has for its object the restoration of health to our suffering fellow-creatures . . . must see, that morbid anatomy . . .

constitutes a study the most essential to their art. . . . I can see no palliative for the presumption of those who profess to administer the remedy, even without the knowledge of the disease. Amongst such a class, however, must those be placed, who are regardless of morbid anatomy.[27]

Hodgkin emphasized the dependence of anatomical pathology on knowledge of the normal structure of the tissues. Although postmortem examinations in rare and unusual cases were more interesting, he said, it was no less important for students and those in practice to witness examinations in ordinary cases. Only from this practice could the student learn to distinguish the almost endless varieties of morbidity that parts and organs assume and to avoid confusing healthy, diseased, and cadaveric appearances (also see chapter 3, note 9). Even the active practitioner needed to keep up his knowledge in order to correct, confirm, and improve his diagnosis. Although many who had neglected this practice had nevertheless benefited their patients and their own fortunes, such success, cautioned Hodgkin, resembled that of a "fortunate gamester."[28]

The study of healthy tissues is an integral part of modern medical education, but in Hodgkin's time many physicians believed that only diseased or damaged tissues need be examined to gain an understanding of the clinical signs of disease and that there was no advantage to pursuing the pathologic changes responsible for the specific symptoms. But Hodgkin offered greater insight: "The changes which disease effects in our different structures and organs, may be regarded as experiments in animal chemistry, performed for us by nature herself."[29]

Comparing the knowledge of the past with that of the present, Hodgkin expressed his preference for the modern works of science. It was not from any lack of respect and admiration for the great men of the past, he said, but

as a falling body comes to the ground with a force compounded of all the forces which have acted upon it in every part of its descent; so one generation, if it perform its duty to that which succeeds it, will transmit, with increase, the knowledge which it derived from that which went before it. The posthumous influence of great names has too often been productive of evil, by exciting idolatry, rather than imitation.[30]

He cautioned his audience against believing that everything valuable in science had been done in their own country and that foreigners had become eminent only by plagiarism.

> The temple of Science is erected on a neutral territory, to which no age, and no nation, can lay a peculiar claim . . . we should feel that we are above national jealousy, and be actuated only by a generous emulation; that, while the fabric is happily advancing by the united labours of many nations, our proportion of the work may be such, as to prove that we are not degenerate.[31]

Lectures on Morbid Anatomy

Hodgkin's lectures were probably the first systematic course in morbid anatomy in Great Britain. The lectures, begun in the 1827 session at Guy's Hospital, were later published in two volumes titled *Lectures on the Morbid Anatomy of the Serous and Mucous Membranes*. Previously, in England, this subject was not a separate course but had been taught incidentally in lectures on special anatomy, surgery, and medicine. His *Lectures* represented the first attempt to treat morbid anatomy as a separate subject for teaching purposes. These two volumes of 943 pages are one of his major works and a testament to many years of scientific hard work. Despite the mention of "serous and mucous membranes" in the title, there are so many lectures on other subjects that the word is a general treatise on morbid anatomy, with many of the author's own observations.

Volume one of the *Lectures* was published in 1836 and was dedicated to his close friend William Stroud (1789–1858), whom Hodgkin met while both were studying medicine at Edinburgh.[32] There was a four-year interval between its publication and that of volume two, part one. This was due to a "serious interruption to my health" quickly followed by his "unexpected separation" from Guy's Hospital in 1837. The latter event deprived him of access to many of the specimens that he had collected and needed for filling in the gaps left in the *Lectures.* He eventually obtained specimens from other sources, and in place of the preparations in the museum, he was able to refer to other collections that he was allowed to examine. This continuing difficulty in obtaining specimens probably kept him from his intention of publishing a third volume (part two of volume two).[33]

Both volumes were reviewed in 1843 and were described as unassuming and full of instruction, with a great deal more than would be expected from their simple title. They were strongly recommended—not for simple casual perusal, but as a work of reference that belonged on the desk of every scientific medical practitioner.[34] Volume one was also published in an abridged American (Philadelphia) edition in 1838 and translated for a German (Leipzig) edition (1843–44). However, the book did not have a wide circulation because of the long delay between the first and second volume and because the work was never completed. Another factor was the popularity of Matthew Baillie's (1761–1823) book on morbid anatomy first published in 1793 (314 pages) and the supplementary atlas of 73 copperplate engravings, noteworthy for their accuracy, and the first of its kind.[35] Hodgkin's book had no illustrations.

Almost entirely descriptive, well-written, clear, and concise, Baillie's book became an immediate and extraordinary success. A second edition appeared in 1797 with foreign-language translations and American editions. Baillie's was the first text of pathology in the English language and the first study in any language to treat pathology as an independent science. Whereas previous works on morbid anatomy were essentially accounts of diseases and dissections, Baillie arranged the various organs of the body in a systematic order of natural structure and described the different morbid conditions of each. The observations and illustrations are mostly of specimens in the medical museum of his uncle, Dr. William Hunter (1718–1783), and of those obtained from his own teaching and hospital practice. Both William Hunter and his younger brother, John Hunter (1728–1793), were lifelong collectors of specimens for teaching purposes. Their museums of morbid anatomy became a standard for the medical world.

The popularity of Baillie's treatise was indicative of the growing acceptance of the anatomical viewpoint advocated by Giovanni Battista Morgagni (1682–1771). Modern pathology began in 1761 with the publication of Morgagni's *De Sedibus*,[36] which Hodgkin described as "one of the most remarkable and valuable monuments of our art."[37] Baillie called it "stupendous." Although organized according to the parts of the body—from head to foot—it is not a modern text of pathology, but a clinical work with anatomic explanations of disease symptoms. This five-volume treatise marked the real beginning of the modern understanding of disease through anatomy because it introduced the anatomic concept of the organ as the seat of disease. For the first time, a detailed analysis of postmortem findings was correlated with clinical symptoms and case histories and explained in terms of localized pathologic anatomy. Baillie wrote his book to overcome the faults that kept medical practitioners from consulting or buying Morgagni's book, namely, disease descriptions with excessive generalization, irrelevant discussion, and great length and expense.[38] Most doctors of Morgagni's time and for years afterward did not think in terms of a localized pathologic process or of specific diseases. General medical thought continued to be shaped and dominated by ephemeral and speculative systems of pathology.

The New Pathology

Pathology—the explanation of morbid appearances—necessarily changes with the advance of knowledge and techniques, but accurate descriptions of pathological changes never become obsolete or useless. One reason offered by Hodgkin for the publication of his own book was that Baillie's descriptions of morbid appearances lacked "that minuteness of detail which is essential to a work destined to teach pathological anatomy."[39] Hodgkin attributed this to the condensed form of the book and the comparatively little attention paid to general anatomy, rather than to any deficiency in Baillie's abilities or opportunities. Unfortunately, despite the groundwork laid by Morgagni, Bichat, Laennec, Baillie, and others, as of 1836 the majority of the medical profession was ignorant of morbid anatomy and did not care to know anything about it.[40]

But why was pathologic anatomy so long in the developing? First of all, normal anatomy had to be understood better in order to distinguish the changes causing death from changes occurring after death. Accurate information about anatomy and physiology was not acquired until late in the development of the healing arts.

The idea that disease processes were localized rather than diffused throughout the body's fluids or nervous system was long ignored or opposed by most practicing physicians. They did not believe that the ultimate explanation for pathologic symptoms was to be found in the observation of gross anatomy, because they did not think that anatomists could distinguish subtle underlying conditions. Nevertheless, anatomists continued to find lesions in particular organs at autopsies and were beginning to suspect that disease processes were really localized.

Surgeons had for several centuries matched their clinical findings with structural changes in the body. They could not operate without visualizing the anatomical change responsible for the disorder. Even physicians who questioned their own need for a knowledge of anatomy believed it was necessary for the surgeons. By coming around to the surgeon's approach to illness, the physician's perception of disease, as well as his relationship to patients and his methods of diagnosis, began a profound but slow transformation. The physician's subsequent adoption of a manual and instrumental approach to diagnosis helped to close the long-standing gap between the two disciplines.

The emphasis on morbid anatomy and the correlation of autopsy findings with clinical disease before death was the great medical advance of the early nineteenth century. This major breakthrough in medical science began with the French clinical school and made its way to other lands. During this period the medical profession got rid of the confusion of theories and systems and concentrated instead on clinical examination supplemented by postmortem study.[41] The profession used to think of "disease" as an entity—a state of being. Gradually, now it began to think of *diseases* and to classify them.

CHAPTER FIVE

Hodgkin's Disease

The Disease

Richard Bright, Thomas Addison, and Thomas Hodgkin worked and taught at Guy's Hospital in London at the same time. Their discoveries resulted in eponymic fame for each of them.

Diseases named for Richard Bright and Thomas Addison are characterized by the correlation of physiological processes during life with anatomical conditions found after death. Bright correlated tissue edema and albuminuria during life with diseased kidneys found after death. Addison observed the peculiar pigmentation or "bronzing" of the skin, pallor, and lack of energy during life and noted their association with the diseased adrenal glands (then called suprarenal capsules) found after death. The correlation made by Hodgkin, however, was made entirely after death. He demonstrated, besides conditions in which lymph nodes or spleen could be diseased separately, a condition in which, after the patient had died with enormously enlarged "absorbent glands" visible in various regions (often the neck), postmortem examination disclosed more enlarged nodes and a greatly enlarged spleen without signs of inflammation. What made Hodgkin's account especially interesting is that he suggested this relationship between spleen and lymph nodes from their gross anatomical appearance at a time when little was known about the functions or cellular structures of either. It is ironic that Hodgkin's disease today is recognized by microscopy of histologic features.

Until the late nineteenth century, few diseases had been given a clear, comprehensive, and definite description by the investigators who first brought them to attention. Hodgkin's disease is no exception. Hodgkin recognized and described a disease entity at a time when pathology was in its infancy and when microscopic examination of tissues was unknown. Although the animal cell had not yet been discovered, vegetable cells had been observed with the microscope by Robert Hooke (1635–1703), and the idea of cellular structure was not entirely unknown. However, the significance of the cell as a fundamental biological building unit was yet to be recognized, and there was no awareness that tissues were aggregates of cells similar in form and function. That the eponym has persisted and that pathologists today are clear as to the nature of the lesion so described indicates that Hodgkin had selected his cases with remarkable perception.

Hodgkin's place in medical history rests on his postmortem description of seven patients characterized by simultaneous enlargement of the spleen (splenomegaly) and lymph nodes (lymphadenopathy). In his examples he did not clearly distinguish between morbid conditions. As subsequently determined, of the seven cases in his report there were probably three, at the most four, cases of the condition that bears his name. His paper "On Some Morbid Appearances of the Absorbent Glands and Spleen" was read on January 10 and 24, 1832, before the Medical and Chirurgical Society and was published in its *Transactions*. Inasmuch as Hodgkin was not then a member of the society, his paper was read by the secretary, Robert Lee, M.D., F.R.S.

There were only eight members and twenty-two visitors present at the meeting of January 10. The names of the visitors at the meeting of January 24, when the remainder of the paper was read, are not recorded.[1] Hodgkin became a fellow of the society in 1840 and a member of the council in 1842–43. He was appointed as one of the Referees of Papers for 1854–55 and elected vice-president for the sessions of 1862–63 and 1863–64.

As Hodgkin states with characteristic modesty in the opening paragraph, he merely recorded a series of findings that must have been observed by every morbid anatomist and directed attention to them. Very likely, he had no idea that possibly in four of his cases he dealt with a peculiar rare disease. "The morbid alterations of structure which I am about to describe are probably familiar to many practical morbid anatomists, since they can scarcely have failed to have fallen under their observation in the course of cadaveric inspection. They have not, as far as I am aware, been made the subject of special attention, on which account I am induced to bring forward a few cases in which they have occurred to myself."[2]

He saw that this enlargement of the lymph nodes was a pathological condition that required separation from cancer, tuberculosis, and other already recognized morbid states. According to Hodgkin, ". . . this enlargement of the glands [lymph nodes] appeared to be a primitive [primary] affection of those bodies, rather than the result of an irritation propagated to them [via lymph vessels] from some ulcerated surface or other inflamed texture."[3] In his two volumes of *Lectures on The Morbid Anatomy of the Serous and Mucous Membranes,* Hodgkin described the "peculiar enlargement of the lymphatic glands" and the need to distinguish it from "the simplest form of scrofulous [tuberculous] enlargement of these glands" to which it "bears so strong a resemblance . . . that it is not always easy to draw the line of demarcation." The enlarged lymph nodes were "quite distinct from malignant disease."[4]

Concepts of cancer or neoplasia were not well developed in 1832, and the terminology was not used in the same sense as it is today. However, Hodgkin was convinced this was a primary disease and not some secondary response to an obscure inflammatory process, because there was no association with pain, heat, or other ordinary symptoms of inflammation.

Hodgkin regretted that most patients did not seek admission to the hospital until the disease had reached an advanced and hopeless stage. He also acknowledged, "A pathological paper may perhaps be thought of little value if unaccompanied by suggestions designed to assist in the treatment, either curative or palliative"; but on this account, he confessed that he had "nothing to offer."[5]

Hodgkin correctly believed that this disease must have been observed by others. After the paper was read, a note from a friend quoted an excerpt from *De Viscerum Structura* published in 1666 by Marcello Malpighi (1628–1694) describing a diseased spleen and disseminated enlargement of lymph nodes in a young girl that resembled this condition. Hodgkin included the Latin excerpt as a footnote in the published report. Considering Hodgkin's scrupulous approach to accuracy and scholarship, it would have been unthinkable for him to neglect to mention that his findings were not original.

There had been other reports of a generalized disease of the lymph nodes distinguished from disseminated tuberculosis or carcinoma. Morgagni described an atypical case of disseminated tuberculosis with large nodes, closely resembling this disease. This and other cases were puzzling because they did not show the usual picture of carcinoma. This was indicated again in 1828 by David Craigie (1793–1866) in *Elements of General and Pathological Anatomy*. Describing the malignant growth of enlarged lymphatic nodes, he pointed out that their anatomical characteristics did not justify the term cancer. It is doubtful whether Craigie recognized the distinctive nature of this disease process, and he made no reference to splenic enlargement.

A second and shorter part of Hodgkin's paper was devoted to seven cases of apparent infarct of the spleen. It began, "Having been led to notice some morbid appearances in the spleen connected with the glandular disease of which I have been speaking, I take the opportunity, before quitting this organ, to advert to another morbid appearance presented by it."[6] But he attached no importance in relation to disease because he thought it was the result of external injury. He noticed it because it had not previously been described.

The paper was published without illustrations, although watercolor paintings of the morbid anatomy of the seventh case borrowed for the occasion were on display while his paper was being read. Hodgkin had come across this seventh case while examining the exceptional collection of pathological drawings made by his friend Sir Robert Carswell (1793–1857), professor of morbid anatomy at University College Hospital in London.

He particularly noticed the color drawing of a greatly enlarged spleen loaded with large round light-colored tan tubercles. He immediately recognized it as a fine example of the morbid condition he had been describing, and his suspicions were confirmed by another of Carswell's fine drawings of the greatly enlarged glands of the neck and axilla of the same patient, shown here in black and white (Fig. 2).[7]

Carswell, an accomplished artist, saw this case at the Hôpital St. Louis in Paris in April 1828 and described it in his notebook. He painted five plates in watercolor to illustrate its pathological features. First published in 1898, these are the earliest known color pictures of the morbid anatomy of Hodgkin's disease.[8] The originals were rediscovered at University College Hospital, London, and three of them were printed again.[9]

Hodgkin did not follow up this association between enlarged lymph nodes and spleen with a critical analysis and published nothing more that might clarify or expand on it. The paper attracted no attention at the time and might have passed into oblivion. But Hodgkin was fortunate. Six years later, in 1838, Richard Bright saw the article. From his extraordinary skills of observation he recognized Hodgkin's cases as belonging to a malignant disease unknown until then.

In a review of diseases of the spleen, Bright wrote: "There is another form of disease, which appears to be of a malignant character, though it varies from the more usual forms of malignant disease; and which has been particularly pointed out by Dr. Hodgkin, as connected with extensive disease of the absorbent glands, more particularly those which accompany the bloodvessels." Bright reprinted two of Hodgkin's cases, one of which had been Bright's patient. This reference and discussion without a journal citation by Bright was buried in the middle of a very long article[10] and did not bring Hodgkin's discovery into the open.

In 1856, Dr. Samuel Wilks (1824–1911) (Fig. 3), who held the same positions formerly held by Hodgkin, curator of the museum and lecturer in pathology in the medical school, was preparing a paper that included a section entitled "Cases of a Peculiar Enlargement of the Lymphatic Glands frequently associated with Disease of the Spleen."[11] He presented ten cases, four from the museum of

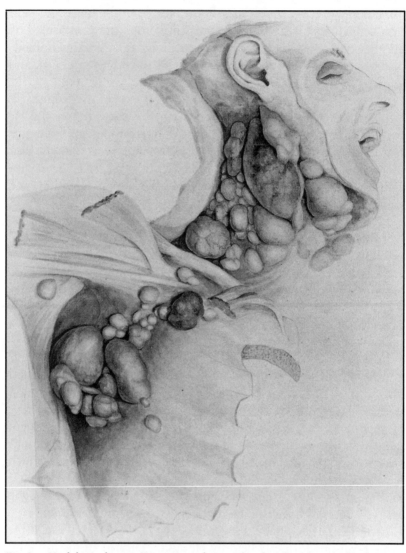

Fig. 2. Hodgkin's disease. Dissection of cervical and axillary lymph glands. Drawing by Robert Carswell. (Courtesy of The Library, University College London.)

Fig. 3. *Sir Samuel Wilks. (Courtesy of the Royal College of Physicians of London.)*

the hospital, which, as it turned out, were part of Hodgkin's original report but were not listed under Hodgkin's name in the museum's catalogue. Not knowing about Hodgkin's paper at the time and apparently not having read about this morbid condition in Hodgkin's two volumes of published lectures, Wilks was clearly under the impression that his own observations were original and "not yet . . . recognised as a peculiar condition, or deserving of a special name."[12] He had no doubt that examples of it were always turning up. Before publishing his report, Wilks came across Bright's reference. When he found Hodgkin's paper, he realized that he had rediscovered the disease which Hodgkin had first described in 1832. At the end of his paper, Wilks acknowledged Hodgkin's priority, adding, "Had I known this earlier I should have altered many expressions which I have used with respect to any originality of observation on my part. . . . It is only to be lamented that Dr. Hodgkin did not affix a distinct name to the disease, for by so doing I should not have experienced so long an ignorance . . . of a very remarkable class of cases."[13]

Neither Bright's comments nor Wilks's report gained any more general recognition for Hodgkin than the original paper. Wilks described another case in 1859 and again cited Hodgkin, adding that it was not always recognized as a peculiar disease and therefore required some distinctive name.[14] Determined that credit for the original observations go to Hodgkin, Wilks wrote a third article in 1865 and left no room for doubt in his title: "Cases of Enlargement of the Lymphatic Glands and Spleen, (or, Hodgkin's Disease,) with Remarks." Opening with a reference to his previous paper, he adds: "Although my own observations were at the time original, I had been forestalled by Dr. Hodgkin, who was the first, as far as I am aware, to call attention to this peculiar form of disease."[15]

Apparently, Wilks recognized even more clearly than did Hodgkin that among conditions affecting the lymphatic nodes and spleen was a distinct pathologic entity. The disease appeared also "to have a likeness to tubercle on the one hand, and cancer on the other. It is, however, as much a disease *sui generis* as any other, and deserves a description of its own. Dr. Hodgkin may himself have been the cause of some confusion, since out of his six cases probably four only are examples of the disease; one is doubtful, and the other is evidently a syphilitic affection."[16]

Wilks concluded that "the disease was of a remarkably uniform character, and quite deserving of a special name; all the cases which I have described having come under my own eye, and resembling in all particulars the first four, which Dr. Hodgkin so many years ago brought under the notice of the profession."[17] This paper by Wilks finally established Hodgkin's disease as a distinct, definite, clinical entity.

In 1877, making no mention of Bright, Wilks took credit for finding Hodgkin's paper, introducing it to the profession, and naming the disease, thus avoiding being "fathered with the discovery."[18] He repeated this account in 1909,[19] forty-four years after he first used the eponym, and has been acknowledged by subsequent writers for his unusual professional generosity in wishing to perpetuate the name of his predecessor at Guy's Hospital, rather than naming the disease for himself or letting Hodgkin's contribution slip into obscurity. He really had no choice, for he had already mentioned Hodgkin's priority in his earlier publication when both Hodgkin and Bright were still alive and undoubtedly read the *Guy's Hospital Reports.*[20] A biographer critical of Hodgkin's work and writing style suggested that the discovery "might just as well, or even better, have been called Wilks' disease, for he gives many more cases and a more perfect description."[21]

Although Wilks gave a more accurate and complete clinical and pathological description than his predecessor, not all of his additional cases were acceptable as Hodgkin's disease. This is not surprising because Wilks also made no microscopic observations. It is remarkable that a pathological disorder originally identified by gross appearances eventually came to be recognized by histologic characteristics. What makes it even more ironic is that Hodgkin was an experienced microscopist as a result of his work with J. J. Lister, whose work with achromatic lenses corrected for spherical aberration in compound microscopes (see chapter 3).

Soon after Wilks's 1865 paper, and apparently unaware of his or Hodgkin's publications on the subject, others began to publish acceptable cases of Hodgkin's disease, as well as to introduce a proliferation of synonyms in the literature. Various writers, impressed by one particular feature of the disease or a point of resemblance to other conditions, confused what little knowledge there was by describing similar cases under different names. Probably no other clinical disorder has had so many different names. The most widely used and accepted of some fifty other names are lymphadenoma, lymphogranuloma, lymphoblastoma, lymphomatosis granulomatosa, and malignant granuloma.[22]

The eponymic designation "Hodgkin's Krankheit" appeared in the German literature as early as 1866.[23] In the same paper the name "multiple lymphadenoma" was also first used for this disease. The term "Hodgkin's disease" was used frequently and interchangeably with lymphadenoma by W. S. Greenfield in 1878.[24] By the turn of the century, the name had taken hold, and Hodgkin's disease was definable as characterized by gradual and progressive but painless enlargement of the lymph nodes and spleen, beginning usually in the cervical region and spreading throughout the lymphoid tissue of the body, forming nodular growths in the internal organs and leading to anemia, cachexia, and death.

Much of the confusion about Hodgkin's disease resulted because the concept of this disease was formulated before microscopic examination was common. During the 1830s, although considerable correction in distortion had been achieved, resolving power was low and the microscope was still a very imperfect instrument. Techniques to prepare specimens for microscopic examination were rudimentary. Plant material, with its relatively rigid walls, lent itself to freehand sectioning, but with softer material, bits of tissue were cut off with scissors, then teased out in a smear or a crush in a drop of water, salt solution, or sugar solution, and examined. Use of water as the medium for examining fresh specimens induced cellular changes that complicated any interpretation. In 1842 Jacob Mathias Schleiden (see chapter 11, note 10) suggested that a heavy razor be used to cut sections, the tissues being held between thumb and forefinger. Modern routine procedures, such as fixation, embedding, accurate sectioning, and differential staining, were not then known. Simple coloring agents, such as iodine, were sometimes used, but the material examined was generally unfixed and unstained. Observing fresh material in spread or squash preparations without differential staining through microscope lenses of low resolution was not easy. The delicate cell membrane, the similar refractive indices of cell wall and cell contents, the granular appearance, and the large variety of cell forms all contributed to difficulties in recognition and identification.[25]

As late as the mid-nineteenth century, the microscope was not generally used by morbid anatomists and histological technique did not exist. Like many innovations, compound microscopes with the achromatic objectives of J. J. Lister did not immediately enter into the mainstream of scientific use.[26] Hodgkin did use the microscope and referred to it in later work (see chapter 11). If he used it in 1832 and did not mention it, it is probably because his observations were inconclusive or indefinite.

The difficulty of cutting sufficiently thin sections was the major obstacle to microscopic examination of solid tissues. This problem was not solved during Hodgkin's years at Guy's, and the understanding of Hodgkin's disease as a pathologic entity awaited appreciation of its abnormal cell structure.

It was the book *Cellular Pathology* by Rudolf Virchow, published in 1858, that removed the inherent limitations of the study of gross materials only. Going beyond Morgagni and Bichat, Virchow considered the cell—which in aggregate comprised the tissue—as the seat of disease. He demonstrated conclusively that disruption of cellular function or, in other words, an abnormal condition, was the basis of disease, just as orderly operation of the cell was the foundation of health. He showed that diseased cells were modifications of normal types. He disproved the notion that cells rose spontaneously from an undifferentiated matrix, and he formulated the doctrine that growth of new cells implied already existing cells.

Not until the cell was recognized as the unit and basis of all structural changes could pathology be an independent science. Diseases were no longer considered merely as groups of symptoms but were defined by structural changes found at autopsy and histologic examination of diseased tissues with the microscope.

When cells were discovered, the great variety of cellular morphology created problems in recognition and identification. These were aggravated by cellular changes caused by aqueous and other media used for examining fresh specimens. During the second half of the nineteenth century, ideas about the nature, scope, and proper terminology of Hodgkin's disease slowly changed. The distinctively large multinucleated cells pathognomonic of Hodgkin's disease as we know it today were described by many observers as the staining techniques improved.

Beginning in the 1860s, "many investigators, in Germany, France, and England (possibly elsewhere as well) . . . recognized and described one, sometimes two, varieties of large cells in patients with a disease characterized especially by enlargement of the lymph nodes and spleen in the absence of a leukemic blood picture."[27] Considerable controversy has surrounded credit for description of the pathognomonic cell of Hodgkin's disease. One name that always comes up is W. S. Greenfield[28] who, in a lengthy paper read before the Pathological Society of London in 1878, clearly recognized giant multinucleated cells and contributed the first drawing of such cells seen under the microscope in a lymph node. The drawing was not very good.

In fact, using modern criteria for these peculiar giant cells, "*none* of the earlier descriptions" or illustrations is fully distinctive or acceptable.[29] Definitive and thorough descriptions of the histopathology of Hodgkin's disease were first given by Sternberg in 1898[30] and by Reed in 1902.[31] Carl Sternberg's illustrations are not equal to his description, and it was Dorothy Reed (1874–1964) who first clearly illustrated the distinctive multinucleated giant cells peculiar to the proliferated tissue growth in Hodgkin's disease. For these reasons the names of Sternberg and Reed are jointly associated with these cells.

Perhaps the greater credit should go to Dorothy Reed, whose accurate description and superior illustrations of these peculiar and typical cells made them recognizable by histopathologists as an integral part of the disease and thereby established Hodgkin's disease on a sound histologic basis. The Dorothy Reed cell, or Reed-Sternberg cell, is a *sine qua non* for histopathologic diagnosis of Hodgkin's disease when it occurs in the proper context of altered tissues.[32] Henry Kaplan has suggested that the time has finally come to call them simply "Hodgkin's giant cells."[33]

Thus, by the start of the twentieth century, the principal clinical features and the chief histologic characteristics had been elucidated and Hodgkin's disease was a definite and clearly recognizable identity. Pathologists were now able to distinguish between Hodgkin's disease and other lymphoproliferative disorders that resembled it in one respect or another. Although comparable large cells may be found in lymph nodes in other diseases, decisive distinction is usually established by precise definition of the characteristic giant cells and by other histopathologic features. By custom, the binucleated mirror-image form of the Dorothy Reed cell is considered diagnostic. This cell, as well as less frequently encountered variants with three or more nuclei, is an end-stage nonproliferating cell. However, the question remained whether Hodgkin's disease was a malignant neoplasm. Not until the 1970s did cytogenetic studies demonstrate that these giant cells satisfy two fundamental attributes of neoplastic cells, i.e., aneuploidy (having more or less than the normal diploid number of chromosomes) and clonal derivation (cells descended in culture from a single cell).[34]

The etiology of Hodgkin's disease was still puzzling. Was it basically an infectious or a neoplastic process? The concept of microorganisms was known by the early 1700s, but that microorganisms caused diseases could not be proved until microscopes were improved and laboratory techniques became available. Long before the identification of cells, clinicians described diseases with considerable accuracy, but their explanation of pathogenesis in terms of humors, vital principles, tension, irritability, and mechanical forces was confusing and inadequate.[35] During the last quarter of the nineteenth century, French and German bacteriologists identified specific organisms in many serious infections. The discovery that bacteria could cause disease created a "microbiological revolution" and led some to seek bacterial causes for all diseases. Hodgkin's disease was no exception.

The relationship between Hodgkin's disease and tuberculosis remained controversial for some time. Investigators wondered whether Hodgkin's disease was an atypical form of tuberculosis or whether tuberculosis found at autopsy in such patients was a superimposed infection. Many of Sternberg's patients with Hodgkin's disease also had active tuberculosis, and he believed for many years that he was dealing with a peculiar form of tuberculosis.[36] As for Dorothy Reed, although histological changes resembled those of a malignant growth, she did not regard Hodgkin's disease as a malignant neoplasm but as a chronic inflammatory process.[37]

Serious efforts were made well into the twentieth century to identify an infective agent as the cause of Hodgkin's disease. One writer was convinced and wrote: "The relentless extension of the disease from gland to gland and from region to region demonstrates very clearly its infectious character, its microbic origin."[38] Although this was a minority view, it had a rational basis and some merit. Evidence for an infectious agent in the pathogenesis of Hodgkin's disease continues to be put forth.[39] But no satisfactory explanation of the cause or development of this disease has yet been offered.

In 1926 Dr. Herbert Fox, a pathologist from the University of Pennsylvania, Philadelphia, obtained tissues from three of the six cases studied by Hodgkin and prepared microscopic sections. Specimens had been kept in alcohol for almost eighty-two years and in formalin for an additional fifteen years. It was evident to Fox from an analysis of the clinical description in Hodgkin's paper that the seven cases were by no means all the same,[40] and he proposed diagnoses of tuberculosis (case 1), syphilis (case 3), and systemic lymphomatosis (case 5). Hodgkin knew that case 1 had tuberculosis and that case 3 had syphilis and had been treated with mercury. But he must have been sufficiently impressed with the enlarged glands and spleen to include them with the other examples.

Using modern histologic criteria, Fox confirmed the diagnosis of Hodgkin's disease in two of the three tissue specimens he examined (cases 2 and 4). The third specimen (case 6) he considered to be an example of acute leukemia or lymphosarcoma. He also accepted the seventh case, provided by Carswell, as an example of Hodgkin's disease on the basis of the extensive clinical history and autopsy report. Although he had given only a gross description, it now seemed certain that Hodgkin had observed and recorded a new disease. After ninety-seven years in preservative solutions, his specimens retained their identity and justified the separation he made.

New microscopic sections of the involved lymph nodes from the original case 2 were prepared again, in 1968, at the Gordon Museum of Guy's Hospital. Binucleate giant cells with huge nucleoli and other cytologic features were readily recognizable as Reed-Sternberg cells even after fixation for 140 years.[41]

Hodgkin recognized the first of a complex of leukemias and lymphomas. Subsequently, beginning in 1845 with the first adequate description of leukemia by Rudolf Virchow,[42] other neoplasms of the lymph nodes were described during the next hundred years. This progress depended on techniques of hardening tissues, imbedding in rigid materials, cutting very thin sections, and using stains that sharply contrast varying cellular elements. The necessary advances took place during the final quarter of the nineteenth century.[43]

Despite the ponderous nomenclature and confusion of classification, Hodgkin's disease has remained a clinical and pathological entity. Pathologists still face problems of classification, staging, and differential diagnosis of Hodgkin's disease and differentiation from the various non-Hodgkin's lymphomas. Pitfalls exist in both classification and interpretation of the various stages in Hodgkin's disease, each with its diagnostic clinical manifestations and spectrum of progressive histologic changes in spleen, lymph nodes, liver, and bone marrow. The histopathology of some reactive and neoplastic lesions of lymph nodes can simulate Hodgkin's disease as well as non-Hodgkin's lymphomas. These lesions include infectious mononucleosis, toxoplasmic lymphadenitis, drug-induced hyperplasia, metastatic neoplasms, viral hyperplasias, and allergic reactions.

Greenfield had described the spreading of the pathological changes to adjacent glands and then "to more distant ones, usually by contiguity."[44] Reed described the progression of the disease to "the neighboring glands, apparently following the normal lymphatic distribution."[45] Even Hodgkin had recognized that the disease spread in some orderly sequence, for he observed that the gross changes in the spleen occurred after those in the lymph nodes. Despite these statements, most clinicians and pathologists, dealing with late-stage cases and confused by non-Hodgkin's lymphoma, continued to consider its spread haphazard and unpredictable. Only recently has this view been proved wrong.[46]

Convincing evidence for the concept of the contiguous spread of Hodgkin's disease was firmly established by Kaplan and his associates at Stanford University. Using lymphangiography (x-ray visualization with contrast medium) to map out the distribution of lymphatic involvement, they showed that Hodgkin's disease spreads in an orderly and direct manner, from one lymph node chain to the next adjacent lymphatic area. It does not spread, as was once believed, in an unpredictable fashion that would make it widely disseminated and inevitably incurable and fatal. Application of localized supervoltage radiation to diseased areas of lymph nodes and, as a precaution, to proximal nodal chains, in conjunction with chemotherapy has been very successful in treating patients with this once inexorably fatal disease.[47]

Hodgkin's disease has been likened to pernicious anemia and diabetes mellitus, as diseases in which major therapeutic and prognostic advances came long before the fundamental nature, etiology, or pathogenesis had been explained.[48]

The unfolding of Addison's disease bears a striking parallel to the explanation of Hodgkin's disease. Not all of Addison's original cases published in 1855 were true cases of this disease, nor were microscopic studies done, nor did Addison follow up on his discovery. The clinical condition was named "maladie d'Addison" by Armand Trousseau (1801–1867), a French clinician.[49]

Retroversion of the Aortic Valves

Hodgkin's original description of lymphadenomatosis was only one of several important contributions that he made to science and medicine. Thomas Hodgkin was not generally recognized for his description of aortic insufficiency five years before Dominic Corrigan (1802–1880) published his celebrated presentation of the same subject.[50] Hodgkin described the postmortem appearances of aortic regurgitation or, as he put it, "retroversion of the valves of the aorta," to the Hunterian Society on February 21, 1827. His paper was not published until two years later, after he reported on additional observations to the society.[51] At that time both presentations were published in the form of two letters. Hodgkin disclaimed any originality for his observation, as he begins in Quaker style:

> My dear Friend, [C. Aston Key]
> Thou wilt probably recollect having pointed out to me, a few months ago, a particular state of the valves of the aorta, which, by admitting of their falling back towards the ventricle, unfits them for the performance of their function.
>
> To avoid circumlocution, and in defect of a better name, I shall designate by the term retroversion of the valves that diseased state which allows of their dropping in towards the ventricle, instead of effectually closing the vessel against a reflux of the blood.[52]

Hodgkin visually observed the strong pulsations of the carotids and noted the double "sawing sounds" and the peculiar thrill (vibration) felt in the pulse. It is extraordinary that his papers attracted no attention, for they gave an excellent, although incomplete, account of the clinical symptoms and the postmortem appearances of aortic regurgitation. Quite possibly the form in which his findings were presented—two parts of a letter published two years after the initial presentation—minimized their impact and kept him from the recognition he deserved.

As often happens when something "new" is described in medicine, there appeared claims of priority as old cases were rediscovered. Descriptions in the literature, unnoticed for more than a century, were unearthed. The best of the very early descriptions and illustrations of the characteristic valvular lesions were from 1705 by William Cowper (1666–1709) and 1715 by Raymond Vieussens (1641–1715)[53] who studied medicine at Montpellier. They clearly described the valvular lesions of aortic insufficiency. However, and this probably is what makes the difference between a discovery and just another case history, neither account led others to look for and report similar cases. Hodgkin was not aware that a specimen with this valvular defect was in Hunter's Museum until it was mentioned during his first presentation by a member of the audience that this was referred to by Baillie's *Morbid Anatomy*.

Hodgkin included this information in a footnote to the published paper.

Hodgkin's paper was also rediscovered by Samuel Wilks, and he once again proposed crediting Hodgkin with priority. However, Hodgkin had made no claim of priority to the observation that the aortic valves can be retroverted. And although he had written the first proper, though incomplete, clinical and pathological account of aortic valvular disease,[54] the profession at that time was not ready to understand it as described by Hodgkin.

Corrigan was not aware of Hodgkin's paper when he fully described the clinical findings and recorded in detail the pathologic appearances of the valves. He also gave a detailed and correct explanation for the altered heart sounds and other signs so clearly associated with the disease. During the years following publication of his paper, aortic regurgitation became known as the "maladie de Corrigan," a name first used by Armand Trousseau in the early 1860s. By the time Wilks reported on his discovery of Hodgkin's paper in 1871,[55] and again in 1878,[56] Corrigan's association with aortic regurgitation was well established. This time the pathologic entity was named for someone else.

CHAPTER SIX

Slavery and Colonization

Contagion, Miasma, and Cholera, 1832

The year 1832, in which Hodgkin described the syndrome that bears his name, was the year of the Reform Bill, giving representation to counties or towns that had sent no members to Parliament. This change was an admission that the wealth of Britain was a product of the towns rather than the countryside. Parliament also made the resurrectionists obsolete by passing the Anatomy Act, which provided for the medical profession's need for educational dissection material. In 1832, cholera struck Great Britain with epidemic force, leaving more than 32,000 dead and threatening public health and safety. Hodgkin expressed his views on combating this scourge. He emphasized the distribution of relief services and charity and the importance of work for the poor. Hodgkin always associated squalor and disease with the lack of employment.

Squalor, filth, and overcrowding, legacies from the Middle Ages, were made worse by the Industrial Revolution. Few bothered about clean air, pure food, and water. The British government provided the poorer classes with almost no protection against the unwholesomeness of their surroundings. The acceptance of laissez-faire principles inhibited governmental regulation of health and industry during the eighteenth century. The laws were inadequate or nonexistent in regard to unfit housing, hazardous industries, adulteration of food and drugs, sale of poisons, animal wastes, and medical licensure.[1]

However, concern for public health existed both in Parliament and in the popular press, where the plight of the poor and unfortunate was vividly described. A by-product of the Industrial Revolution was a consciousness that the environment could be controlled. Illness and poor health were no longer regarded as inescapable burdens of life on earth. Such fatalistic attitudes became unfashionable in an age of progress. The dominant idea of progress led to the belief that man could overcome disease even as he could control the other forces of nature.[2]

The progress of public hygiene and welfare in England from 1800 to 1830 lagged, however. The dominant conservatives regarded all appeals for social reform as subversive, possibly a backlash against the excesses of the French Revolution, and the war with France drew attention from domestic affairs. Concern about disease reappeared with the fear of cholera. Then the interest of government, the public, and the medical profession in public hygiene suddenly increased, along with demands for investigations, clean-ups, and general sanitary reform.[3]

The mystery of its origin, its sudden onset and high rate of mortality, and its ominous spread across continents and overseas made cholera the most feared of all diseases. Endemic in India for centuries, cholera penetrated the Russian land mass in 1829 and moved along the river systems into central and western Europe during 1830–31. Then it moved with merchants, pilgrims, and armies on the march.[4] The epidemic in central Europe excited much interest and fear in England, where until then cholera had been regarded as an Asiatic disease and was as much a mystery as plague had been five centuries earlier.[5]

Since there was ignorance of the transmission of cholera and the means of its prevention, intense controversies among physicians, press,[6] and public were frequent. Physicians recommended quarantine and isolation and stressed the need for sanitary improvements. This simultaneous advocacy of sanitation and quarantine revealed confusion concerning the etiology and transmission of cholera. A frequently expressed opinion was that Asiatic cholera was an aggravated form of common cholera, a reassuring and flexible term descriptive of dysenteries and diarrheas. This opinion implied an indigenous origin, not imported and not contagious. Common cholera sounded less threatening than a new and spectacularly deadly disease. Adding to the confusion was the lack of distinction made by physicians among the terms contagious, infectious, and epidemic.[7]

Quarantine helped sometimes, but direct contact was not necessary to contract cholera, which moved erratically and might skip over whole areas without contact. As the epidemic of 1832 spread, the dominant contagionist view was replaced by anticontagionist views, invoking the agencies of noxious airs, evil humors, or "miasmas" emanating from within the earth or released into the air by mud, sewage, filth, or other decaying and putrid animal or vegetable matter. These concepts called for sanitary measures.[8]

Quarantine and contagion were discredited for social reasons by a society dependent on freedom of movement for trade and commerce. Contagionism was a doctrine requiring government controls and quarantines. To merchants and industrialists this meant disruption of trade and economic loss. Anticontagionists were welcomed as reformers and liberals opposed to government interference. Furthermore, anticontagionist doctrines permitted the churches to regard cholera with religious fatalism as an unpredictable visitation rather than a contagion against which one could take precautions.[9]

Since the concept of disease specificity was not generally accepted, social and moral factors were assigned a role in the cause of cholera. Alcoholism was often blamed, along with neglect of religion and prayer. If not directly imposed by Divine Providence as a form of well-deserved punishment for individual sin or collective national guilt, the onset of cholera was undoubtedly the result of a weakened physical constitution due to transgressions of God's physical, moral, and spiritual laws. This explanation made pain and death legitimate and more bearable. The idea of predisposition to cholera reinforced a weak point in the atmospheric theory by explaining how some came down with the disease while others, who breathed the same air, did not.[10]

Medical knowledge being what it was, prayer was probably the most effective preventative available to the middle classes. The calming influence of religion had a social as well as a medical effect, for it gave many the courage they needed to carry on with their responsibilities in the face of sudden death. The full range of religious responses to the cholera was evoked by an official day of fasting, prayer, and humiliation, observed on March 21, 1832. The working-class radical press derided the whole affair, pointing out that asking the poor to fast was superfluous.[11]

A germ theory of disease had no practical application at the time because it could not explain cholera among people who had no contact with the sick or the failure of many people in intimate contact with the sick to develop the disease. Pathogenic micro-organisms were not known, and their transmission in food and water, and by human, insect, and animal carriers, was not understood.[12] Scientific standards of 1832 provided no guidance in the planned and orderly accumulation of scientific knowledge. Effective research was hampered by professional rivalries, the inadequate resolving power of available microscopes, the absence of solid nutrient media on which pathogenic bacteria could be grown, and lack of statistical techniques to analyze the epidemiological data. Consequently, when cholera returned in 1848–49, it struck in the same places and found the same state of unpreparedness.[13]

Cholera arrived in Great Britain for the first time in October 1831 by ship from Hamburg. It broke out in Sunderland, a seaport near Newcastle. Moving like a contagion, it reached London in February 1832. Its connection with unsanitary living conditions and polluted water supplies meant that most of its victims would be poor. The epidemic exposed urban misery and sharply emphasized the inequality between the social classes. Living in filthy crowded rooms on inadequate diets, the poor suffered the severest cholera attacks.[14]

The epidemic struck England during the final stages of the Reform Bill of 1832 and intensified social tensions. The middle class saw cholera as a poor man's disease and did not panic and run. They stayed in their offices and counting houses. The ruling class saw cholera as a threat to the social and economic well-being of the community and reacted sharply with public health restrictions and cholera hospitals, which the poor saw as a far more serious threat to their legitimate rights than that posed by the cholera.[15]

No one wanted cholera hospitals in his part of town, and no one wanted to go into the hospitals. The poor man feared that he would be murdered there and dissected by the doctors. Rapid burial of cholera victims added to this unrest by interfering with traditional funeral and mourning customs. In many places the public health measures of the authorities and physicians met with violent resistance and rioting.[16]

Many suspected that the alarm over cholera was a government hoax created by the antireformers to produce counterrevolutionary excitement and to distract attention from reform agitation and the wretched living conditions of the working poor. Radical leaders attacked the government's special "cholera powers" as invasions of private rights and a thinly disguised assault on reform. The cholera itself was challenged as an imaginary and bogus humbug that the ruling class foisted on the people and a scheme to make money for the medical practitioners and druggists.[17]

Such was the state of affairs and intellectual climate when, soon after cholera reached England, Thomas Hodgkin published a pamphlet in which he offered his own suggestions for dealing with the epidemic, "as one who has long taken a lively interest in the means of promoting the public health."[18] The pamphlet has an interesting title page (Fig. 4). The long title is printed in nine separate lines of type set in six different sizes and two styles. And, oddly for a publication directed to the "Public in General," it is prefaced by a Greek quotation from Homer's *Iliad* and one in Latin from Cicero's *De Republica*.

Although not committing himself as a contagionist or a noncontagionist, Hodgkin admitted the merit of the conflicting evidence supporting both points of view. Nevertheless, he strongly objected to quarantine measures or any plan of isolating cholera patients into special wards or hospitals set aside specifically for that disease. He feared that grouping of patients might aggravate or spread the disease to other patients and their attendants because "the protective principle which many individuals possess must be greatly impaired, and the extension of the disease necessarily promoted."

HINTS

RELATING TO THE

CHOLERA IN LONDON:

ADDRESSED TO THE

PUBLIC IN GENERAL,

BUT ESPECIALLY TO THOSE WHO POSSESS INFLUENCE IN THEIR

Parishes an' Districts.

A LETTER TO A MEMBER OF THE BOARD OF HEALTH.

BY

THOMAS HODGKIN, M.D.

Εἰ μιν θάνατόν γι φύγωμιν.—Hom. *Iliad.*

" Neque enim hac nos patria lege genuit aut educavit ut nulla quasi alimenta expectaret a nobis, ac tantummodo nostris ipsa commodis serviens totum perfugium otio nostro suppeditaret."—Cic. *de Republ.*

LONDON:

HIGHLEY, FLEET STREET; J. & A. ARCH, CORNHILL;
HARVEY & DARTON, GRACECHURCH STREET.

1832.

Fig. 4.   *Title page of Hodgkin's pamphlet on cholera.*

He mentioned that fever patients at Guy's Hospital were systematically dispersed throughout the different wards without any fear of ill effects.[19]

Hodgkin knew that communicable diseases, such as smallpox and scarlet fever, required additional factors besides the contagious principle to become widespread or particularly severe and fatal. Since this combination did not come together in all places simultaneously, epidemics were usually progressive. But for this circumstance, cholera might long since have broken out in the London area, because people either recently recovered or who had been in close contact with sufferers were constantly arriving from infected foreign areas. Therefore, he questioned the effectiveness of quarantine after the appearance of symptoms, especially the quarantine of ships carrying coal and other vital supplies whose delay could add to the miseries of the poor, particularly in winter, because of the scarcity and cost of fuel. Quarantine, warned Hodgkin, would produce hardships for manufacture and commerce. Yet he urged the prohibition of large crowds of people at fairs and on other such occasions where many people came together "for idle and useless, if not for dissolute and corrupting, purposes."[20]

These views of Hodgkin placed him in the large center of moderates, the so-called contingent-contagionists, who tried to compromise on the evidence before them. They believed that cholera was contagious under some circumstances, as one of many possible factors could cause the disease. But, by condemning quarantines, they showed their true convictions and came down on the side of the anticontagionists. Hodgkin's concern for the poor did not alter his upper-middle-class economic philosophy and liberal political loyalty. Most physicians at the time were liberal and bourgeois and favored anticontagionism. As a result, they, as did Hodgkin, emphasized the commercial and maritime damages brought about by contagionist-motivated quarantines.[21]

The connection between bad living conditions and cholera was too obvious and too dramatic to be overlooked. To prevent or mitigate the spread of cholera, Hodgkin believed it necessary to change the living conditions of the poor. The affected individuals were poorly clothed, undernourished, and subject to lengthy periods of exposure to bad weather. He attributed the privations of food, clothing, and fuel of these wretched inhabitants to lack of employment. Hodgkin pointed out that food and clothing were as essential as cleanliness in counteracting the spread of the epidemic. He recommended the cleaning of the streets, as well as the interior and exterior of houses in the districts inhabited by the poor, where he saw starvation, sickness, and accumulated filth.[22]

Hodgkin was convinced that the misery, distress, and ill-health of the poor, as well as their wretched housing and dependence on charitable institutions, were all due to their being unemployed. Aware that many cases could be relieved only by charity and that experienced beggars were able to divert to themselves a disproportionate amount of the money intended for the most needy and deserving, Hodgkin devised a plan for distributing relief more efficiently. He wanted a full-time staff to make inquiry and follow-up visits to the urgent cases. He also suggested that relief articles, such as food, coal, and clothing, be distributed by vouchers to be redeemed in designated shops "at extremely low prices, rather than be actually given away. The relief so afforded" not only would reach more people and last longer, but would also "tend to ensure the proper application of the smallest sums which the poor may be able to raise." The "visitors" could also give advice about cleanliness and household management, practices too often neglected by the poor through carelessness rather than necessity.[23]

The scientist in Hodgkin also recognized the opportunity presented by the cholera epidemic. He emphasized the importance of careful observation and accurate recording of all available data relating to the disease, information that could improve existing knowledge of the laws that appear to regulate widespreading epidemics in general. He hoped to discover the "distinction between those circumstances which promote exemption from the disease, and those which favour predisposition to its attacks—a knowledge which can scarcely fail to be of useful application, should we be again threatened by a like awful visitation."[24]

The working class, said Hodgkin, was a valuable national resource whose unemployed status was a financial loss to the community and the nation. Since money given as charity left nothing behind in exchange, greater good would result if the charitable money was used to provide employment to those capable of working. "Why should not Charity, as well as Avarice and Ambition, turn over her capital, instead of being limited in her exertions, and restricted to unproductive consumption?" Hodgkin's work projects for the unemployed were the construction of railroads and pedestrian walkways.[25]

The cholera epidemic of 1832 exposed the organizational tensions and structural weaknesses of the medical profession. The squabbling and indecision within its ranks, endless debates over etiology and treatment, and hospital rules that blocked admission to cholera patients, all combined to reduce the status of the medical man in the eyes of the public.

Cholera became a political subject for newspapers, journals, Parliament, the churches, professional and other societies, charitable institutions, radicals and agitators, and the various agencies of local government.[26] Simple statistical data collected during the second outbreak in 1848–49 provided evidence that the disease could be transmitted by drinking water contaminated with the excreted waste of cholera victims. John Snow (1813–1858) made this connection in 1849[27] before the work on microorganisms and infection by Louis Pasteur and Joseph Lister, and before the cholera bacillus (*Vibrio cholerae*) had been discovered by Filippo Pacini (1812–1883) in 1854.[28] Snow reasoned that cholera was propagated by a *specific* living water-borne, self-reproducing cell or germ. Many were interested, few were convinced. The College of Physicians dismissed the idea that certain microscopic bodies caused cholera.[29]

During the third epidemic, in 1853–54, Snow surveyed more than 300,000 individuals living in districts supplied with water by two companies. He demonstrated convincingly that cholera was transmitted in the drinking water supplied from the Thames River in the vicinity of the sewer outlets.

A revolution in the understanding of disease followed the development of bacteriology later in the century and rapidly shifted the emphasis in public health from statistical analysis to biological investigation. Cleanliness was still a protection against disease in general, but now that many diseases were known to be caused by specific agents, it was necessary to know the cause and mode of transmission.

Slavery and Colonization

The drama of the cholera epidemic of 1832 was overshadowed by a turning point in British history. The Reform Act of 1832 gave evangelicals, nonconformists, and radicals a more effective voice than before. High on the agenda of the new Parliament were the issues of abolition of slavery and emancipation of slaves. Britain, once the leading carrier of slaves, had undergone a crisis of conscience, and many Britons believed that the suppression of slavery and the slave trade was connected with their own moral redemption.[30]

There was no slavery as such in the British Isles, but a practical problem concerned slave servants brought into the country by planters from the West Indies. The issue was settled in 1772 by the legal decision that an escaping slave could not forcibly be removed from England to what would be certain vengeance in the colony. As a result of this ruling, a slave became a free man the moment he set foot in the British Isles. Slavery in the overseas colonies was unaffected, but the decision automatically freed more than 10,000 Africans in London and the provinces, who, as flamboyantly dressed and heavily powdered flunkies at stately homes and town mansions, were status symbols. They found themselves destitute because few households wanted them as wage earners. Many concerned people realized that since a free black man would become no more than a second-class citizen in a white society, colonization in a free government of their own was the only solution. Colonization appealed to those who respected private property because it did not mean the abolition of slavery. Many plans were proposed for the resettlement of liberated slaves in Nova Scotia and Sierra Leone on the west coast of Africa. It was a humanitarian response to a newly created problem of color. Guilt would be relieved, responsibility discharged, and a social inconvenience disposed of.[31]

There was much controversy between advocates of abolition and supporters of colonization in Africa. Although most Englishmen sympathized with American abolitionists' opposition to colonization, Hodgkin supported colonization and the new nation of Liberia. It was seen as a haven for freed slaves from the strong, widespread prejudice in America and as the best means of ending slavery itself. However, colonization required voluntary emigration of freed slaves, and the abolitionists advocated immediate and universal emancipation. As a result, Hodgkin and the colonization societies appeared to be in conflict with the Anti-Slavery Society while agreeing with its ultimate objective of the extinction of slavery. This was an impassioned issue. The abolitionists charged the American Colonization Society with perpetuating slavery by aiding emigration of freed slaves, thereby depriving them of their rights as native-born citizens.

In 1832 Hodgkin, who was a vice-president of the Pennsylvania Colonization Society, wrote the first of three pamphlets answering the objections and misrepresentations made against the American Colonization Society. The pamphlet, originally written as a letter, was refused publication by the Anti-Slavery Society and so Hodgkin printed it privately. He warned that "general, immediate, and unconditional emancipation would be an act of cruelty, rather than kindness, to the Blacks" and would present them

> with a gift which would be far from a blessing to them. They have been so long accustomed to consider labour and slavery as synonymous, that it is extremely difficult to obtain any thing like regular labour from an emancipated Black, whilst remaining in our colonies, and surrounded by his brethren in a state of slavery. It is essential that the slave, in his progress towards freedom, should be taught that exertion and liberty are not incompatible with each other: he will then become a more useful member of society as a freeman than as a slave; and his former owner will find that his purchased and voluntary exertions are far more productive than those which he had been accustomed to extort from him by any species of coercion.[32]

Hodgkin suggested a more gradual procedure, whereby the slave is allowed to buy back his freedom in the way a debtor pays back with a suitable period of labor to his creditor, in the manner of an indentured servant.

Hodgkin compared the prejudice in the United States against people of color, whether slave or free, with an example from English history. "There seems to be a strong tendency in man to hate those whom he has injured." He explains that "our forefathers, the common ancestors of ourselves and of the Americans, entertained a stronger prejudice against the Jews than the Americans at present do against the Blacks; and that having enriched themselves by their wealth, they either killed or banished them."[33]

Child Labor

Hodgkin's interest in oppressed peoples was not limited to the overseas territories. At home he was involved in the fight against a subtle form of slavery and abuse—child labor, with its many odious parallels to the overseas variety. The excesses of the factory system, spawned by the Industrial Revolution, fell harshly on the thousands of children employed in the cotton, silk, worsted, and flax mills throughout Great Britain. In the latter part of the eighteenth century, pauper children were practically sold into slavery as indentured workers to factory owners and worked for sixteen hours a day, frequently with irons around their ankles. They slept in filthy beds in nearby barracks in relays and were in other ways mistreated and exploited.[34]

In 1832 a group of concerned citizens formed a Society for the Improvement of the Condition of Factory Children to serve as a rallying point for all who had at heart the interests of the young persons. As chairman pro tem of its committee, Thomas Hodgkin was the signator of a single sheet[35] (undated, but issued in 1832) soliciting funds from the public in support of this cause, as well as the public's cooperation by launching numerous and urgent petitions in favor of a bill newly introduced in Parliament. The bill would prohibit children under nine years of age from working in a factory and would limit older children to ten hours of actual labor daily.

An earlier bill, stalled by repeated hearings in committee, died when Parliament was dissolved. The factory owners opposed the legislation and tried to wear out the friends of the children with expense and delay by calling for additional hearings, hoping thereby for the public to cool or be distracted by other issues. They would then introduce such modifications into the bill that would make it nearly or completely ineffective.

The appeal to the public cited the early age at which these young people, mostly females, were sent to work, many under eight years of age—the duration of their work, for twelve, fourteen, and even fifteen hours a day, with only half an hour for meals, besides occasionally working the whole night—the heated and corrupt atmosphere in which they were confined for long periods—and the promiscuous association of the sexes, which combined to make their occupation very injurious to their health, destructive to their morals, and in many cases, fatal to their lives.

The society was short-lived and achieved little. Even though William Allen was its chairman, this was not mentioned in the three volumes of his official biography. In general, Quakers played no prominent part in the movement to limit factory hours for children. Except for Thomas Hodgkin and a few others, wherever Quakers did appear in the controversy, they were indifferent or almost always in opposition. Even those in Parliament were hostile to attempts to limit the hours of factory children. Their attitude was fairly representative of Quakers. When the ten-hour bill finally passed in 1847, some Quaker factory owners tried to subvert its intentions by means of a shift system. This hostility to factory reform did not mean insincerity or hypocrisy by the Quakers in their humanitarian efforts. People with noble motives absorbed the ideals and assumptions prevailing within the social class and the period in which they lived. Freedom was uppermost among these ideals, and they did not understand that it was absurd to apply this ideal to the relationship between factory owner and employee.[36] Even reformers are usually aware of only a few of the many abuses of the social structure in which they find themselves and wish to improve.

With the new balance of power, Parliament passed the Emancipation Act of 1833, which freed the slaves in the British West Indies—to take effect the following year. The slaveholders were compensated with £20 million, less than half the value of the confiscated property. The financial settlement was a compromise between sentiment and equity. The approximately 800,000 slaves, the backbone of the economy of the West Indies, were not immediately and unconditionally set free. They had to pass through a transitional period of apprenticeship to accustom themselves, un-

der appropriate restraints, to the responsibilities of their new
status. The apprenticeship system, which had the approval of many
philanthropists, in practice differed little from slavery. Reports of
abuses led Parliament to discontinue this interim program. Finally,
on August 1, 1838, all slaves in the British West Indies were set
free. Later, similar steps were taken in other British possessions.[37]

In 1833 Hodgkin published a second article on the advantages
of colonization and the successes of the American Colonization
Society. The sixty-three-page pamphlet (Fig. 5) sold for one shilling
and leveled some revealing criticism against William Lloyd Garrison (1805–1879), the editor of the Boston-based *Liberator*. This
antislavery weekly newspaper advocated immediate emancipation
and opposed African colonization.

Hodgkin charged that Garrison was waging a vitriolic campaign
of distortion, misinformation, and out-of-context quotations
against the American Colonization Society. Garrison claimed that
the society was organized in the interests of slavery and that, in
offering itself as a practical remedy for that system, it was guilty
of deception. In refuting the unjust charges, Hodgkin summarized
the objectives of the American Colonization Society as follows: the
elimination of slavery indirectly by voluntary liberation; the suppression of the African slave trade by the establishment of civilized
settlements of free American blacks along the west coast of Africa;
to benefit Africa by the introduction of civilization and Christianity.[38] He pointed to the contradiction in the free states of America,
where the free colored people suffered from the most unjustifiable
prejudices and were subjected to scorn and contempt. In Africa
the black man became a member of a community in which he was
free and equal. Relocation of liberated slaves to northern free
states did not improve their condition, because only the most
menial and unproductive work was available to them, if even that.
Hodgkin compared this migration to the North to the large influx
of the Irish into England that had flooded the labor market.[39]

Hodgkin pointed to the success of the American Colonization
Society's projects in Liberia and urged British involvement in a
similar enterprise to establish new markets for the sake of British
prosperity and nationalism. British presence and influence on the
west coast of Africa would allow Britain to participate in the

AN

INQUIRY

INTO

THE MERITS

OF THE

AMERICAN COLONIZATION SOCIETY:

AND

A REPLY TO THE CHARGES BROUGHT AGAINST IT.

BRITISH AFRICAN COLONIZATION SOCIETY.

THOMAS HODGKIN, M.D.

Cupio me esse clementem.—Cic.

LONDON:

J. & A. ARCH, CORNHILL;

HARVEY & DARTON, GRACECHURCH STREET;

EDMUND FRY, HOUNDSDITCH; AND S. HIGHLEY, 32, FLEET STREET.

R. Watts, Printer, Crown Court, Temple Bar.

1833.

Price, One Shilling.

Fig. 5.   *Title page of Hodgkin's pamphlet on the American Colonization Society.*

benefits from colonization before inroads were made by other European powers. British-sponsored colonies, said Hodgkin, could be settled by freed blacks from America and the West Indies and eventually joined by the local natives to become new trading partners for Britain's products. Eventually, they would obtain Britain's protection while retaining self-government on the American model.[40]

Hodgkin was a capitalist. He thought of business, trade, and profits. Emancipation was one thing, colonization was another. To Hodgkin and those in the evangelical movements, there was nothing wrong with colonialism. This imperialist vision was entirely acceptable and morally desirable because it served humanitarian ends. The natives in the overseas British territories would benefit from British moral authority and legal justice. Their ignorance and paganism would be overcome by teaching "the simpler peoples the benefits of Steam, Free Trade and Revealed Religion."[41]

The plan for the new colony originated with Hodgkin's good friend and Quaker philanthropist Elliott Cresson (1796–1854) of Philadelphia, whom he had met in London in July 1825. Cresson had come again to England in 1831 seeking financial support for the American Colonization Society and its projects in Liberia. Finding some sentiment for colonization on the part of other distinguished Englishmen, he organized a British African Colonization Society as a counterpart to the American-based organization, to establish a colony of American blacks at Cape Mount north of Liberia. In soliciting financial contributions, Hodgkin offered the prospect of participation in the formation of a new state. The cost would be ten guineas per settler. Those donating £100 before the land was appropriated and went up in price could give their name to a parish or hamlet.[42]

The British African Colonization Society faced the same opposition from the Anti-Slavery Society as did the American Colonization Society. Hodgkin countered that "the energetic language of the Liberator" had not freed one slave but created opposition against Garrison because he was suspected of stirring up the blacks, who constituted a large majority of his subscribers.[43]

Cresson's efforts were also hampered, and he was subjected to unfounded personal attacks and abusive language by the opponents of the Colonization Society. He had come at an inopportune time coincident with the completion of the campaign to end slavery in the British Empire and was emphatically rejected by British abolitionists. They had been convinced by Garrison that colonization was not a genuine antislavery program, but a scheme to export unwanted blacks.[44] Consequently, they regarded colonization as proslavery and viewed Hodgkin and his organization with hostility and suspicion.[45] Garrison proposed a public debate between himself and Cresson. Cresson agreed, but his supporters, fearing that such an occasion was more likely to arouse painful feelings than to elicit the truth, suggested a private conference. Garrison refused, offering no explanation.[46]

Hodgkin was loyal to the American Colonization Society. He corresponded with its leaders, entertained them in London, and defended them from malicious falsehoods by abolitionists in England and the United States. In 1834 he wrote a third pamphlet, repeating much of the information about the British settlement plans.[47] He included a letter from a Quaker spokesman in North Carolina who related the activities of the society and some new instances of Garrison's literary harangues. Hodgkin defended and documented the progress being made in Liberia and pointed to the failure of Sierra Leone (first settled in 1787 by freed slaves shipped from England), which had met with more difficulties, experienced more crime, and achieved less success than the American colony.[48] Hodgkin suggested that to promote British honor and interests, the planners of the new colony should cooperate with the Americans in Liberia and follow their example.[49] The British African Colonization Society was a short-lived organization, from 1834 to 1835, and its plan for a colony was never realized.

CHAPTER SEVEN

Poor Laws

Poor Law Relief

One of the first programs undertaken by the new Whig government was a reform of the poor laws in 1834.[1] Thomas Hodgkin's efforts to improve the quality of medical relief to the poor and his association with the medical officers providing these services under the poor law are not mentioned in his obituaries and have been generally overlooked. However, his pamphlet on the procedures of selection of poor law medical officers provides a valuable contemporary record of the inefficiencies of the system.[2]

Prior to 1834, relief services to the poor were administered by 15,000 separate and autonomous parishes, varying widely in size, population, financial resources, and criteria by which assistance was granted. The system of relief dated from the reign of Queen Elizabeth I. The Tudor monarchy was concerned not with the settled, able-bodied, dependent poor, temporarily out of work due to a bad winter or a seasonal economic depression, but with the roving vagabonds and beggars who posed a threat to civil order. By providing work-relief, the Elizabethan poor law of 1601 aimed to keep the poor at their place of origin and to discourage them from vagrancy. This law required each parish to relieve the aged and helpless, to raise unprotected children and teach them a trade, and to provide work for the able-bodied unemployed through a tax on all households. It was administered by unpaid local officials who dispensed food or money and supervised the parish poorhouse (almshouse).[3]

By the latter part of the eighteenth century, a mobile work force was needed for the growing industrial society, and by 1832, a new type of able-bodied poor had evolved. These were the inadequately paid laborers whose wages were supplemented by payments of relief when earnings fell below a standard of subsistence based on the price of bread and the size of the laborer's family. This allowance blurred the distinction between wages and relief and led laborers to expect parish relief when temporarily out of work.[4]

The commissioners planning the new poor law claimed that workers lost incentive when subsistence no longer depended on labor and made no effort to save money. They became, in the moral judgments of government planners, idle, indolent, ignorant, lazy, dishonest, fraudulent, worthless, dissolute, and degraded. Poverty, they maintained, was the fault of the poor and had remained unchecked through the overindulgence and laxity of the government. The commissioners hoped to end pauperism, i.e., reliance on charity. They believed that poverty, as distinct from pauperism, was inevitable and not the proper object of poor relief. Relief was intended only for the indigent—those unable to work or earn enough for their subsistence.[5]

Legal relief for the poor was seen as an incitement to idleness and an obstacle to self-help. The new law intended to draw a distinction between the pauper and the poor to save the working poor from the dependency that brought with it the vices and degradation of character that, more than material impoverishment, typified pauperism. To this end, the relief offered to an able-bodied pauper was made significantly inferior to the purchasing power of a laborer at the lowest end of the salary scale and would be available only in the workhouse (i.e., poorhouse)[6]—a regulated institution in which people of working age were put to work. The threat of confinement in the workhouse[7] was intended as an added deterrence to seeking relief and an incentive for the able-bodied to return to the work force.

Poor Law Medical Officers

Medical relief was not specifically provided by the old poor laws, but parochial authorities readily allowed medical aid for the sick and infirm without inquiring into the circumstances. By 1834, about half of the parishes in England had a medical officer. Because there was no understanding of the relationship between poverty and disease, neither the commissioners' report nor the subsequent law took special note of medical needs and assumed that home medical aid to the old and infirm, the orphan and the widow, would continue as before. Here too, the poor law commissioners were determined not to allow medical relief to be better in quality or quantity for the able-bodied pauper than the wage earner could buy on his own. Otherwise, relief would be seen as a reward for indolence and an inducement to the working poor to neglect the health insurance plans of sick clubs and friendly societies and to fall into a cycle of idleness and vice and end up as paupers on relief.

Edwin Chadwick (1800–1890), who was largely responsible for writing the new poor law, wanted to strengthen social discipline, cut back on the distribution of wealth to the nonworking population, and enlarge the national economy by forcing the poor to work in it.[8] Eventually, when Chadwick initiated the public health reform movement, it was from the awareness that sickness due to insanitary surroundings was a major cause of poor law expense. He understood the relationship between insanitary environment (housing, external sanitation, drainage) and excessive sickness and realized that it would be cheaper in the long run to provide money to remove the basic causes of disease than to spend without any limit for the relief of individual cases of illness. Public health projects were designed for group prevention and became a problem of statistics and engineering rather than of medicine, which Chadwick knew was of limited value in halting the transmission of communicable diseases.[9]

The way it was set up, the poor law was administered locally by a Board of Guardians. No one was legally entitled to any kind of relief who had any property or any means, or was not in a state of absolute destitution and in danger of perishing from want if relief was withheld.[10] An additional obstacle in obtaining relief, besides the parish guardians, was the Relieving Officer, a nonmedical intermediary between patient and doctor. These laymen decided whether relief was justified. They were guided more by a commitment to fiscal economy than by the humanitarian instincts and medical judgment of the patient's needs.[11]

This denial of independent medical judgment indicated the low regard in which the general practitioner, even if certified as apothecary and surgeon, was held by the public. In many areas the doctor was considered little better than a tradesman and below the local magistrates. It was a reflection of attitudes toward private practice, where social background and manners determined the choice of physician and the extent of confidence in his medical ability. It might as well be social criteria, considering the questionable value of much of medical treatment and the difficulty of judging its quality.[12]

The rigid specifications of relief entitlement produced an unfortunate by-product. The "respectable" poor would not apply for aid because of the disgrace and social stigma attached to pauperism. Thus, they were without a doctor's care, or they had to resort to inferior treatment by a quack, a druggist, or an inferior practitioner, many of them employed for the sake of economy; or, it was inadequate treatment from good doctors because of the insufficient payment.[13] By contrast, the voluntary hospital, supported by charity, provided decidedly better medical services to the *deserving* (working) poor without requiring a legal status as a pauper.

Before 1834, parish authorities employed a local medical man to treat the poor and agreed to pay him a lump sum annually irrespective of the number of patients he treated and out of which he supplied all drugs and equipment. They usually employed the man who would accept the lowest fee, without much regard for his qualifications. Medical men went along with this unfair advantage because of the competition and the fear of losing the appointment (considered to be a sideline), which would be detrimental to private practice. This system was continued after 1834, and although hiring for the lowest fee was abolished in 1842, evasion was widespread. Positions were advertised at rates so low that only a struggling or inexperienced doctor, or one who wished to eliminate competition, would accept it.[14]

This state of affairs led Hodgkin to write a pamphlet criticizing his colleagues for neglecting the medical care of the poor. He rejected the plan of "farming out" parish medical appointments to the lowest bidder—those applicants who offered to accept the greatest number of patients or visit the largest district for the smallest salary. What often happened, as Hodgkin pointed out, was that a medical man with a large practice and high reputation took on the assignment of attending to the poor of a parish for a trifling sum. He did this partly to keep competing rivals out of the district, but chiefly to be able to hire young assistants for their good apprenticeship fees. Despite the serious evils of this practice, Hodgkin realized that if the duties were not delegated to young and inexperienced hands, the practitioner would probably cut down on his high-demanding but low-paying parish duties in order to give greater attention to his own private practice. The result was that the poor would receive no care or "defective medical advice founded on imperfect data" relayed by relatives and neighbors.[15] A survey published by the poor law commissioners in 1837 revealed that, of 1,830 poor law medical officers, 327 had never taken an examination in surgery, 313 had never been tested in medicine, and 233 had not taken any professional examination at all.[16]

There were other problems besides the lack of qualified credentials. The poor law service attracted frustrated men who were less than devoted to their responsibilities or were unsuccessful in private practice to which they still gave their time. The London-based commissioners sought to attract capable men by encouraging payment of adequate salaries and by investigating and dismissing inefficient or inhumane officials. Their efforts were only partially successful due to foot-dragging by the local boards, which resented and resisted government interference in regional affairs.[17]

Since the costs of relief were paid by local taxes, the willingness of the Boards of Guardians and ratepayers to provide the funds was almost entirely determined by immediate economic conditions. During economic slumps the guardians maintained salaries at a low level. If no medical officer could be found to accept such a position, it was not unusual to ask one practitioner to take on two or more medical districts. The small salaries led to a perfunctory mode of dealing with case assignments, and medical relief was given in a grudging spirit.[18]

The Boards of Guardians were so miserly in releasing money that poor law medical officers had to provide the drugs for their pauper patients out of their own pockets. Since patients always expected drugs, medical officers had to choose between quality and cost. As a result, patients got the cheapest medicines, when they received anything at all. In addition, effective medication was diluted or adulterated and offered for paupers at reduced rates from respectable pharmaceutical houses.[19]

Not only did low pay promote official incompetence and embezzlement but it also gave these underpaid officers a hold over the boards. Because of difficulties in filling these low-paying jobs, the guardians were unwilling to lose a long-serving and inexpensive officer, even when they were dissatisfied with his poor service or where disciplinary action was clearly in order for mistreatment of the indigent. The boards, deferring to social status, simply accepted the word of the accused officer rather than the complaint of the pauper. In most cases, the Boards of Guardians were inept at investigating abuses and often tried to conceal them or otherwise protect their employees out of misguided loyalty. Official dismissals reflected only the most flagrant offenses or bad relations between guardians and the medical officer.[20] There was a similar reluctance on the part of guardians to investigate paupers' complaints of abuses by the lay officers of the workhouse.[21] Guardians did sometimes victimize a conscientious officer for "too great liberality" to the sick paupers.[22]

Although dedication and concern for the poor by the poor law medical officers as a group were no doubt sincere, there were numerous instances of callous, negligent treatment and brutal disregard of pauper patients, especially if the patient had no poor relief order—even in cases of life-threatening obstetrical emergencies.[23] The stinginess of the Boards of Guardians and their arbitrary rejection of medical recommendations, in the interests of saving money, contributed to the abuses.

Reformers understood that the poor, able to support themselves in health, were unable to handle medical expenses when illness interrupted their regular wages and created immediate and serious problems.[24] But reforms were usually rejected as being motivated by the doctors' self-interest. The guardians were pledged to a reduction of expenses, and the middle and upper classes lacked the understanding that society would benefit economically and socially from a healthy laboring class. Furthermore, an efficient health service was not in step with the underlying principles of the new poor law or with the desire or ability of the community to pay for it.[25] In 1840, medical relief was only about 3.3 percent of total relief expenditures and remained proportionately unchanged for decades.[26]

Selecting and Remunerating Medical Officers

Hodgkin offered a remedy for the issue of financial compensation of medical officers holding public positions. Salary was to be fair and adequate, decided on beforehand, and be kept separate from the selection process. Selection of a medical officer should depend solely on medical or professional ability as determined by an oral, written, and practical examination and a review of the candidate's moral character. Hodgkin's plan to improve the standards of the medical officers attending the poor was to hold public examinations, in order to publicize the qualifications necessary to become an accomplished medical man. This would lead doctors to keep up with medical science and standards of practice. Competitions would safeguard against the appointment of men with defective ability or with nothing more to recommend them than manners and address or connection and patronage.[27] Hodgkin also wanted the term of office to be five years, with reappointment discouraged. He believed this was long enough to make a favorable impact in the job and derive the maximum advantage from association with the public post, especially the opportunity that it afforded for accumulation of valuable records that would benefit the public and profession. Since private practice did not lend itself to such research, Hodgkin wanted these opportunities to be available by rotation to others. Besides, a longer term would be tiresome and cause the practitioner to become negligent and careless in his duties.[28]

> Not only a serious blow would be given to the strong holds of professed quackery, but the public would attribute less than they do at present, to the pestle and mortar—to bottles of coloured water— to the gold-headed cane—to a solemn and ominous expression of countenance—to quaint and technical phraseology—or even to those kind and assiduous attentions, which, though justly commendable in themselves, and not to be dispensed with in the intercourse with the sick and their anxious relatives, are unavailing substitutes for sound knowledge and skill.[29]

Hodgkin pointed out that graduates from medical schools are not differentiated between those who passed their examination in a creditable manner and those who barely managed to get by. With degree in hand, they all started at the same level as candidates for public favor. Therefore the proposed additional local examinations would help evaluate applicants for public office. He cited the system on the Continent, especially in France, where nearly all the public medical posts, from the lowest dresserships to the highest professorships, were filled on the basis of rigorous competition (*concours*). There were many candidates for the frequently held examinations. The advantages of this system, he argued, could be seen from the many distinguished doctors and important contributions made to medical science by France.[30]

The new poor law did not anticipate the need for new social services made necessary by the Industrial Revolution and the growth in population of London between 1801 and 1841 from one to two million.[31] The flow of workers from the rural areas to the better-paying jobs in the towns and cities was accompanied by deteriorating conditions of public health and sanitation followed by mounting crime, poverty, illness, and mortality rates. The hospitals, by failing to adapt, develop, and expand, were unable to meet this growing crisis in health care for the working urban poor. While the population grew by leaps and bounds, the hospitals excluded many categories of patients or illnesses and continued to function as relatively small, conservative institutions providing, at best, symbolic care. This was fostered by an outmoded mindset on the part of the hospitals' supporters and governors, for whom the modern image of the voluntary hospital providing a community with comprehensive care had no relevance. They saw the hospital as a monument to Christian charity and concern.[32]

The direct response to this new community need was another of the outstanding achievements of medical philanthropy in the late eighteenth and early nineteenth centuries—dispensaries for the poor. Their plan and design were mainly determined by the shortcomings of the hospitals. The first dispensary was opened in London in 1770 and was followed by fifteen more before the end of the century, in addition to others in the provinces. Medical practice was making its first attempt to reach the mass of the people.

A dispensary was a charitable out-patient institution where medicines were dispensed and medical advice given free. Seriously ill patients were visited at home. Dispensaries were governed and financed like the voluntary hospitals. Subscribers had the right to issue letters of recommendation to patients who were proper objects of charity: in other words, those too poor to pay for medical care but not so destitute that they should be sent to the poorhouse. Although letters were not usually required by the hospitals or dispensaries in cases of accidents and emergencies, they acted as a barrier to many needy cases suffering from medical rather than surgical conditions. As a result, while both institutions aimed to provide free care for the industrious and deserving poor, medical cases predominated at the dispensaries, surgical cases at the hospitals.[33]

Provident Dispensaries

There were also the provident (self-supporting) dispensaries, which Hodgkin considered to be the best and most economical means of supplying prompt and efficient medical assistance to the working classes. These prepaid clinics were maintained by individuals or families who joined them and provided support with small annual payments in advance. In return, the subscriber obtained medical advice and medicine promptly, without recourse to a letter of admission, without fear of a burdensome bill due to lengthy illness, and from his free choice among the medical men attached to the dispensary. At the same time, the profit-sharing arrangement of this "group clinic" afforded an equal assurance to the participating medical practitioner that he would be paid for his services.[34]

Because parishes and charitable institutions occasionally purchased tickets of admission for treatment of the sick poor by a provident dispensary, Hodgkin stressed that a clear distinction should be made between this class of patients and regular subscribers. Administration of the provident dispensaries should be kept separate from that of the poor laws; otherwise, it would defeat the purpose of "promoting a prudent fore-thought amongst the working class" should they believe they were not receiving the advantages of subscribers and were not being treated as separate from and better than paupers. Hodgkin also pointed out that where parishes did utilize the self-supporting dispensary, the reduced demand on the time and effort of the district medical officer would make that position more attractive to the more experienced and accomplished practitioner. The self-supporting dispensaries, continued Hodgkin, were a strong force acting to maintain and uplift the moral character, since they were designed to avert those calamities which began with illness and ended in the total degradation of entire families that once were respectable in their poverty. Self-supporting dispensaries, he added, were instrumental in maintaining independence and in encouraging planning for the future by the poor and working classes and were as useful and necessary to the mechanic and laborer as fire insurance is to the wealthy property owner.[35]

Medical Officers' Associations

After passage of the new poor law in 1834, the profession of medical practitioners decided that something had to be done to improve the relationship between doctor and community. Unable to rely on the London-based corporate elites (physicians, surgeons, apothecaries) to represent them, general practitioners in the provinces formed their own organizations to express their opinions on issues of national health policy. The most important of these societies was the Provincial Medical and Surgical Association, founded in Worcester on July 19, 1832, by Dr. (later Sir) Charles Hastings. Initially a local organization with fifty members (1,700 by 1844), it became the core of a network of local societies that extended over the greater part of England and Wales and was renamed the British Medical Association in 1856. Although its purposes were originally scientific, it was soon caught up in the melee of national medical politics as spokesman for the provincial practitioners in the movement to bring reform and order into the haphazard regulation of medical schools and medical practice by the London-based independent licensing bodies. The major issues were standardization of medical qualifications, registration of practitioners, and restriction of unqualified practice (see chapter 12).[36]

It was at one of the meetings of the association's special Poor Law Committee, formed for looking into the poor law medical services, that the Convention of Poor Law Medical Officers was founded in 1846. It was the earliest organized effort by the poor law medical officers at lobbying the government and the public for recognition of their status and professional needs. As its chairman, the convention chose Thomas Hodgkin because of his interest and writing on issues of public health and his calls for improvement of medical services for the poor, as well as in the quality and status of the medical officers providing them. He served until the convention's dissolution ten years later. During this period he was involved with questionnaires, petitions, deputations, and other public relations and information activities.

The medical officers wanted to focus public attention on the evils that existed in the administration of poor relief. Announcements were inserted in the London and provincial daily press revealing current cases of hardship and injustice and the suffering of the poor and their doctors because of the terribly inadequate salaries. They wanted permanent appointment, payment proportionate to their duties, professional standards, and responsibility to a professional authority consisting of a medical board and inspectors. They felt strongly that lay supervision and control was oppressive, and they complained that the vexatious conditions and miserable pay under which they served were not conducive to bringing maximum benefit to the poor, who would be the ones to suffer in the long run. Adding to their financial hardship and their image as tradesmen was a holdover of the old poor law requiring the medical officer to provide all drugs and medical supplies out of his salary.[37]

Early in 1850, a committee of the convention, consisting of Hodgkin and several others, called on the president and secretary of the Poor Law Board. They requested that a fixed standard of payment be established for medical services at an average of six shillings per case throughout the country. Hodgkin's group asked that poor law duties and sanitary obligations be combined and carried out under the General Board of Health. They asked to be paid for extraordinary services during the recent cholera epidemic (1848–49) but were told that the Poor Law Board had no authority to order payment for services required by the Board of Health in an epidemic. No promises for redress were made, and the deputation was thanked for its many valuable suggestions.[38]

A publicity release from the poor law medical officers, signed (and probably drawn up) by Hodgkin, as chairman, pointed out the startling figures that a staff of over 3,000 professional gentlemen acting under the Poor Law Board, administered relief to nearly three million people and received on average a payment of about two shillings per case. The board had actually suggested a further reduction of salaries. Such lack of appreciation for professional services, complained Hodgkin, was inappropriate when an annual salary of £1,500 is paid to a secretary of the board "for doing that which occupies but a moderate portion of his time." Hodgkin went so far as to suggest that members of the medical profession use their personal influence with individual members of Parliament whom they saw as patients to bring about an improvement in the system of poor law medical relief.[39]

But the majority of poor law medical officers did not get involved. Nor was public sympathy for poor law patients readily aroused by doctors' demands, which, although reasonable, had a self-interested ring. Very few developed the single-minded interest in the poor law service that might have led to effective pressure for change. They lacked initiative and the cohesion, participation, and support from among their own numbers that later made the British Medical Association such a potent force. They tended to see their difficulty in terms of money—but instead of demanding a specific salary befitting a full-time professional, they concentrated on increasing "fee-for-service." This made them out to be essentially part-time employees whose main interest was advancement through private practice. Faced with a lack of unified cooperation, and because public opinion was not favorable at that time, the committee of the convention discontinued its activities early in 1851.[40]

A few years later Hodgkin supported plans to seek increased funding from Parliament for medical attendance on the poor and for administrative reforms at the local district level. He urged unity and cooperation by the medical men throughout the kingdom and again asked them to publicize these proposals with members of Parliament who were their patients.[41] New organizations and leadership sprang up during the next two decades.[42] Their perseverance, increasing agitation, and countless appeals achieved important gains and eventual recognition in 1871. Reform came about because the medical profession was itself becoming more self-conscious and aware of the importance of its work. With the rise in professional standards and the progress of medical science, doctors refused to tolerate the conditions around them. The medical journals, especially *The Lancet*, gave nationwide publicity to complaints, notices of meetings, and other news calling for improvements in the poor law and public health. This information could not have been distributed as rapidly, as widely, or as cheaply by the medical officers themselves.[43] The General Medical Register (see chapter 12) established in 1858 helped clarify and standardize medical qualifications and gave new status to the medical profession and new strength to the work of its organizations.

CHAPTER EIGHT

Physicians, Surgeons, Apothecaries

Statistics

Advances in pathology after 1800 required more exact clinical observations, but clinician-pathologists were skeptical about therapy and were more interested in descriptions of symptoms and identification of diseases than in cure. Physicians made vague use of quantitative terms, claiming that a given drug benefited "most" of their patients, but they were reluctant to submit their insights, cumulative wisdom, and intuition to dull numerical tests. Record-keeping did not fit the self-image of physicians as theorists and philosophers.[1] Furthermore, for clinical data to be of value, it was needed in large amounts. This was available only in large hospitals—nonexistent before 1800. In addition, studies on therapy required that the disease be identified. Since practitioners brought up in the older generalized pathology denied the existence of specific diseases, there was nothing for them to count or measure.[2]

Prospects for clinical statistics of distinct diseases began to improve after 1800 as larger hospital services became available, notably in Paris. By about 1820 there was a growing awareness that generalized theories in pathology could not explain the specificity of localized lesions that were identifiable and measurable.

However, studies were still defective because sample size was usually too small or not representative.

The first systematic use of clinical (as distinguished from vital) statistics was made by the French physician Pierre Charles Alexandre Louis (1787–1872).[3] To establish his own data base, Louis performed over 5,000 postmortem examinations. He applied his method particularly well in the correlation of symptoms and organic changes found at autopsy in tuberculosis (1825), but he is best known for his two-volume clinico-pathologic description of typhoid fever (1829), which gave the disease its name.[4]

Numerical Analysis

Louis's numerical analysis of the effects of bloodletting in inflammatory diseases, particularly pneumonia (1835), showed that the course of the disease was not affected by the timing or the number of bleedings and that the benefits of bloodletting were not as great and as striking as was commonly believed. He, as well as Hodgkin, urged selective use of this measure and a continuing inquiry into its merits for treating other diseases. This centuries-old ineffective and harmful practice was eventually discontinued.[5]

Hodgkin met Louis during his student year in Paris, when Louis was accumulating data and developing his ideas on medical statistics, and was quickly won over to the significance of numerical analysis. Hodgkin understood the value of this application of clinical data and incorporated Louis's teaching into his own lectures.[6] Louis believed that the fallacies of *a priori* theories such as the *systems* of disease and the arbitrary *doctrines* of treatment were easily exposed by good statistics. He dismissed any data characterized as *often* or *sometimes* and insisted on exact figures.

Louis's method of clinical teaching was based on comprehensive and systematic record-keeping and numerical comparison of all indicators of illness (age, profession, nutrition, previous diseases, patient's comments), as well as all phases of a disease (causes, symptoms, progress, duration, severity, frequency, therapies). It was necessary to avoid hasty conclusions from a limited number of cases and to rely on large amounts of data in order to eliminate individual factors and establish conclusions with reasonable certainty.

Louis's *numerical method* utilized simple arithmetic. He compiled his observations in tabular form and then drew inferences about the value of a particular therapy or the connection between clinical phenomena. However, he was not an accomplished statistician and did not employ the calculus of probabilities to make allowance for "probable error." Although he recognized the importance of large numbers of cases, Louis, like his contemporaries, actually reached his conclusions from relatively small numbers of observations because there was no criterion for judging what amount was significant. He did not understand the significance of numerical average and did not know how to establish the precision or validity of his results. Consequently, he treated as significant small statistical differences that were really meaningless.[7]

It was obvious to Hodgkin that many variables in the study and diagnosis of disease were suitable for tabulation in determining their significance: relative susceptibility to a particular disease according to sex, symptoms and their frequency, value of a particular therapy, duration of recovery, or occurrence of death. He understood that the observer who trusted transient impressions of the cases as they occurred would be biased by the striking character of some particular cases that had recently come to his attention and therefore would lead to exaggerated or erroneous conclusions.[8]

Some information, such as pulse and temperature, Hodgkin thought, might be expressed "not merely in numbers, but in forms which speak to the eye . . . by lines or curves similar to those employed by meteorologists"[9] to keep track of changes in the weather. He believed that statistical analysis of the observations of symptoms would redeem medical science from its habit of conjecture and exert a positive influence on medical practice. However, Hodgkin was no iconoclast. Although emphasizing the significance of numerical analysis, he recognized the shortcomings of the statistical method and discounted the claims that it made medicine an exact science.[10]

Despite increasing recognition after 1835 of their importance, statistical methods received only limited use in clinical and pathological studies in France during the next few decades because of inertia and lack of information.[11] French physicians were mainly interested in individual patients, and French mathematicians were not interested in medical applications. As a result, the initiative passed to Great Britain, where the science of medical statistics had its origin and early development. During the boom in scientific societies in the 1830s, the Royal Statistical Society was founded (1834). Hodgkin was elected a fellow in 1844 but did not contribute to its journal.

Animal Experiments

The numerical method is applicable to animal research. Although this kind of investigation was something Hodgkin did not enjoy doing, he carried out a study for the British Association for the Advancement of Science (BAAS) "On the Effects of Acrid Poisons" that involved live animals and reported it at the annual meeting in 1835. The main purpose of the study was to help judicial inquiries and add to the knowledge of the pathology of the mucous membrane of the alimentary canal. Experiments were described of the effects of poisons, usually arsenic, on the stomach and intestinal canal of dogs and horses.

Hodgkin admitted to "painful feelings accompanying experiments on inferior animals" but believed these were justified "when the object in view promises to be an advantage to man" and is carried out "with the least expense of life and with the least possible amount of suffering." Hodgkin experienced much difficulty in choosing the animals for these experiments and tried, as far as possible, to take only "those lives which for other reasons it was either necessary or desirable to sacrifice." He made several attempts with cats, which he calls "supernumerary and worthless animals" and which were more easily obtained than dogs. But due to "their extraordinary tenacity of life and the readiness with which they reject from the stomach whatever offends it," he was unsuccessful in attempts to poison four of them with arsenic and stopped using them for experiments.[12]

Hodgkin had no objection to using the data of animal experiments when made by other physiologists, but because of his own sensitive nature, he preferred not doing them himself. Had anesthesia been discovered and in use at the time, he probably would have had no objection to performing the experiments. He admitted it might be thought that he should have done more work on a particular subject, but since these experiments would have involved some degree of cruelty, they would have been painful for him to undertake as well as to his audience to hear described.[13]

Guy's Hospital Reports

A major outlet for medical research made its debut in 1836 as Guy's Hospital embarked on an innovative program of publication. The intent of the *Guy's Hospital Reports* was to extend the hospital's vast store of information "beyond the narrow limits of oral instruction" and bring it to the entire medical and scientific profession.[14] *The Lancet*, no friend of Guy's Hospital, greeted the first issue with sarcastic criticism.[15]

Hodgkin is well represented in the first volume with four papers. One is a joint report[16] on a monstrous fetus that Hodgkin had obtained and forwarded to Sir Astley Cooper because of the latter's interest in unusual specimens. Hodgkin commented on the then current belief by embryologists that the human fetus in its progressive development passed through the final stages of the different classes of lower animals. The different degrees of imperfection in abnormal fetuses were supposed to be due to the accidental cessation of development at different periods. Although there are a few examples to support this nineteenth-century view that "ontogeny recapitulates phylogeny," it is not true in most cases and is generally not accepted as a modern concept. The other papers contain contributed autopsy reports[17] and his comments on a bony tumor in the face.[18]

It was a busy year for Thomas Hodgkin. In addition to the inaugural volume of the *Guy's Hospital Reports*, volume one of his *Lectures on Morbid Anatomy* was published. He also presented a provisional committee report on connections between veins and the lymphatic system[19] to the British Association for the Advancement of Science. The British Association was a relatively new forum for the presentation and publication of scientific activities. Its establishment in 1831 was in part a reaction against the practices of The Royal Society, at that time composed mainly of individuals who in no way participated in scientific research. Even with the founding of the British Association and a half-dozen specialty science societies, most English scientists of that period remained amateurs as far as occupation was concerned (see chapter 11, note 27).

In volume two of the *Guy's Hospital Reports* (1837), Hodgkin described an unusual urinary calculus removed after death from the bladder of a two-year-old boy. He discussed the appearance of some of the urinary calculi in the museum at Guy's and added numerous drawings.[20] With the start of 1837, Hodgkin was well on his way to a satisfying, productive career and professional prominence. He entertained high hopes of moving out of the theater of morbid anatomy and up to the patients' wards and a clinical appointment at Guy's Hospital. He couldn't begin to suspect that his career, until now centered on morbid anatomy, would go into an abrupt and premature decline.

Refusal of Fellowship in College of Physicians

There were many contributing factors. One of these certainly was his refusal of the distinction of fellowship offered by the Royal College of Physicians of London in June 1836. The status and prestige enjoyed by the Royal College of Physicians derived from its jurisdiction over all who practiced medicine as *physicians* in the City of London and within a radius of seven miles. This authority, granted by Henry VIII in 1518, placed the university-educated physicians on the top rung of the three tiers of the medical hierarchy: physician, surgeon, apothecary.[21] Its role in the delivery or—more correctly—nondelivery of health care during the subsequent centuries helped shape the development of medical practice and medical education in Great Britain. The physicians, few in number and charging high fees, were never a large enough group to care for all the sick people in the London metropolis. If not for the apothecaries, the population would have received no medical attention.[22] As intermediary between physician and patient, the apothecaries had learned about the uses of herbs and other drugs and developed their own independent practice of medicine,[23] not only by preparing and selling medicines but also by visiting the sick and prescribing for them as well.

As for Hodgkin, his displeasure with the Royal College of Physicians derived from the fact that not until 1834, with only a few exceptions, was anyone elected to its fellowship who was not a graduate of Oxford or Cambridge university with the Doctor of Medicine degree. The Royal College of Physicians even excluded the graduates of the University of Edinburgh, which had been the great school of medicine of the British Isles for nearly a century. Inasmuch as Oxford and Cambridge required an oath subscribing to the articles of the official state church, they did not admit Catholics, Jews, Quakers, and other Protestant nonconformists. Consequently, the great majority of fellows of the Royal College of Physicians were members of the Established Church of England.

At any one time the total membership of the college was not large. By 1836, there were only 265 members, of whom 164 were fellows.[24] It was a greatly coveted honor and one that conferred a high social status and many privileges. Those graduating as M.D. from universities other than Oxford or Cambridge were eligible only for admission to examination by the Royal College of Physicians to practice as licentiates (a lesser designation) of the college within the metropolitan district of London. It was impossible to be appointed as a physician to a major hospital in London without an M.D. degree and fellowship or the license of the Royal College of Physicians. Permission to practice was granted to examinees who, according to Hodgkin's genteel sarcasm, afforded "proofs that they were as competent to cope with obscurity, and knew as much of the *ars conjecturalis* [an art guided by guesses] as themselves."[25]

The mystique of an Oxford/Cambridge (Oxbridge) education was that it developed "character" or "moral" superiority and upheld the dignity and respectability of the profession of physic. It was more important for its social value than its intellectual content. The identification of the Royal College of Physicians' fellowship with Oxford and Cambridge assured the physicians that they had the same status as their well-to-do patients. The upper classes appreciated the advantages of the classical learning acquired by an Oxbridge education and chose for their doctors those who had experienced the same education. The College of Physicians was seen not as a vehicle primarily in the service of medicine, but as a means to maintain and enhance the physicians' status in the social milieu they inhabited and gain respect from colleagues and patients.[26] This was important because medicine, as a profession, did not enjoy great prestige during the first sixty years of the nineteenth century. Society preferred the Church, the Law, and Government or the armed forces—in that order—as suitable occupations for a gentleman.[27]

In 1834, the Royal College of Physicians repealed its by-laws that limited fellowship to graduates of either Oxford or Cambridge university. Although this membership restriction based on religion was removed, it was replaced by a new one. Consequently, a Committee of Associated Licentiates of the Royal College of Physicians was formed, which included Hodgkin and other eminent physicians, who sought to overthrow the new by-laws. In their petition to Parliament on August 17, 1835, they protested the "injustice towards the majority of physicians practising in London," which tends "to injure and degrade the order of Licentiates," and challenged the legality of the new by-laws to the charter granted by Parliament. They objected because the new rule limited the number of licentiates eligible for election to fellowship by the total membership to a slate selected by a council. They contended that personal and political prejudice would lead to favoritism. Hodgkin's group wanted the full membership of fellows to have the right "to propose or vote for any or every Licentiate into the Fellowship."[28] The college did not accede to their petition.

As a result, when on June 25, 1836, Thomas Hodgkin and fourteen other licentiates were invited to become fellows in the Royal College of Physicians of London, the first to be selected under the new by-laws that obviated the religious affiliation, Hodgkin and his friends Sir James Clark (Scottish Presbyterian) and Neil Arnott (Catholic) and three others, despite the honor, refused from conscientious motives to accept the invitation.[29] They believed that it carried an invidious and exclusive distinction and that its acceptance would imply approval of a discriminating practice and be regarded as a betrayal of their associates in the movement and of other licentiates who were not selected.

This perception of the unfair exercise of its powers by the Royal College of Physicians had led to another involvement by Hodgkin and many of the same liberals, dissenters, nonconformists, and reformers. Neil Arnott (1788–1874), Sir James Clark (1788–1870), Henry (later Lord) Brougham (1778–1868), Sir Charles Locock (1799–1875), and George Birkbeck (see chapter 4) were prominently associated with Hodgkin in a movement for the formation of an officially recognized, broad-based, and wholly nonsectarian institution in London in arts, science, and medicine, for students barred from Oxford and Cambridge universities because of religion or lack of means. These ancient seats of learning had muddled along and become inefficient and unproductive as a result of their insularity and pretence to elitism. They paid little attention to physics and chemistry and the other new branches of learning that were needed for a rapidly industralizing society. Despite concerted protests against their reactionary status quo, they resisted reform of their discriminatory practices on religion, which denied admission to thousands of potential students.

By 1825, a rapidly growing urban middle class, with a large representation of dissenters, was generating mounting pressures for establishment of new and alternative facilities for higher education in London. At the same time there was rising public concern over the state of medical education in London and a suspicion that the quality of the health care being administered was not as good as it could be. Teaching was still based on the private medical schools and apprenticeship to the physicians and surgeons in the large hospitals. The system gave rise to a great deal of nepotism in hospital appointments. What was clearly needed was a long, systematic, and comprehensive curriculum leading to a degree. Another motivation for new facilities of higher education was the realization of the scientific inferiority of England, especially London, compared to Paris and other continental centers.[30]

University of London

London was one of the very few European capitals to be without a university. The idea for a modern nonsectarian University of London, unhampered by the social and religious exclusiveness of the universities at Oxford and Cambridge, was first proposed in 1825 and set into motion the following year. But once again the issue of religion created controversy. This was an all-important question, because success depended largely on nonconformist support. Opposition to the "God-excluding seminary" was immediate and vocal.

Eventually, it was agreed to have no religion in the curriculum, and "the London University" on Gower Street opened in October 1828 with some 300 students. However, Church and Tory interests opposed this arrangement and were able to deny the new institution the right to confer degrees. Meanwhile, a rival school, King's College, which did require instruction in Church of England doctrines, opened in 1831. The two colleges competed vigorously and bitterly for the privilege of granting degrees. Finally, on November 27, 1836, a royal charter was granted establishing "the University of London" with a chancellor and a senate of persons eminent in science and literature appointed for life, as a nonteaching body empowered to conduct examinations and confer degrees in arts, law, and medicine on the students of King's College and the Gower Street College, now known as University College London."[31]

Hodgkin was actively involved in the affairs of the University of London and wrote a plan for its future constitution and reorganization of its administration. In 1837 he was one of the first appointed to the senate of the new University of London. Having supported the formation of a University of London from the beginning, he could now play a role in the academic functioning and growth of an institution where dissenters, Quakers, and members of other religious minorities could receive a university degree without having to leave the country. Among the thirty-five others named in the royal charter where John Dalton, Michael Faraday, and Hodgkin's friends James Clark and Neil Arnott. Hodgkin served in the university senate until his death.

The very idea of a University of London was a challenge to the ascendancy of the Tory party, which was then based on the graduates of Oxford and Cambridge universities. But the liberals, who championed free speech, insisted that the institution of the new university would do more to crush bigotry and intolerance than all the bills passed through Parliament.[32]

University College London became the first institution in England to provide a university education for students intending to become general practitioners. It closed the gulf between medicine and surgery by offering medical students a planned and integrated curriculum in medicine and surgery. Students would no longer have to wander from one school or hospital to another attending courses given independently of one another. It was now all in one facility.[33] This institution raised the standards of medical education in London.

When it was proposed in 1833 that the University of London should grant medical degrees, Guy's Hospital Medical School felt itself to be especially threatened. The Court of Committees passed a resolution stating that if the University of London were enabled to grant "Degrees in Medicine . . . such a privilege would be of great injury to the Medical School of this institution."[34] The treasurer was authorized to prepare a petition to this effect to be presented to the House of Commons if he considered it desirable to do so. If the resolution was delivered, it had no effect. The University of London obtained its charter and its privileges. Hodgkin's involvement with the new university and his refusal of the College of Physicians' fellowship could not be easily overlooked, and they certainly were contributing factors in souring his relationship with the chief executive of Guy's Hospital.

CHAPTER NINE

Conflict and Controversy

Aborigines' Protection Society

The short reign of William IV (1830–1837) came to a close, and he was succeeded by his niece, Victoria. That year, 1837, was doubly significant for Thomas Hodgkin. It marked the founding of an organization to which he had given much thought since first proposing it nearly twenty years earlier, when he was an apprentice with Glaisyer and Kemp in Brighton (see chapter 1). This was to be a society for safeguarding the rights and culture of the primitive tribal peoples all over the world and for providing them with the skills to help them bridge the gap with modern civilization. But, before the year was over, bypassed for a promotion largely because of his involvement with this society and its objectives, Hodgkin resigned from Guy's Hospital.

Hodgkin's resignation from Guy's Hospital in September 1837 followed on the heels of what was the pivotal event of his life—the rejection of his candidacy for promotion to assistant physician. These two events were the final outcome of a disagreement with Benjamin Harrison, Jr. (1771–1856) (Fig. 6). Harrison, the formidable treasurer and chief administrative officer at Guy's, was also on the seven-man policy-making committee of the Hudson's Bay

Fig. 6.   *Benjamin Harrison, Jr. (Courtesy of the Wellcome Institute Library, London.)*

Company. Therein lay the origin of this conflict with Hodgkin and Hodgkin's new organization, the Aborigines' Protection Society.

Early in 1837, Hodgkin, together with a small nucleus of other political moralists, organized the Aborigines' Protection Society in response to revelations of cruelty to aborigines in various parts of the British Empire. The group included Richard King (1811?–1876), William Allen, William Stroud, Thomas Fowell Buxton (1786–1845) and a few others. From the start, Hodgkin was recognized as "the Father and Founder of the Aborigines Protection Society,"[1] but the founder best known to the public was Buxton. A member of the Church of England, and of Parliament from 1818 to 1837, he succeeded William Wilberforce in 1824 as leader of the antislavery party in the final phase of the campaign in Parliament to abolish slavery. Buxton had the most political experience and was the logical choice to be the first president of the society.[2]

The Aborigines' Protection Society was part of a great complex of progressive-issue organizations that came into being as a result of the activity for emancipation. Some of the beneficial goals that these groups pursued were education, peace, temperance, women's rights, prison reform, famine relief, voting and political reform, and abolition of capital punishment. There were overlapping memberships and interlocking committees. The members were often connected in their business enterprises and in many cases—especially the Quakers—were related by marriage. The incentive to establish an organization to look after the interests of aborigines had already been in existence for some years. It evolved from the momentum of the abolition victory, gained in 1833, when Parliament's attention turned to the related problem of protection for the aborigines. Aborigines were defined as any indigenous population with an inferior culture due to ignorance of Christian values and resistance to the superior customs of the colonizers.

Buxton had secured the appointment of a Parliamentary Select Committee on Aborigines, in July 1835, to investigate frontier fighting in South Africa between Boer settlers and native tribesmen. Also on the agenda were questions of justice and civil rights for the natives in British settlements and neighboring tribes. Testimony by numerous witnesses revealed a picture of villainy, cruelty, and murder, superimposed on the deficiences of a nonexistent colonial policy in the wake of expanding British power. The committee issued recommendations for dealing with legal and territorial problems between settlers and natives. Following the dissolution of the committee early in 1837, Hodgkin took the lead in reorganizing the informal group that had followed and supported the committee's activities into a permanent body that would monitor all colonization schemes and government directives affecting native tribes and promote measures for their protection and improvement.

Benjamin Harrison, Jr., and the Clapham Sect

Benjamin Harrison, Jr., whose father held the office of treasurer of Guy's Hospital from 1785 to 1797, served without salary from 1797 to 1848. During this long period the hospital and school flourished under his autocratic rule. Known as "King Harrison," he had virtual dictatorial power at Guy's Hospital.[3] This was the benefit of his membership in the "Clapham Sect," a group of wealthy evangelical reformers and humanitarians who lived in and near the village of Clapham, to the southwest of London, and worshipped in the local anglican church. As dedicated Christians, they were driven by a sense of religious conscience to do good works. This is apparent from their diaries and reminiscences. However, their critics charged that their concern for the welfare of overseas natives betrayed an indifference to, or even a wish to, divert attention from the sufferings of other groups nearer to home.[4]

Although they believed in helping the poor, the underprivileged, and the handicapped, their self-righteous humanitarianism preferred to retain the class distinctions that came with wealth and not to disturb the traditional order of social rank. Their efforts were mainly spiritual, with "more emphasis upon the salvation of souls than of bodies" and an inclination "to congratulate the poor on their poverty, because it made easier their path to heaven."[5] They were at their worst when they sought to close down all Sunday entertainment and when they created a vicious anti-Catholic movement out of traditional fears and the resentment of Irish immigration.[6]

Harrison's humanitarian activities also reached out to the American Indians. Described as "a noted and active philanthropist" with a "humanitarian spirit," he had started a steady flow of books to the Red River settlement (near Winnipeg) as early as 1816. In 1820 he had arranged for the appointment of a chaplain. Harrison also supported a proposal for a regular mission, and this led to the appointment of a schoolmaster for the Indian children in the district.[7]

Members of the Clapham Sect were among the governors of Guy's. The governors oversaw the operation of the institution, defined administration policy on discipline, the types of cases to be admitted, fund-raising, and expansion and construction of new facilities. They also served under the hospital's charter as trustees of the rent-yielding landed endowments and philanthropic contributions, which often came from their own private means. They were prominent in public life and presided over major banking and commercial interests in London. Their political and business interests coincided with those of Benjamin Harrison, Jr., and they readily accepted his recommendations on hospital and school policies and appointments.

Harrison's power and influence at Guy's were so effective that even the Charity Commission of 1837, set up under the Acts of George III, found no irregularities or abuses. The commission's 1840 report commended his scrupulous and disinterested integrity, but noted the absolute and uncontrolled authority that he enjoyed in the administration of the hospital and its finances and in the naming of lecturers, from whom the physicians and surgeons of the hospital were usually selected.[8] Although final appointment of physicians and surgeons to the hospital staff was made by election of the governors, Harrison's recommendations were very influential.

Assistant Physician

When Dr. Henry James Cholmeley (1777–1837), physician to Guy's Hospital, died, Dr. Thomas Addison was expected to advance from assistant physician, a post he held since 1824, to physician. This would create a vacancy in the position of assistant physician, and Thomas Hodgkin, with many years of faithful and dedicated service at Guy's, expected to be rewarded with the clinical appointment to the hospital staff. It would mean a step up the professional ladder—from the dissecting room to the clinical wards—a move "upstairs" to a post that provided greater income from student lecture fees than what he earned from the limited enrollment in his elective course on morbid anatomy. There was no salary for the assistant physician during Hodgkin's time.

The assistant physician was required to live in the vicinity of the hospital and be in attendance daily. In addition to outpatients, he saw to the patients of any of the physicians who were absent and occasionally filled in for them on admission day. Hodgkin had been doing this for Thomas Addison for eight years, unofficially, but with the treasurer's approval and without reimbursement.

Although Hodgkin's medical and scientific credentials were outstanding, he came before the selection committee with additional and very undesirable baggage. Some of it had to do with his membership in the Society of Friends, his involvement with the University of London, which competed with Guy's for medical students, and his Mechanics' Institute lectures to the poor and working class of Spitalfields on the causes of illness and some basic facts of hygiene to protect one's health. This was a radical idea. What might they demand next? For Harrison, who represented the conservative establishment, this added up to a portrait of a dissenter and reformer. In addition, there was his recent illness, which suggested poor health. It was also believed that Hodgkin was a poor lecturer because he attracted a small class. However, pathology was not a popular subject and the course was an elective and not required by the colleges for examination. It met three times a week at 6:30 P.M., which may have been an inconvenient time.

But there were other reasons why the treasurer and associates may not have supported him. There was Hodgkin's limited medical practice, suggesting a lack of interest, as well as his habit of undercharging his patients or charging nothing at all. This came in for considerable criticism from the colleagues. He, in turn, in keeping with his Quaker principles, could be very outspoken in his criticisms of his colleagues, a trait that did not endear him to some of them. And there was his refusal, the previous year, of the honor of fellowship offered by the Royal College of Physicians.

Conflict and Controversy

It is impossible to say what one thing tipped the scales, but ultimately, the rejection of Hodgkin's promotion was undoubtedly related to the association of Benjamin Harrison, Jr., with the Hudson's Bay Company and Hodgkin's liberal political activities. Hodgkin's study and criticism of the effects of "civilization" on indigenous populations due to the encroachment of European settlers began at a young age. He kept up with these interests and activities during his years at Guy's, and his sympathies were well known to his associates.

Hodgkin had a committed interest in the affairs of freed black slaves and educated Indians and entertained them in his house. They were held up as symbols of what the future might bring. As one of the founders of the Aborigines' Protection Society, whose object was to prevent the exploitation of the natives of the colonies, he spoke out vigorously in his speeches and in his writings against the oppressive measures then being employed by the colonists against the Indians of North America. Hodgkin's publicly expressed views and sympathy for the Indians, for whom he advocated full rights of British citizenship, brought him into conflict with some of his colleagues.

The chief interest of the Hudson's Bay Company was the fur trade rather than the well-being of the native hunters. Undoubtedly, since management decisions were made several thousand miles from where they were to be carried out, events in the territories must have had a greater effect on the contacts and dealings with the Indians than instructions or policies originating in London and transmitted by lengthy sea and overland voyages.

Because of Harrison's financial interest in the Hudson's Bay Company's fur trade with the Indians and Hodgkin's humanitarian activities on behalf of oppressed and underprivileged peoples everywhere, the two men were eventually led to a direct confrontation. A clash was inevitable between the domineering Harrison, who tolerated no opposition, and the independent Quaker who felt compelled to speak out against what he perceived to be injustice. Hodgkin was a man of diverse nonmedical interests and radical opinions, and this rarely is a recommendation to anyone who wields power and makes appointments. Considering Harrison's dedication to the company and his autocratic personality, he could be expected to take personally any criticism of company policies or practices. Hodgkin, to his own great misfortune, provided these criticisms. They were based on observations made by Richard King during an expedition to the Arctic Ocean, and they came at the worst possible time, only months before the sequence of events leading to the election of a new assistant physician.

In 1833, Richard King, who had qualified as a surgeon at Guy's in 1832 and knew Hodgkin, sailed on a Royal Navy expedition to the Arctic Ocean as surgeon and naturalist. The expedition had been fitted out by public subscription and government grant. The original objective of the trip, headed by Captain (later Sir) George Back (1796–1878), was to find and assist Captain (Sir) John Ross, who had sailed with his party to the polar regions in 1829, and whose fate at that time was unknown. Ross's expedition had become icebound in the Arctic during their search for the northwest passage. Captain Back and King also planned to map the coastline of the northeastern extremity of the American continent at the request of the Royal Geographical Society. News of Ross's rescue by a whaling ship and return to England in October 1833 reached the Back expedition the following April. They were now able to direct their entire attention to the secondary objective of geographical discovery.

Before leaving, King asked Hodgkin for suggestions of what to look for on the trip. Hodgkin sent a list of questions pertaining to the local plant and animal life, the seasonal variations in mortality of the inhabitants, geological formations and mineral deposits, and the effects of meteorological phenomena on the natives and the members of the expedition. However, Hodgkin's chief interest was in the ethnology of the aboriginal tribes. Noting that these Indian tribes were rapidly disappearing, Hodgkin, who was very concerned about their threatened extinction, urged King to collect as much information as possible about their origins, customs, traditions, languages, religions, and life-style. He wanted large numbers of observations and verification of important observations obtained from secondary sources, such as missionaries, traders, and interpreters. Aware of the sufferings of the natives at the hands of self-styled Christians, Hodgkin stressed that a more liberal policy toward the Indians would be advantageous to fur company and Indians alike. An improvement in their condition would not only be good for commerce, but would be a stabilizing factor in the region by adding to territorial security against American and Russian expansion.[9]

King's description of the deplorable living conditions of the Indians brought about by the fur trade in the territory confirmed Hodgkin's fears. The natives had fallen into an abject state and were suffering from rum and venereal disease. In his letter to Hodgkin from Fort Reliance in April 1833, King wrote that improvement of the Indians' condition could be accomplished only by the strong arm of government. He added that "as long as the Hudson's Bay Company exists this noble race must remain in status quo." King asked that "out of respect to our Treasurer," this not be mentioned for the present.[10]

King returned to England with Captain Back in 1835 and subsequently published his own account of the expedition, in which he described the ruinous aftermath of the contact between North American Indians and Europeans. He told how the introduction of firearms had made them forget the use of the bow and arrow, the spear, and the various other modes of trapping their game. They were extended more credit than they could repay by their hunting excursions, which placed them more deeply in the power of the trader. The Indians were also plied with liquor, and in their drunken frenzy became murdering savages, attacking relative, friend or enemy.[11]

According to King, the Indians no longer enjoyed their happy independence, in feasting, dancing, and other pastimes. They now went begging in the most humiliating manner, for guns and ammunition, which the fur trade had made essential for their existence. They had fallen into so debased a state that their sacrifices and religious solemnities were entirely suspended and their funeral and matrimonial rites completely neglected.[12]

They had, by force of example, been taught every vice that could bring about their degradation, but had received no instruction in any skills that would have added to their comforts and conveniences. Their land was taken away from them by force or fraud and they were cheated and taken advantage of by those engaged in the fur trade. The pitiful low price paid for the furs by the agents of the Hudson's Bay Company enabled only the more active hunters to eke out a barely survival existence and led "to the death of the more aged and infirm by starvation and cannibalism." It was quite apparent that the company's trading practices had changed the survival patterns of the natives. They had been hunters and now became fur trappers and traded beaver skins for provisions and guns. King remonstrated, "Surely that honourable company which by royal charter is permitted to reap such golden harvests might appropriate a small fund to rescue from starvation the decrepit and diseased, who in their youthful days have contributed to its wealth."[13]

Complaints about the treatment of the Indians were not new. As far back as 1649, an anonymous pamphlet (*Tyranipocrit Discovered*, printed in the Netherlands) attacked the English government for robbing the poor Indians of their goods and then "decking our proud carcasses, and feeding our greedy guts with superfluous unnecessary curiosities."[14]

Captain George Back, who received the Gold Medal from the Royal Geographical Society in 1837, made no mention in his account of the misery and desolation of the Indians that so distressed Richard King. Hodgkin wrote to the Geographical Society that the contrast between the two reports highlighted the indifference by society-at-large to any efforts for improvement of the Indians' condition, when there is no profit to be made, "unless fashion or some other equally unworthy motive apply temporary stimulus." Hodgkin suggested that Back's report might be an example of the power of special interests "in causing silence respecting evils which need strongest appeals for redress."[15]

King's application to the Geographical Society for another expedition to the unexplored regions of the northern coast of

America was rejected. Dr. Hodgkin, as a member of the society, wrote a letter on behalf of King's proposal.[16] Recalling the limited success and the high cost and risk of previous arctic voyages of exploration, Hodgkin recommended, as a more economical and promising option, the less dangerous overland expedition proposed by Richard King in this book. King consistently spoke out for polar exploration by land rather than by sea. Hodgkin analyzed the disadvantages inherent in travel for a large company of men, especially the large boats needed for inland waterways. He favored the small group with the least necessary baggage, proceeding and subsisting off the resources of the land in the manner of the natives and traders in the region. Hodgkin's plea gained no support, and he turned to Benjamin Harrison, Jr. It was a mistake.

In December 1836, Hodgkin wrote a long letter to Harrison in which he sought his financial support for a new arctic expedition to the northern shores by King. In addition to new knowledge about the Indians and their way of life in this little-explored region, other objectives would be to obtain many new specimens for the museum of the medical school. The reference to specimens for the museum may have been Hodgkin's attempt at making the project more acceptable to the treasurer. However, Hodgkin did not stop there but continued in his characteristically forthright manner by expressing his concerns about the native population and making a strong plea for a change in policies of the Hudson's Bay Company. It should have been clear to Hodgkin that he was going out on a limb by relying solely on Richard King's commentary. With his polite but strongly worded letter of criticism, he was risking gravely offending an important and powerful figure. King was later openly critical of the way he had been treated by the admiralty in connection with another rescue expedition, on which he sailed in 1850. The newspapers were sympathetic, but his reputation for eccentricity and excitability hindered his advancement, and he died in obscurity.

In contrast to some of his other writings on social issues and scientific topics, Hodgkin's letter to Harrison is remarkably clear and direct in language. Hodgkin defends King's revelations about the fur trade. He describes King as an accurate observer and faithful narrator who could neither avoid seeing nor fail to describe the existence and operation of activities that demoralize and depopulate those vast regions subject to the authority of the Hudson's Bay Company. From their offices in London the directors of the company cannot see the process of deterioration for themselves, while their agents are not likely to report it. As long as rich cargoes continue to arrive and make the company prosperous, neither the governors nor the shareholders will suspect, or care to inquire about, conditions in the territory. Only through the observations of an enlightened and unbiased traveler, continues Hodgkin, is the truth likely to be revealed. When the truth about the fur trade finally does come out, it will seem no less appalling in its ultimate results than the slave trade itself. In defending his friend, Hodgkin was repeating the criticisms that King had made in public statements and before a parliamentary committee.

> A lively interest in the fate of Aboriginal tribes which I have now cherished upward of 20 years, makes me feel intensely on this subject, and will, I trust, be a sufficient apology for my having sought to arrest thy attention respecting it. Of the mass of the members and directors of the Company I know little or nothing, but I cannot believe that Benjamin Harrison, whose life is almost entirely devoted to institutions which have for their object the relief and amelioration of his fellow creatures, will either regard the subject with indifference, or have his attention fixed upon it without conceiving the means which may correct and retrieve the evil, or that he would advocate the cause in vain, were he to undertake it.[17]

Hodgkin holds out the probability that concern for the well-being of the inhabitants of the regions and the institution of a humane and Christian policy would lead to an increase in the variety and productivity of furs and other resources. Cargoes would be increased in number and in value, and all this would add to the income and power of the company.

One can well imagine the impact that this communication had on Harrison. On January 5, 1837, Harrison responded to Hodgkin that the statements of Richard King were false and that he was astonished that Hodgkin could find no better authority than that of King on which to "have entertained an opinion of a person whose conduct in other situations in life has been under your immediate observations."[18]

Hodgkin, stunned by this sharply worded protest, denied any hostile intent. A few days later, Harrison asked Hogdkin to meet with him and reviewed his own longtime commitment to the welfare of the Indians and his financial support for their churches and missions.[19] Harrison attributed King's criticism to his rejection for a position at Guy's and added that the company had considered the previous expedition to be very poorly organized. Hodgkin did not question Harrison's involvement on behalf of the natives but maintained that the fur trade was having a destructive effect on the Indians. Hodgkin conceded that King might not have been completely informed but had reported only what he saw. It is doubtful that this disagreement was lightly dismissed by Harrison.

Examples of Harrison's philanthropy might at first glance cause one to question the validity of the rumor (reported in 1892) that the treasurer would have no officer of the hospital who drove about with a North American Indian.[20] But these opposing attitudes are not difficult to reconcile. Is it not conceivable that Harrison would want to help the natives to discover the white man's God while they remained in their native habitat on a distant shore but became uncomfortable when one showed up in his own front yard?

The Indian reportedly seen with Hodgkin was probably a Chippewa chief falsely accused of assault. Hodgkin contributed to his bail and, after acquittal, raised funds for his return to America. Hodgkin also provided supplies and advice for starting a school for his tribe. These events were probably the origin of the story about Hodgkin driving around London with an Indian.[21] In later versions Hodgkin's companion has also been described as dressed "in his full costume"[22] and as "a half-naked North American Indian."[23] Whether or not it was the same Indian, either way, the effect on Benjamin Harrison, Jr., was sure to have been the same. Another popularly held impression that has survived is that Harrison objected to Hodgkin because he drove about with a "coloured man" sitting next to him.[24]

In March 1837, Hodgkin experienced a sudden attack that left him numb on one side and confined him to bed for several weeks of rest. He described it as "a febrile attack with protracted derangements of the alimentary canal which has considerably reduced my strength."[25] Richard Bright, one of several physicians consulted, believed Hodgkin was suffering from overwork. The exact nature of the illness (probably neurologic in origin) is not known, but the family medical history reveals a pattern of illness and related symptoms. His brother, John, Jr., was frequently ill. His nephew and namesake experienced convulsive seizures, and another nephew was diagnosed an epileptic. Narcolepsy and epilepsy appeared in subsequent generations.[26]

Friends and relatives recommended that he refrain from all activities and retire to a calm and relaxed environment to convalesce. Such an atmosphere was available in the peaceful and familiar surroundings of his relatives in Lewes, Sussex, at the home of Sarah Godlee Rickman, his childhood sweetheart. Widowed the year before, she had returned to her family home with her two children. Under Sarah's companionship and attention, Hodgkin's disturbing symptoms of headache, unusual sensations in hand and foot, intermittent fever, and gastrointestinal disturbance gradually subsided, and his mental and physical state improved.[27] Their friendship renewed, Hodgkin once again entertained thoughts of marrying his cousin despite the threat of expulsion from the Society of Friends.

Election Campaign

Then, quite unexpectedly, Hodgkin learned of Cholmeley's death on June 15, in a letter from Dr. H. M. Hughes, a colleague at Guy's. Hughes was supportive of Hodgkin's candidacy and had written so that "you may have an opportunity of acting as you think right with the slightest loss of time,"[28] and he offered to help. Hodgkin urged Hughes to apply also and even suggested where he could seek support.[29] Hodgkin immediately announced his candidacy for the expected vacancy in a letter to the treasurer,[30] and adding that, if appointed, he would like to stay on as curator of the pathological museum to which he had given so much effort.

Hodgkin wanted the appointment very much—so much so, in fact, that to avoid damaging his chances, he took a step very much out of character for him. He asked to have his name removed from a letter of support he had written to the Reform Association complaining of religious bias by conservatives when it came to employment of dissenters. The letter was published anonymously.[31] Undoubtedly, he did this to avoid alienating Harrison and the governors, who for the most part supported Tory policies. As time went by, Hodgkin gradually came to understand why he would probably not get the position. As he became less assertive in his own cause, there was an increase in campaigning by his supporters, especially John Hodgkin, Jr., by now a prominent lawyer. But Hodgkin's friend Dr. William Stroud sensed failure and advised him to withdraw from contention for reasons of health. John Hodgkin, Jr., on the other hand, did not agree and told his brother that Stroud's "friendship for thee may warp his judgment & increase his natural timidity & caution."[32]

Dr. Hughes had written that Addison considered it "most impolitic" for Hodgkin to be away for so long.[33] The delay in returning could make it appear that he was not fit for the position for reasons of health. At this point there was a rumor that the vacant position might be shared between Hodgkin and Benjamin Babington. His supporters advised Hodgkin to return to London.

Hodgkin hurried back. Apparently there was something to the rumor. His brother had conferred with Harrison on August 2 and was left with the impression that Thomas Hodgkin could have half of the appointment but would have to give up the museum.[34] On the afternoon of August 5, Harrison presented Hodgkin with his proposal. Two assistant physicians should be appointed, but only one should give the clinical lectures and receive the fees.

The other post was curator of the museum but otherwise was somewhat vague. By now Hodgkin would have been willing to give up his post at the museum if it meant becoming assistant physician, but not if it was only as window dressing. Hodgkin regarded the plan "in no other light than as virtually passing me over." Two days later he wrote to Harrison that the projected plan of having two assistant physicians is "an act in which I could not with justice to myself concur." The treasurer's response, as noted by Hodgkin, was brief and to the point: "Then I shall appoint Dr. B. alone."[35]

There was still a month to go before the governors were scheduled to vote, and Hodgkin's brother and friends initiated a major drive on his behalf. However, Hodgkin seemed to be reconciled to disappointment. In a letter to the steward of Guy's on August 9, he specifically disassociated himself from any efforts being made on his behalf because these would be "diametrically opposed to the object for which I am now most anxious—vis. to prove that, tho' I have failed to obtain the post which I have, for years, laboured to merit, I am sincerely endeavouring to bear the disappointment with equanimity and Christian patience."[36]

As the election drew near, Hodgkin's mood vacillated between resignation to failure and renewed hopes. His supporters and especially his brother stepped up their activities and enlisted prominent Quakers and others. Dr. James Clark and Sir Moses Montefiore agreed to help. Letters were written, governors were visited, and a committee was formed to plan strategy. John Blackburn, a Liverpool surgeon and former student of Hodgkin's, prepared a statement on behalf of former students, supporting the appointment of Hodgkin.[37] Mock confrontations were staged within the group of supporters, as objections that had been voiced during the preceding months were reviewed and responses prepared.

A statement by Samuel Gurney, a prominent Quaker, and John Hodgkin, Jr., was prepared without prior consultation with Dr. Hodgkin and was printed for distribution to the governors. The statement reviewed the many qualifications and accomplishments of Thomas Hodgkin that had brought fame and credit to the hospital and the school over the period of many years. They also noted that Dr. Babington was a comparative newcomer and had done little or nothing for either institution. In summary, the statement added that Hodgkin's services "can only have been sustained by the confident anticipation, which he has so long been tacitly permitted to entertain, of being appointed to the honorable post, which the governors have now the opportunity of conferring on him, with its attendant and consequent advantages."[38]

However, there is some question as to whether the statement was sent to any of the governors or perhaps not at all. Sixteen hand-fashioned envelopes, three addressed to governors, the rest without names but clearly intended to carry the document in question, were found in a packet of old papers in the home of a Hodgkin descendant.[39]

Throughout all this maneuvering there hovered a realistic anticipation of failure. It was an exercise in futility as they went through the motions, letting the drama play itself out to its inevitable conclusion. Although he was convinced that he would not receive the appointment, Hodgkin's sagging spirits and hopes were buoyed by the enthusiasm of his supporters.

Rejection and Resignation

On August 31 he was formally notified by the registrar of the hospital that a General Court would be held on September 6, for the election of the new assistant physician. As late as September 2, he wrote to his brother that he would readily withdraw from contention if only his qualifications for the position were acknowledged. Hodgkin realized how tense and uneasy his work environment would be if he were elected over the treasurer's objection. He expected there would be constant fault-finding by Harrison and his loyalists on the hospital staff. Finally, he resigned himself to the judgment of his family and friends, saying: "Anything like flinching from want of nerve would be an ungrateful return for your kindness. I am therefore prepared to act the part which you may assign me—or to withdraw with perfect satisfaction when and how you may think fit."[40]

The final scene took place on Wednesday, September 6, 1837, when the president and governors of the hospital met to select an assistant physician to replace Dr. Addison, who had been advanced to physician at an earlier meeting. There were seven applicants. Doctors Hodgkin, Barlow, Hughes, Babington, and Whiting were presented individually to the governors. Doctors Barrett and Rees were unable to attend. After Hodgkin's letter of application was read, he was interviewed by Harrison in a manner more suited to an interrogation than an interview. The outcome was a foregone conclusion.[41] The treasurer then intimated to the court that Doctors Barlow, Hughes, and Whiting had withdrawn their petitions— probably advised to do so—and the vote was held. Twenty-four ballots were cast. Babington received twenty-one and Hodgkin three. There were two abstentions.[42] Because his sense of personal disappointment was so great, he felt unable to stay on in any capacity at Guy's Hospital.

> The proceedings of yesterday leave me no alternative but to resign the offices of Curator of the Museum & Demonstrator of Morbid Anatomy immediately. I had previously proposed to take this step at a later period in order that I might not leave important work unfinished: but, in my present position, it would be not only painful to my feelings but inconsistent with the duty which I owe to myself to hold office any longer.[43]

Babington, The Successful Candidate

The offer of duplicate jobs (in title) to Babington and Hodgkin was probably a compromise that Harrison thought a fair response to the heavy active campaigning by many of Hodgkin's prominent supporters. Had Hodgkin accepted, he might have gotten a share of the lectures. Babington did not lecture much in the school but was a careful clinical teacher in the wards and a successful practitioner.[44] Quite possibly, Hodgkin would have been appointed to the next vacancy. This occurred in 1840, when Babington was advanced to physician. However, after waiting for twelve years, Hodgkin was unwilling to accept a compromise.

What about the five other unsuccessful candidates? How did they fare? George Hilaro Barlow, the first editor of *Guy's Hospital Reports*, and Henry Marshall Hughes were both appointed assistant physician in 1840. Barlow was appointed physician in 1843, while Hughes had to wait until 1854 for this distinction. Hughes acquired a great reputation for his aptitude with the stethoscope and in the recognition of the physical signs of disease and wrote a popular book on these topics. George Owen Rees was made an assistant physician in 1843, the year of Bright's retirement from Guy's. Rees's work from the very start was in the study of pathological chemistry.[45] In 1838 he showed how sugar could be isolated from blood and was the first to demonstrate the presence of sugar in the blood of diabetic patients and to measure it. He also carried out extensive researches for Bright on the presence of urea in the blood. Barrett and Whiting received no appointments.

Hodgkin's failure to be appointed to the staff was the cause of much controversy, speculation, and concern. The impression at the time was that Hodgkin was too independent and liberal a spirit to live under the despotic rule of "King" Harrison and "His Majesty," as *The Lancet* called him. It was believed that Harrison regarded Hodgkin's interests outside of medicine very unfavorably. Students and friends of Hodgkin charged the treasurer with having rejected Hodgkin because of personal dislike and religious and political prejudice. No doubt Harrison objected to Quaker involvement in the political issues of the day.

Apparently, Hodgkin was popular with the students, for a large number of them protested with a memorandum to Benjamin Harrison, Jr., expressing their dissatisfaction, and the following unsigned letter appeared in *The Lancet* on September 16, 1837:

GUY'S HOSPITAL.—(*From a Correspondent*).—To those who are acquainted with the management of affairs at *Guy's Hospital*, little surprise will be created by the appointment of Dr. BABINGTON to the office of physician, left vacant by the death of Dr. CHOLMONDE-LEY [Cholmeley], and the consequent displacement of Dr. HODGKIN. Many years of severe duty at Guy's, as curator of the Museum, as lecturer on pathology, as demonstrator of anatomy, with the most profuse adulation of the treasurer during that period, and continued avowals of extravagant admiration of everything as it existed in that institution, would seem to present strong claims in favour of Dr. HODGKIN, but King HARRISON thinks otherwise. It seems that Dr. HODGKIN is a *Dissenter*—that he is supposed, under the rose, to be liberal in politics, and, above all, he is one of the members of the new London University! Is it wonderful, then, that the distinguished medical acquirements of Dr. BENJAMIN GUY HARRISON BABINGTON should supersede every other consideration or claim? *Sic volo, sic jubeo.*[46]

The editor commented: "Why, yes, this is rather hard treatment, considering the services rendered to His Majesty, from the time of the death of Stephen Pollard to the present moment." This reference was to the libel trial of Bransby Cooper vs. *The Lancet.*

There was another show of support for Hodgkin by the students. Although it did not succeed, it revealed the mood of the medical class. The incident was described years later in answer to a correspondent's rejection of a proposed testimonial for Hodgkin (see chapter 13, note 30).

> SIR, — I write to you not so much for the purpose of answering "Justus," who would more correctly have subscribed himself "Malevolus," in his criticisms on Dr. Hodgkin's career, as to inquire from you with whom I can communicate on the subject of the testimonial. I, as an old Guy's student, shall feel proud of joining with my professional brethren in testifying regard for one whose enlarged benevolence, untiring industry, and comprehensive scientific acquirements, have shed a lustre on English medicine.
>
> Nearly twenty years ago, when the doctor was driven from Guy's Hospital, with far more injury to the school than to his own reputation, a very general feeling pervaded the medical class that there ought to be some recognition of his services to the profession and the school. I was deputed to draw up a memorial, in the writing of which I carefully avoided any allusion to the unworthy treatment he had received. After our address had been engrossed, I placed it on the table of the clinical-room, and it was in course of signature, when my old but I must add irritable friend, Mr. Browell, the steward, rushed into the room on hearing of the meditated treason, and, without waiting to read a line, crumpled up the parchment, dashed it on the floor, and threatened the direst vengeance against the perpetrators. I have long since forgiven him; he did what he considered his duty, in his own way. I have not heard of him for some years, but if he is still on the serene side of nature, I hope he is enjoying, in a happy old age the *souvenirs* of an active and well-spent life.
>
> Should some old friend of mine lurk under the title of "Justus," I hope he will pardon the liberty I have taken, and excuse my warmth in defending a very learned and deserving member of our profession.
>
> I subscribe myself your obedient servant,
> Dukinfield, November, 1856.   Alfred Aspland.[47]

His old friend and personal physician Dr. William Stroud and a former student, John Blackburn, urged him to go public with the grievance, but instead, Hodgkin withdrew from society. His intense disappointment triggered a prolonged period of depression. This was nothing new. Throughout his life Hodgkin experienced periodic bouts of nervousness or anxiety, as well as depression and moods of pessimism. It probably affected his physical well-being. In early October he suffered a relapse of his earlier intestinal illness and had to give up all outside activity. Because of his health he left the city.

Hodgkin's resignation from Guy's brought to a close the most productive scientific portion of his career at the early age of thirty-nine. Part I of the second volume of his *Lectures* did appear three years later, but the material for it was accumulated before 1837; Part II was never published. On the title page of volume two, Hodgkin lists his many memberships in foreign scientific societies and academies of medicine. These were in Rome, Siena, Paris, Marseilles, Brussels, Ghent, Heidelberg, Philadelphia, Massachucetts [sic], Catanea, Palermo, and the Sandwich Islands. Not included are his memberships in many scientific societies in England. At the end of this listing of affiliations, he adds Licentiate of the Royal College of Physicians in London, and then he adds one more. In a larger-size type than the others, he mentions, Formerly Lecturer on Morbid Anatomy at Guy's Hospital. Was this lengthy compilation of foreign societies an attempt to compensate for the personal and professional disappointment suggested by the word "Formerly" in the final line?

His small private practice at home grew somewhat at first, now that he had more time for it, but he still provided gratuitous advice to those friends who imposed upon him. From strangers he took only small fees. There was little reward, monetary or otherwise, from this practice of medicine. His heart was not in it either, cut off as he was from sources of pathologic specimens and thereby deprived of the opportunity to advance and develop his profession. Since Hodgkin was not a staff physician to Guy's Hospital, he was dependent on his colleagues for his postmortem material and for information about the patients while they were alive. From these examinations he obtained the specimens for the museum, and they formed the basis of his own observations and publications. It was this kind of cooperation that provided the data for his famous

1832 paper on absorbent glands (see chapter 5, note 2). Of the cases described, two of the patients, when in the wards, were under Bright, one was under Addison, two under Morgan, and one was a patient of Back.

Hodgkin didn't let the unfair treatment at the hands of the hospital administrators affect his feelings toward former colleagues, with whom he retained close friendships. He referred to T. W. King, who followed him as lecturer and curator, as "my much-valued friend and able successor."[48] In 1840, Hodgkin dedicated volume two, part I of his *Lectures* to "my friends" Thomas Bell, surgeon-dentist, and John Morgan, surgeon and lecturer, both of Guy's Hospital. In a brief note, Hodgkin added that their highly-valued friendship continued, with undiminished value, to survive his separation from Guy's Hospital. He also acknowledged the kind and respectful attention of the students.

This does not mean that Hodgkin got along on the most cordial terms with everyone. His critical attitude could be irritating to his associates. As a Quaker, he preferred to speak out, even when a tactful oversight would have been more appropriate. On one occasion in 1834, naming no names, only the streets on which they lived, he chided some staff members for not attending meetings of the Physical Society. Hodgkin thought that they lived close enough and added that their presence would heighten the interest and importance of the meetings.[49] Undoubtedly, this was spoken with the best of intentions, but it was not diplomatic to do so at an open meeting, especially since Hodgkin was president of the society at the time.

There was no personal rivalry involved for the position of assistant physician. The relationship between Hodgkin and Babington remained warm and cordial. It was unlucky for Hodgkin that, when at last a vacancy did occur, it was the son of William Babington (1756–1833) who was the leading candidate. The elder Babington had been on the staff of Guy's from 1795 to 1811 and was one of the most distinguished and respected physicians of the time, greatly admired for his personal qualities.[50] Benjamin Guy Babington (1794–1866) (Fig. 7) inherited his father's modesty, charm, and personality, and all his life he enjoyed the same

Fig. 7. *Benjamin Guy Babington as a young man. (Reproduced by kind permission of the President and Council of the Royal College of Surgeons of England.)*

immense popularity. Like his father he gave freely of his time and
advice to those who couldn't pay.

One can readily find fault today with the treasurer's preference
for the popular son of an admired and distinguished physician at
Guy's Hospital rather than the more brilliant but outspoken social
radical Hodgkin. However, this was a clinical appointment, and
Babington, an authority on cholera, was also known for his
knowledge of fevers, which in those days was the major reason for
admission to the hospital. The position involved care of patients,
and Hodgkin had established a reputation as a morbid anatomist.
Babington certainly fulfilled the medical requirements and was a
worthy candidate. Although Babington's research activities could
not compare with Hodgkin's record of publications, and he spent
most of his time in private practice rather than at Guy's Hospital,
he was a fellow of the Royal College of Physicians and of The
Royal Society. He later achieved other honors as the first president
of the Epidemiological Society and president of the Royal Medical
and Chirurgical Society.

Hodgkin had faced an impossible task in seeking the position
and never really had a chance. Not only did he risk further
antagonizing the authoritarian Harrison, who did not like him,
but he couldn't attack his chief opponent because of past associa-
tions with Babington's family. Babington's father had been the
Hodgkin's family doctor and had treated the chronically ailing
Elizabeth Hodgkin during her final illness. Hodgkin had performed
the autopsy on William Babington in 1833 at the family's request
and on one of Benjamin's young sons in 1828. Babington also had
the right family connections. At Guy's he assisted his brother-in-
law, Dr. Richard Bright (whose first wife was Babington's sister,
Martha), with laboratory examinations of blood and urine in his
researches on diseases of the kidneys. If all this weren't enough,
Harrison was Benjamin Babington's godfather.

At this critical point in his career, Hodgkin's independence, his
lack of deference for authority, and his participation in so many
controversial and nonmedical activities finally outweighed his reputation and achievements as a physician and pathologist. The man
who "was universally beloved . . . amiable and genial . . .
overflowing with fun and good humour," and whose "benevolence

was carried to a fault,"[51] was preferred to the outspoken character, champion of the underdog, and political and social moralist.

As for Babington, he too had his professional ups and downs. He has never been adequately recognized for his invention and first use of the laryngoscope in 1829. This instrument made it possible to see the larynx by means of a reflecting mirror in the mouth. Babington's instrument, which he called the *glottiscope*,[52] resembled the modern laryngeal mirror and was exhibited at a meeting of the Hunterian Society on March 18, 1829. By an odd coincidence, the only other contemporary notice of Babington's invention was made in one of Hodgkin's lectures at Guy's Hospital. Hodgkin, with his rigorous classical background, rejected Babington's term and referred to the instrument as "the *speculum laryngis* or *laryngiscope*, invented by my friend Dr. Babington in 1829."[53] Babington appreciated the change. The slightly altered spelling came later.

Babington used the instrument on his patients and at least one professional colleague[54] over a period of several years, but he left no records and eventually abandoned its use. Hodgkin's brief report passed virtually unnoticed. The instrument was reinvented twenty-five years later in Paris by Manuel Garcia (1805–1906), a Spanish singing teacher. Garcia was unaware of Babington's work but was interested in the anatomy of the vocal organs.[55] Once the laryngoscope came into general use, Babington received some belated acknowledgment as the original discoverer.[56]

Babington missed out on another chance for eponymic fame when he was the first to report on a hereditary form of epistaxis (hemorrhage from the nose).[57] When this is associated with a network of dilated capillaries and small blood vessels with a tendency to bleed, most often in the nose or mouth, the condition is called hereditary hemorrhagic telangiectasia and is usually known as Osler's disease, or the Osler-Rendu-Weber syndrome.[58]

Babington's life had two other parallels to the life of Thomas Hodgkin. The first was his resignation from Guy's Hospital because of a disagreement with the administrator, not Benjamin Harrison, Jr., this time, but his successor, Bonamy Dobree (d. 1863). He left because of new regulations at the hospital that deprived the students of privileges that they had long enjoyed.[59] He considered this to be an infringement of the custom and contract between students and hospital administration. The objectionable restrictive orders dealt with after-hours visiting for dressers, obstetric residents, and students. It was intended to put a stop to all-night partying and other forms of disorderly and boisterous behavior, which could keep the dressers from effectively treating casualties the following morning. These rules were later rescinded.

The other parallel was the final event in Babington's life. His death occurred on April 8, 1866, four days after that of Thomas Hodgkin. A bladder ailment and difficulty in passing urine led to a suppurative inflammation of the kidneys which proved fatal. Hodgkin's and Babington's obituaries appeared on the same page of *The Lancet*[60] and the *British Medical Journal*.[44]

The circumstances of Hodgkin's departure from Guy's Hospital cast a cloud over his tenure at the institution. There may have been a conscious effort by some to erase the record of Hodgkin's contributions to Guy's Hospital. His presentation on the stethoscope was removed from the proceedings of the Physical Society (chapter 1, note 78). The organization of an innovative Clinical Report Society for student record-keeping of bedside observations was credited by the editors of the *Guy's Hospital Reports* to Mr. Blackburn of Liverpool;[61] this claim was repeated in a later issue (volume 6, 1841). Hodgkin, the real guiding force behind the creation of this society and its first president, was completely ignored. In 1854, Hodgkin referred to the suppression of this fact in a preliminary note when he published a lecture that he had given to the Physical Society of Guy's Hospital in 1834.[62] However, the truth is preserved in the minutes of the Clinical Report Society, where Richard Bright and Thomas Addison acknowledged Hodgkin's role and initiative in founding the society.[63]

CHAPTER TEN

The Oxford Case

Resumption of Activities

The unsuccessful outcome of Hodgkin's campaign for the post of assistant physician, and his subsequent resignation from Guy's, brought on a relapse of his earlier illness with all the same symptoms and a bout with depression. It was a major setback for Hodgkin, coming so soon after his episode of nervous exhaustion and intestinal disorder. He had looked forward to a career as physician at Guy's, with some time for philanthropy and social reforms, but Harrison's hostility had put an end to that goal. Now, without a base for medical research, Hodgkin had to pursue private practice, an activity he was poorly suited for by intellect and personality. Plagued by his forced retirement and incapacity, Hodgkin's mood changed from day to day. His depression generated morbid thoughts of imminent doom, and for a time he thought that he was close to death and would not recover. He told no one of this, but a note found among his papers many years later showed the extent of his anxiety. "It is with the consciousness that my present malady is of a very uncertain & precarious character & that though it may on the one hand admit of amendment & continuance of life for months or even years, on the other

163

it may with little or no further warning deprive me of sensorial power if not of life."[1]

The illness and depression once again alarmed his friends and relatives. His medical colleagues urged complete physical and mental rest. This time he remained in Lewes for six months. By the end of July 1838, after recuperation from surgery for hemorrhoids, Hodgkin was well enough to plan a trip to the Continent, but with a friend and not alone, because of persisting symptoms. His family and friends hoped the travel would speed his recovery from the stress and strain of the past eighteen months.[2] Back in London in early 1839, Hodgkin was ready to resume his many varied activities, including some that were a little out of the ordinary even for him—insanity and high treason. He also got publicly embroiled in a very personal dispute with the elders of the Society of Friends over the consanguinity marriage rule.

Advocacy for Aboriginals

Hodgkin got back to work with a long article on his favorite constituents, the aboriginal populations. It was his first publication since leaving Guy's Hospital. In describing the exploitation and demoralization of the Indians of North America, he picked up where he had left off in his letter of December 1836 to Benjamin Harrison, Jr. Now, he specifically criticized the Hudson's Bay Company for "withholding any thing which can tend to bring their system into discredit."[3] Hodgkin rejected ideas voiced by others that the Indian was not capable of rising above his primitive condition and was doomed to extinction by the spread of civilized society. Their existing state of barbarism, he said, was not necessarily permanent and unalterable. Nor was intellectual improvement by no means impracticable. Hodgkin gave numerous examples, both past and present, of European civilizations that successfully advanced from the level of barbarous savages similar to that of the North American Indians. He mentioned Greece, Germany, and Ireland, whose inhabitants during early periods of their history progressively emerged from various stages of barbarism. He pointed to Russia as an example of what could be accomplished on a large scale within a comparatively short period in advancing from barbarism to civilization.

For the North American Indians, Hodgkin proposed the fullest participation in the rights of British North American subjects: the right to hold property; encouragement for advances in religion, education, and the arts of civilized life; advanced education for the better students to enable them to become teachers; formation of a system of police or civil government suitable to the Indian character, which would lead to their settlements becoming integral parts of the province in which they were located; and extending the advantages of British laws and protection to Indians beyond the present frontier, for the mutual benefit in security and commerce. These were fine-sounding concepts, but they offered no working formulas. They were a restatement of the noble goals of enlightenment to which he assumed all men of goodwill aspired. But they didn't fit in with British imperial and economic objectives.

The Southern Retreat

At about the same time as he was preparing this essay for publication, Hodgkin, not known for any special connection with the study of mental diseases, although he may have had some contact with mental patients at Guy's,[4] met with a group of prominent London Quakers to plan a mental asylum for Quakers in southern England. A committee of six, including Hodgkin, issued a prospectus on July 17, 1839. "The Southern Retreat" was to be a counterpart to the already famous York Retreat in the north. The main reason for a new asylum was the expensive and fatiguing travel by Friends in southern England to reach York. The new institution would also enable Quakers to avoid sending insane relatives to asylums not connected with the society, where their religious peculiarities might subject them to additional emotional stress and physical suffering.

In 1813 Samuel Tuke (1784–1857), Quaker philanthropist, tea merchant of York, and grandson of William Tuke (1732–1822), the founder of the York Retreat, set in motion the first great psychiatric revolution when he published a description of the retreat and its successful experiences with mild treatment and moral management. The retreat and the book were influential in Great Britain and elsewhere in improving hospital treatment of the insane. For this, Samuel Tuke is remembered as one of the great figures in nineteenth-century treatment of the mentally ill.[5]

The first physician appointed by Samuel Tuke was Thomas Fowler (1736–1801), an Edinburgh graduate, after whom Fowler's solution of potassium arsenite was named because he introduced its modern medicinal use. Tuke and Fowler knew that pharmaceutical remedies were inadequate to cure or to relieve insanity. It was this ineffectiveness of medicines that made it possible for sympathetic laymen such as William Tuke to be as capable of directing asylums as medical men. York Retreat did not neglect medical treatment but had found that emetics, bleedings, blisters, and cathartics were not successful, and, except for warm baths, there was less confidence in the medical approach.

The York asylum for Quaker insane had been opened on May 16, 1796, and operated under a philosophy of religion combined with humanitarian concern for minds closed to the Inner Light. The retreat's avowed aim was to accord the insane the dignity and status of sick human beings. Implicit was a rejection of the "beat and bleed" therapies, so conventional in many institutions, as cruel and ineffectual, and substitution of mild and gentle treatment and moral management (psychological support). The moral management of insanity constituted all those means which, by operating on the feelings and habits of the patient and inducing self-esteem, would exert a beneficial effect and restore him to a sound and natural state. A key element in this mild management of body and mind was to draw the patient's attention away from thoughts and feelings connected to his disordered state and to stimulate the activity of superior motives. Experience showed that the regimen of religion, sound diet, and useful labor could be used successfully with some insane patients to replace the debasing and brutalizing coercion of the then current "terrific system" as it was called, which controlled them by repression, depletion, and restraint.[6]

Depletion of body fluids exhausted the patient and was accomplished by bleeding (venipuncture or leeches), vomiting (emetics), and evacuation of bowels (purgatives). This extended the prevailing humoral theory of medical practice to the treatment of mental illness. Medical practitioners believed that the different patterns of illness were merely changes in the status of the humoral system. Therapy was directed to restoring harmony to body fluids, whatever the name given to the disease.

The new institution planned for the south of England was to be a business funded by a sale of investment shares, and net proceeds from patient fees were to be divided among the shareholders. The prospectus sought to raise £20,000 for a property through the sale of 400 shares of £50 each, transferable, with a limit of 20 shares per investor. Individual dividends were not to exceed 7½ percent annually on capital invested, with surplus, if any, going to the improvement of the establishment. There was to be a guarantee-list for those who did not wish to buy shares but who wanted to support the institution by guaranteeing any losses by the shareholders during the first seven years of operation. The Southern Retreat intended to copy the practice of the York Retreat of accepting wealthy patients at higher rates, not only from the Friends but from other religious groups as well.[7]

The new asylum did not plan to neglect human kindness, moral emphasis, or the psychological side of care, but its approach to mental illness—according to the prospectus—was to be the "too much neglected branch of medical treatment of mental and cerebral disease." It intended to restore a more traditional medical regimen along with greater use of medication, close bedside observation, research, and cadaveric examination. Here we see the influence of Hodgkin.

For Hodgkin this project had extra added attractions, since it would allow him to be involved as humanitarian and scientist. Hodgkin was a religious man, but he was also a careful scientist and undoubtedly was intrigued by the scientific side of this abnormality. He wanted more certainty and had more confidence in medical solutions. He believed that greater reliance on the medical treatment of mental diseases, supplemented by thorough pathological examinations, would advance medical knowledge.

The potential for research opportunities at the Southern Retreat may have been a factor in Hodgkin's leadership role in the planning. His scientific curiosity concerning mental illness centered on the physical changes in the brain as observed by pathological investigation and correlation with the clinical findings of disease during life. In his lectures on morbid anatomy, Hodgkin emphasized the correlation of clinical with pathological study of disease. He stressed the need for "personal acquaintance with disease," based on observation at the bedside followed by a careful examination of the effects of disease, as revealed by the postmortem inspection.[8]

The institution was to be located near London and run by Achille-Louis Foville (1799–1878), an experienced alienist and noted pathologist, who was also a longtime friend of Thomas Hodgkin. Their friendship went back to the time of Hodgkin's studies at the Necker Hospital in Paris during 1821–22. The two were probably drawn together by a mutual interest in pathology. Hodgkin's fluency in French also gave the friendship an added dimension. In his major work on the anatomy, physiology, and pathology of the cerebrospinal system, Foville acknowledged Thomas Hodgkin in the preface. "My excellent friend Doctor Hodgkin from London has found ways of helping me despite the distance that separates us."[9] Foville believed that madness was not incurable and that some cases could be successfully treated by a medical approach.

Because of the close association of Samuel Tuke with York Retreat, it was understandable that he might have been less than enthusiastic or even hostile to the proposal of a rival Quaker asylum whose philosophy of treatment and care ran counter to his own. A letter of August 21, 1839, from Hodgkin to Tuke touches on this potential for conflict.

Although I am aware that thou hast felt some doubt as to the present necessity for a lunatic asylum in the South of England in some respects resembling your Retreat and destined for the reception of members of the Society of Friends yet I believe that there are few if any persons who will feel more interested in the progress and results of the Institution should it be formed than thyself. . . . In its progress I think we may be excused if we occasionally apply to thee for advice and assistance.[10]

Hodgkin continued at some length on the importance of Foville to the new asylum and that if not confirmed he soon might accept another offer in France. Hodgkin wanted Tuke as an ally and knew that he could deflect any criticisms of the undertaking within the Society of Friends, including suspicions of Foville because he was a foreigner. He asked Tuke to write a letter of support for Foville, but there is no record of an answer.

By July 1840, £12,250 had been subscribed, but the following May, after two years and fifteen recorded meetings, the project had to be abandoned. All moneys less minor expenses were returned to the subscribers. Hodgkin had pledged five shares at £50 each and paid £50 on account. He recovered £49 13s. 2d., for a small financial loss.[11] There were several reasons for termination of the project, chief among which was failure to obtain a suitable location for the building. Another was the loss of Foville, because of the delays, to the Royal Asylum in Charenton. There he succeeded Jean-Etienne-Dominique Esquirol (1772–1840),[12] his former teacher at the Salpêtrière and the first to outline the main forms of insanity, as chief medical officer. Other contributing factors were the suspicion, even hostility, of some Friends toward the project and to Foville because he was a foreigner. Foville lost the Charenton post in the political revolution of 1848.

If nationality was a factor, the bias was shortsighted and self-defeating. Whereas the Germans were applying psychology to the understanding of mental illness, and the English were improving conditions and treatment in the insane asylums, the French, during the first half of the nineteenth century, were in the lead in the treatment of mental disorders. This was the result of progressive laws, teaching, and the transformation of the beggar prisons, where mental patients had usually been kept since 1656, into mental hospitals. These advances had been initiated by the internist Philippe Pinel (1745–1826), who, by freeing some of the insane from their chains at Bicêtre in September 1793, symbolically converted this prison into a hospital and liberated the treatment of mental illness from the confines of systems and hypotheses. He replaced bleeding, purging, and other such depletion practices with moral treatment, a firm but benevolent attitude, and work therapy.[13]

Inasmuch as the Southern Retreat never came into being, we can only speculate as to the kind of medical treatment and research that might have been conducted there. It is doubtful whether Hodgkin contemplated any more effective use of the pharmacopoeia of the day. Some of the most frequently used remedies were opium, antimony tartrate, sulfate of magnesia, calomel, and cinchona bark (see chapter one, note 53).

Hodgkin was influenced by the French clinicians and believed, as they did, that many traditional therapies were truly absurd, useless, and even more harmful than good. He conceded the therapeutic value of mercury but believed that it had probably done much more harm than good. He warned against resorting to mercury in difficult-to-treat diseases with no idea of its action on the principle that a doubtful remedy is better than none, especially when that remedy is a decided poison. In his own medical practice he recommended procedures followed by those physicians and teachers known as eclectics. Their aim was to select from the various systems and theories of medical practice only those facts verified by observations. Such a school would not teach medicine as a perfect and fixed science. He believed that the physician should try to help the convalescing patient regain his normal bodily functions and that this was best accomplished by assisting nature itself as the immediate agent of cure, with good diet, fresh air, and rest.[14] However, Hodgkin was well aware of the limitations of medical practice and that his specialty in particular was often unable to suggest the best form of treatment.

The Oxford Case

Following the start-up efforts to establish the Southern Retreat, Hodgkin was caught up in a new issue involving insanity, but this time it was in an entirely different capacity. He was asked to give expert testimony for the defense in the trial of Edward Oxford, an eighteen-year-old bar-boy who had fired two pistols in quick succession at Queen Victoria while she was out riding with Prince Albert in an open carriage on June 10, 1840. Arrested immediately, the boy made no attempt to escape and admitted simply that he had done it and would go quietly. He could give no explanation for his action, and there was no evidence of delusion or other sign of insanity.

The boy's mother, unable to pay for a legal defense, applied for financial assistance to the Society for Abolishing Capital Punishment. It agreed to take the case, but believing the boy must be insane, from the very senselessness and foolishness of his act, the society's barrister decided on a plea of insanity, or more specifically, "unsoundness of mind," and called a number of expert medical witnesses to testify to that end. All the medical witnesses for Oxford gave their services without payment. Apparently, Hodgkin was included because he opposed the death penalty. John Conolly (1794–1866), who knew Hodgkin at Edinburgh University, was chosen to represent the most advanced opinion in the field of mental illness. He saw this as a duty not only for humanity but for science as well.[15]

Conolly's graduation thesis, *De Statu Mentis in Insania et Melancholia* (1821), showed his interest in working for improvement in the status of lunatics and advancing knowledge in this important branch of medicine. Although there is no evidence that Hodgkin introduced Conolly to Samuel Tuke during the latter's visit to Edinburgh in May 1821, it is very likely that he did or, at least, that Conolly asked to meet Tuke. Conolly certainly knew of Tuke's work in the treatment of the insane and the management of asylums and made flattering reference to it in his thesis. Conolly's work in the mental health field had an important influence on the development of modern clinical psychiatry in the first half of the nineteenth century.[16]

Hodgkin, Conolly, and others on the defense team visited Oxford in Newgate prison and were satisfied with their impression of the defendant. Conolly noted a peculiar depression in the boy's forehead, which he had never seen except in persons who were either idiotic or otherwise unsound. They were all convinced that, in spite of his essentially rational behavior, Oxford was not of sound mind. Taking into account the hereditary trait of his forehead and that his father was a lunatic and his mother little, if any, better, they were confident of convincing the jury, if not the lawyers, that Edward Oxford was not responsible for his actions.

The defense's plan was to keep the facts simple, to present them in language the jury could understand, to avoid all definitions of insanity, and to let the lawyers fight it out on the legal questions. It was a wise move. The Crown was determined to convict the prisoner of its most serious crime—high treason. Counsel ridiculed defense witnesses as philanthropists mistaken about the meaning of legal insanity. So confident was the prosecution of conviction that it indicted Oxford on only that single count. This was an error in strategy, because the only evidence that the pistols contained bullets was Oxford's admission to the police. No bullets were found.

Oxford was quickly brought to trial, only one month after the crime. In court Hodgkin testified that, considering the boy's family history, the apparently motiveless act itself, and his manner of amused indifference and unconcern throughout the trial, he would not hesitate to call him insane. Even the judge in his summation noted that such nonchalant conduct seemed scarcely compatible with a right condition of mind. According to Hodgkin, the evidence clearly pointed to a "*lesion* of the will . . . a form of insanity, in which flagitious acts, sometimes only eccentric acts, are committed. It means more than a loss of control over the conduct. It means morbid propensity."[17] He thought that committing a crime without any apparent motive was an indication of insanity. Hodgkin apparently believed in the existence of "moral insanity," a term coined by his friend, the distinguished mental health specialist and noted anthropologist Dr. James Cowles Prichard (1786–1848),[18] to characterize a new group of mental disorders and distinguish them from such other forms as delusions and hallucinations.

Prichard divided mental diseases into three main classes: feeling or sentiment, understanding, and the will. Because propensities were closely allied to passions and emotions, Prichard combined disorders of feeling with those of the will, i.e., active, or moral powers, and named this disease moral insanity. It was thus a form of mental derangement consisting in a morbid perversion of the feelings and the active powers, without any illusion or error impressed on the understanding.[19]

In Hodgkin's opinion,

A form of insanity under which individuals are led to the commission of acts of great atrocity without any of the ordinary inducements which influence the acts of human beings, and from which they receive no restraint from the considerations which tend to deter those who, however depraved, are not insane, is so fully admitted by the best writers on insanity, and by those who have had the greatest practical acquaintance with the insane, that, however difficult of admission the proposition may at first appear, its truth can admit of no reasonable doubt.[20]

In such cases, proofs of insanity drawn from the individual's acts, unrelated to the crime committed, may be entirely missing.

It was Prichard who first focused attention on the many mental disorders characterized only by disturbances of affect and behavior and which had been largely neglected. But he included a wide range of cases that today would fall into other categories. At the time it was a considerable advance to equate with insanity those cases that exhibited no delusions and hallucinations, features long and still considered the distinguishing characteristic of the mad, as well as cases showing no loss of the use of reason.[21]

Prichard believed that the varieties of moral insanity are perhaps as numerous as the modifications of feeling or passion in the human mind. Succeeding generations gradually trimmed away the mental conditions Prichard had included in the larger class until at the present time "moral insanity" is represented only by its offspring, the "psychopathic personality," a term that covers lack of psychological understanding and excuses the failure of therapy.[22]

The defense asked for a not guilty verdict because the pistols contained no bullets, and also on the ground of insanity in view of the hereditary trait, manners and appearance, cerebral configuration, absence of adequate motives, and the assumption that Oxford had given in to a morbid and uncontrollable impulse. The prosecution ridiculed the idea of moral insanity and would not admit the existence of morbid impulses.

The judge instructed the jury that acquittal on ground of insanity was the only verdict it could possibly arrive at. Oxford was found not guilty on the ground of insanity and was sent to the wing for criminal lunatics at Bethlehem (Bethlem) Hospital. In 1863 he was transferred to the new Broadmoor Asylum. Eventually he was released on condition that he leave England and never return. He migrated to Australia.

Oxford was imprisoned under an act that provided for custody of persons charged with treason, murder, or felony and found to have been insane at the time of the offense, and hence acquitted. That act had been hurriedly passed in 1800 following a not guilty verdict by reason of insanity in the case of James Hadfield, who had fired a loaded pistol at George III. At the time, attempted murder of the sovereign or the heir-apparent was a treasonable offense. However, there was no legal basis to hold an insane assailant even though he would have been a danger to the community and to himself if released.[23]

Many people thought that since at no subsequent time did Oxford give any overt evidence of unsoundness of mind, he could not have been mentally unsound at the time of the act for which he was tried. However, this assumes that insanity is not curable.[24] The same crime today usually produces the same verdict and for as little scientific reason, since understanding of the psychopathology of such impulsive acts has not materially improved. This case showed the importance of medical witnesses using the plainest language and the commonest terms in order to bring evidence within the understanding of the jury.

Earlier legal precedents placed the burden of proof of the defendant's sanity, when it was brought into question, on the prosecutor.[25] This judicial position was reaffirmed in the Oxford case. But only three years later, in 1843, there occurred a major change in criminal law for the insane, and a landmark ruling that reverberates in courtroom dramas to this day. It was the result of an assassination attempt that succeeded. The outcome of that trial was a new set of judicial guidelines for ruling on the insanity plea. Daniel McNaughton (whose name appears in sixteen variant spellings),[26] a wood turner from Glasgow, was tried for the murder of Edward Drummond, the private secretary to Sir Robert Peel, the prime minister. When the examining physicians on both sides agreed that McNaughton had been suffering delusions of persecution, the case was stopped and the jury found the accused not guilty on the ground of insanity. This unexpected verdict alarmed the public about the dangers to ordinary citizens from the acts of madmen. The memory of Oxford's recent acquittal of attempted murder was still fresh in the public's memory. Legal authorities became equally concerned and uneasy about the uncertainties of the criminal law, which in the past had accorded different treatment to insane assassins, including confinement without trial and execution.

The House of Lords convened a panel of the fifteen chief judges of England to consider and clarify questions regarding the criminal responsibility of persons afflicted with insane delusions. What the judges came up with is known all over the English-speaking world as "the McNaughton Rules."

The key rule stipulates that to gain acquittal on the ground of insanity, "it must be clearly proved that, at the time of committing of the act, the party accused was labouring under such a defect of reason, from disease of the mind, as not to know the nature and quality of the act he was doing, or, if he did know it, that he did not know he was doing what was wrong."[27] In effect, the accused is presumed to be sane until clearly proved otherwise by the defense. In practice, the question put to the jury is whether the accused at the time of the act knew the difference between right and wrong. This has come to be known as the "right and wrong" test, and it remains to this day the sole test of criminal insanity in England and in many American states. The question of whether the defendant must prove his insanity or the prosecutor must prove his sanity has produced precedents and rulings that vary from state to state.[28]

The inability to distinguish between right and wrong as the *sine qua non* for legal insanity was a return to earlier interpretations of legal insanity—that only perfect or total madness could excuse one from legal responsibility. Since it seems to satisfy the basic community demand that whoever does wrong and knows what he is doing should be punished for it, it has resisted change even though ever since its introduction the rules have been criticized by lawyers and psychiatrists, and courts have varied in their interpretation. Had McNaughton and Oxford been tried under these rules, they might have been found sane and sentenced to death.

The panel of judges, in its reversal from the more liberal approach to legal insanity, was undoubtedly influenced by the fact that a murder was actually committed this time and that the victim was close to the prime minister, as well as by the overall ominous atmosphere of political and economic crises that posed an imminent threat to the English social structure. There was agitation for more electoral reform; more welfare to relieve poverty, hunger, and despair; protests against child labor; and ongoing disputes between advocates of a protectionist trade policy and those who wanted free-trade worldwide. Consequently, the judges came up with a new and narrower definition of the law of insanity and rejected the flexibility of past legal precedents for dealing with individual cases.[29]

It was a difficult time for Hodgkin. Although he had recovered sufficiently from the emotional shock and physical letdown of the rebuff from Harrison and the governors to resume his scientific and humanitarian activities, the circumstances of his departure from Guy's still left a bitter residue. This is clear in a letter to his Philadelphia friend, Dr. Samuel G. Morton, as he explains his inability to cooperate in a work of mutual interest: "The interruption to my health & the unjust & unkind treatment which I received from the Treasurer & Governors of Guy's Hospital have deprived me of some facilities which I hoped to take advantage of in thy service as we had several interesting American crania of which I might have procurred & forwarded [some to thee]."[30]

Marriage Prohibited

Before long Hodgkin opened himself to more disappointment and emotional stress when he again gave serious thought to marriage with his cousin Sarah. The childhood romance of Thomas and Sarah had been rekindled after her return to Lewes following the death of her husband. She was a comfort to Hodgkin during his illness throughout those difficult months preceding the selection of assistant physician, and he may have delayed his return to London because of her presence. She buoyed his spirits, wrote letters for him, gave encouraging advice, and in many ways filled the role of close friend and confidant. Despite opposition from his family, he spoke out against the Quakers' marriage rule and published a pamphlet strongly critical of the prohibition against marriage between first cousins. He attempted to show that the historical bases for the rule were no longer pertinent, but his main emphasis was that the Scriptures did not provide any spiritual authority for the rule. Attacking the issue head-on, he said:

> When a Christian Church adopts a law respecting marriage, by which it binds its members, under pain of expulsion, accompanied with a stigma of moral delinquency, it may reasonably be supposed that the grounds for such a law are to be found, in express or implied terms, in the Christian Code, as delivered by our Saviour or his apostles. But it is in vain that we search in the New Testament for any trace of the law in question.[31]

He cited examples in the Old Testament of marriages between first cousins expressly commanded by the Almighty, through Moses. He believed the rule was doubtless one of the traditions of the corrupted Church, when prohibitions opened the way for lucrative dispensations, and might be traced to the priestcraft and barbarism of the Middle Ages. (He made numerous unflattering references to the Church of Rome, in an uncharacteristic, but possibly desperate, attempt to play on feelings of prejudice.) With the coming of the Reformation, this restriction was discarded. The ministers of Protestant Churches not only sanctioned the marriages of first cousins in their congregations and families but formed such unions themselves. Hodgkin also rejected the argument that such marriages are "physiologically improper" because they "tend to promote debility of mind and body, and a predisposition to various diseases" in succeeding generations. Hodgkin apparently ignored the admission usually made by Friends that there was a high rate of insanity among their members and that it was attributed to generations of intermarriage. As for the contention that these marriages were generally unhappy, marked as they were by the displeasure of the Almighty, this, he believed, would be extremely difficult to prove by any valid statistics.

Utilizing his numerous contacts in the Geographical, Ethnological, and Aborigines' societies, Hodgkin collected information on the effects of inbreeding in Arab horses and in isolated human communities, such as remote Indian settlements where marriages of close relatives were inevitable. He continually requested explorers and travelers to distant lands to record any pertinent observations.

Allowing that the early members of the Society of Friends were favored with divine assistance in composing the regulations of the society, Hodgkin questioned, nevertheless, whether succeeding generations should "ascribe an equal degree of importance to every step which they took," and not examine and compare the circumstances of the times. Hodgkin pointed out that when this rule was formed, the Friends were little known and greatly misrepresented. Quaker marriages, solemnized in their own manner without a priest, were held suspect by the general community and denounced as licentious. It was therefore expedient that they should be especially prudent and defer to the scruples of the time. However, such marriages had been practiced in every age and in all lands despite any legal restrictions. Though once deemed scandalous due to papal influence, they were now, he noted, allowed by the law of the land and by the Established Church and were sanctioned by the example of Queen Victoria herself.

Hodgkin pursued all possible avenues in his protest. He cited the action of William Penn in 1682 in sanctioning and recommending marriages of close relatives and the forbearance of the society with respect to violations of more serious rules, such as those dealing with marriage outside the Friends, failure to pay debts or tithes, and use of firearms.

Hodgkin noted that the rule was not uniformly enforced and that couples expelled from the society for breaking this rule had later been readmitted. Furthermore, the rules governing marriage were different for Friends in other countries. He even predicted that the prohibition against marriage of first cousins would promote celibacy and marriages out of the society.

Hodgkin published his pamphlet again a year later with additional notes and a preface because, apparently, his arguments had not been answered or even fully considered by the elders. He wanted to make it clear that it was not his intention to disparage the early Friends, who undoubtedly were expressing the sentiments of the age in which they lived. However, he wanted the elders to consider whether they were justified in withholding from others that liberty of conscience that they valued for themselves and in claiming for themselves an authority that exceeded that of the Scripture. As long as the rule existed, said Hodgkin, it was an encroachment on individual liberty, and its supporters should understand the injury it might cause.[32]

None of this did him any practical good and must have alienated him from many of his Quaker friends. The pleas were again rejected by the elders. Hodgkin could not bring himself to give up the Society of Friends. His Quaker upbringing had sustained him throughout his life and formed the basis of his character, beliefs, and behavior. He may have disagreed strongly with the rulings of the society, but he respected its authority, even though Sarah would have married him whatever the outcome. Since he could not change Quaker law, he passively submitted. Other factors as well played a role in Hodgkin's decision, namely, an unwillingness to go against his father's wishes and fear of alienating his brother.

With the passage of time, marriage between first cousins became more tolerated, and in 1860 the ban was lifted. It had been the leading cause of expulsion from the Society of Friends. By the 1880s, half of all Friends who married were marrying non-Quakers.[33] These changes came too late for Thomas and Sarah. Although they continued to see each other at family events, their romance had come to a quiet end. (Sarah's death on April 20, 1866, came less than three weeks after that of Thomas.)

Appointment to St. Thomas's

For a brief period in the early 1840s, Hodgkin was back in an academic hospital setting. In May 1842, St. Thomas's proposed a reunification with Guy's Medical School, but Treasurer Harrison rejected the overture. Realizing that reunion was not possible, St. Thomas's decided to reorganize and seek a charter of incorporation as a collegiate establishment. In July, nearly five years after leaving Guy's, Thomas Hodgkin was invited by St. Thomas's to assist in a reorganization of its medical school, which had fallen on hard times through a series of internal quarrels and resignations of several lecturers. St. Thomas's was no longer the main competition for Guy's. That role was being filled by the new medical school of the University of London.[34] Guy's and St. Thomas's continued their separate ways for the next 140 years. In 1982 they were reunited as the United Medical and Dental Schools of Guy's and St. Thomas's Hospitals, a part of the University of London.

Although somewhat wary of this new opportunity because of his long absence from the lecture room, Hodgkin was confident he could do for St. Thomas's what he had done for Guy's. He became Curator of the Museum and Lecturer on the Theory and Practice of Medicine. He also lectured on morbid anatomy. Hodgkin redesigned the medical lectures and assigned them to staff physicians who were specialists in their fields. The rotation of lecturers was a welcome change of pace for the students. As for the museum, Astley Cooper's specimens were still there, but few additions had been made since the break with Guy's, and the catalogue needed revision and updating. Hodgkin improved the museum and the record-keeping. He also introduced a Society of Clinical and Practical Observation and evening discussion groups, which were well received.[35]

Hodgkin's ponderous lecture style had not changed. His writing has been described—not without justification—as being diffuse and wandering, as well as excessively detailed. But there were occasional bright spots when his rhetoric would glide effortlessly along the printed page, as for example, these remarks in his introductory lecture to the students at St. Thomas's. Made a century-and-a-half ago, they remain relevant in today's highly structured and multifaceted medical curriculum. They are worth repeating not only for their content but for their literary style as well. We may

> point to the descriptions of disease, as furnished by accurate observers from the most remote times, for the proof, that whilst Nature has been consistent with herself in her abnormal and unhealthy, as well as in her physiological phaenomena, the same symptoms have in all ages been noticed; and practitioners, however discordant in their

doctrines, have obtained success by somewhat similar means. Hence, though new facts of great value have been added to our stock of knowledge; though most important additions have been made to the list of our Materia Medica, we have nevertheless the same diseases to contend with, for which our forefathers prescribed; and though we may desire to be more successful than they, we must still employ analogous means, but direct them with greater accuracy. I have made these remarks to warn you against the possible error of paying too little regard to the writings which time has sanctioned; and against being too much engrossed by productions of the present day, in which it must often happen, that what is new is not true.[36]

Hodgkin wrote in elaborate sentences and complicated paragraphs. It was a literary style characteristic of nineteenth-century rhetoric. For example, in the following excerpt he tells the students of St. Thomas's that they will be more interested in a lecture that is given by a research investigator: "The intensity of interest is necessarily increased when the hearer listens to the announcement of views and facts proceeding from the very lips of him whose perseverance and sagacity have been exercised in the field of original research, in which he has succeeded in gathering fruits to enrich the common storehouse."[37]

In another such example from the same lecture, Hodgkin correlates career mobility with prior performance as a student: "Permit me, however, to observe, that very important results are contingent on the mode in which the Student's part of the Professional career is past. With but few exceptions, the character of the future Practitioner is determined by it. All the advantages of connection and patronage, with which some may enter upon practice, may be lost;—or the difficulties and trials which attend their absence, and at times occasion almost overwhelming discouragement, may be surmounted, and nobly triumphed over."[38]

His stay at St. Thomas's lasted only one year. Something also went wrong there, and he and other lecturers were dropped from the school's prospectus. Hodgkin was informed in writing on July 28, 1843, that lectures on the Theory and Practice of Medicine and those on Pathological Anatomy would be given by other appointees. It is impossible at this time to find out exactly what happened, and the records of St. Thomas's provide no evidence as to the reason for Hodgkin's dismissal. Very likely, the reorganization had not produced the anticipated improvement in enrollment, and the internal dissensions had persisted. Hodgkin, always available with unsolicited advice, probably got caught up in the maneuvering for turf and power and, unable to stay clear of the controversy, may have come down on the wrong side. Another rejection, another disappointment, another humiliation.[39]

There were no more teaching positions in Hodgkin's future. In 1844 he filled a vacancy as consulting physician at an institution for diseases of the skin (see chapter 11) with which he was affiliated for the rest of his life. In 1847 he was appointed to a salaried post as medical officer for the National Provident Insurance Company, where he was responsible for examination of applicants and claimants. He had held this position earlier but resigned in 1837 when his health deteriorated.

How much he was hurt by his experiences at Guy's and St. Thomas's is apparent from a letter to an old friend, in which he complains:

> I have very recently been greatly annoyed by the singularly uncourteous & unhandsome conduct of the managers of the Medical School at St. Thomas's, which, during the last year, has absorbed a large portion of my time attention & labour. Miserable intrigues, of which I regret to say that some members of our profession were at the bottom, have been carried on so as to erase my name from the list of Lecturers without consulting me on the subject, or assigning a reason.
>
> Thou knowest that the people of Guy's used me very ill, but those of St. Thomas's have been still more regardless of even the form of courtesy.[40]

A sympathetic letter from a friend described the shameful treatment by the managers of St. Thomas's as another example of "the emptiness and instability of earthly relations and merely human friendships—how instructive are these lessons! but how painful, how agonising and how humiliating."[41]

After he left St. Thomas's, Hodgkin ceased to have any affiliation with any hospital. He continued to see patients, but his practice, not being large, gradually began to recede into the background.

Now he could give more time and effort to general scientific subjects and to the wide range of liberal causes that he had pursued even while at Guy's, such as the promotion of social reform, furtherance of humanitarian projects, and justice for all oppressed and underprivileged peoples of the world. His seemingly endless energy was directed to problems of slavery, resettlement of freed slaves, the fate of primitive peoples overseas, and the general problems of the poor and socially oppressed at home, particularly issues dealing with public health, medical care, housing, and employment. And although he still wrote on medical topics, the emphasis began to shift to nonmedical subjects.

A tabulation of his publications according to subject matter bears this out.[42] From 1822 through 1837, he authored twenty-five papers with clinical themes and fourteen that were sociological or essentially nonclinical in content, albeit of interest to the medical profession. From 1838 until his death, the division into these two categories of subject content was seventeen and fifty-nine, respectively. A ratio of almost two-to-one in favor of clinical publications was reversed to a ratio of three and a half-to-one in favor of sociological papers. His output, on average, for the two periods was almost the same, namely, 2.4 and 2.7 papers per year, respectively.

CHAPTER ELEVEN

Hodgkin's Comic Relief

Theories of Medical Practice

As late as the early part of the nineteenth century, medical practitioners distinguished diseases according to symptoms and anatomical location of the complaint. They believed that, essentially, there was one disease state, a humoral derangement, and that different patterns of illness were merely changes in the status of the humoral system. Medical knowledge was so limited that, hoping to discover the *one cause* of all diseases, doctors espoused widely different systems of medicine without fear of contradiction. The usual characteristic of a system was its monistic view, which attributed one underlying cause to all diseases, and the belief that they all could be treated by one method. As a result, there was little progress in identifying and treating particular diseases.[1]

Therapy was directed to restoring harmony to body fluids, whatever the name given to the disease.[2] Unsatisfactory fluids were removed by bleeding, purging, sweating, blistering, and vomiting. Depletion of body fluids appeared to have a beneficial action. By exhausting the patient, it exercised a sedating or calming effect. If a deficiency was believed to exist, the patient was treated with diet and drugs. The routine of medicine had been to treat everything with something and not to trust to the healing powers of nature.

It was taken for granted that unless treated promptly every disease might end fatally. Almost everything that could be thought of for the treatment of disease was tried at some time or another and may have continued in vogue for years or for centuries. It was human experimentation by trial and error—ending in error.[3]

Dogmatist, Empiric, Eclectic

The replacement of dogma, speculation, and theoretical rationalism by a study of the evidence is a gradual process and often depends on the slow and far from uniform incremental advances in affiliated sciences and arts. Consequently, occult ideas, theological presuppositions, and speculation about the nature of disease existed side-by-side with measurements, experiments, and new theories well into the nineteenth century, with residues of dogmatic practices of the past persistently hanging on.

Hodgkin categorized medical practitioners into two major camps: empirics and dogmatists—each totally opposed to the other. As a result of mutual recriminations, *dogmatist* has come to mean one who is arrogant, teaches in a style of absolute authority, and despises experience; *empiric* has come to signify an ignorant pretender, synonymous with quack or mountebank.[4] As for medical dogmas and empirical facts, Hodgkin quoted his former teacher at Edinburgh, Dr. James Gregory, who found at least ninety-nine out of a hundred of these dogmas and facts to be false or stark nonsense, and more than that proportion of the remedies of dogmatists and empirics to be as insignificant and dangerous. Our medical facts, said Gregory, "are less to be trusted, and often much more dangerous than our medical theories."[5]

The inevitable outcome of these two styles of practice were methods of treatment that were diametrically opposite, sometimes even for the same patient, leading to confusion by the student and loss of confidence by the public. Hodgkin did not dismiss outright the opposing claims of conflicting medical theories and methods of treatment but conceded that each had something favorable to offer for the successful treatment and should be studied and understood.[6] To avoid being misled by false medical theories and axioms, he recommended that practitioners become personally acquainted with physiology and pathology by conducting their own experimental investigations, and he cautioned against relying exclusively on information obtained by others.[7] For Hodgkin, the physician's first priority was "to become acquainted with the characteristics of diseases. For this purpose, it is essential that they be accurately and intelligibly described."[8]

Hodgkin sought his facts with the aid of the microscope, and in 1843 he gave an early example of its application in morbid anatomy. "Microscopic examination affords us the means of becoming acquainted with the most intimate structural peculiarities, and is therefore the counterpart of chemical analysis, which relates to the elements which enter into their composition."[9] The paper is also notable because Hodgkin mentions his visit in the fall of 1838 to Berlin, where Professor Schwann gave him a demonstration of the nucleated cells. These had been described by Schwann and Schleiden as performing an important and essential part in the formation of vegetable and animal tissues.[10]

Cancer Transport and the Microscope

Hodgkin used the microscope to study the structure of cancer and other adventitious structures and noted: "The most practiced eyes, and the best instruments, have been employed in these observations, and the results obtained have been so generally in accordance, that, notwithstanding the doubts which are attached by some to microscopic inquiries, they may be received with confidence, although from the optical characters of the objects themselves, their examination is often difficult."[11] Hodgkin was an experienced microscopist when he wrote this in 1843. It is doubtful whether he could have made the same statement in 1832 about the "best instruments" available then when he described the gross appearances of glands and spleen in what later came to be known as Hodgkin's disease. Had he made microscopic observations then and seen something that he could describe "with confidence," he would have done so. As it was, this was still a new technology in

1843, and Hodgkin admitted that examination with the microscope was often difficult.

Hodgkin appreciated the beneficial use of surgery in the treatment of cancer and advised: "That in operating for the removal of a tumour of this class, it is extremely important to leave behind none of those minute cysts which often form granules in the surrounding cellular membrane, though it may appear to be in other respects perfectly healthy: this appears to be a mode of extension of the disease, independent of inflammation."[12]

In his studies of malignancies with the microscope, Hodgkin showed an awareness of the cellular level of pathology and the manner in which cancer spreads. Hodgkin believed that the presence of cancerous matter in the lymphatic system and circulating blood was not due to formation or preexistence but was an indication of transportation.[13] More than likely the blood vessels were in some way connected with the spread of the disease.[14] The transport system of the body was Hodgkin's long-lasting interest. His first scientific paper, "On the Uses of the Spleen," was published while he was a student at Edinburgh.[15] He followed this up with a graduation thesis that was concerned with the absorbing function of the spleen and whether this took place through the lymphatic vessels or through the veins.

An example of the successful use of surgery in a case of possible malignancy included Hodgkin's detailed examination of the secretion in a large ovarian tumor. His observation with the microscope revealed no particled material, crystals, or large nucleated cells generally found in cancerous matter. He designated the growth as not malignant and placed it in the category of serous cysts. In his opinion, a growth originally not malignant does not degenerate to malignancy, but since the additions of subsequent growth may take on one or more of the various forms of a malignancy, he recommended early and complete removal of nonmalignant ovarian cysts.[16]

Hodgkin also understood that cancer may long remain confined and later break out of bounds.

> The long period during which the disease may remain strictly local seems to indicate that in the healthy system there is some barrier to

the ready transfer of the newly-formed morbid molecules to the different parts of the body; but, on the other hand, when the disease has shown itself in different parts, the striking similarity presented by the molecules taken from each of them, strongly favours the idea of family connection, and consequently of transfer.[17]

Hodgkin continues, "Are we to suppose that some pre-disposing cause favours the production *de novo* of the disease in each of these parts," or rather that some of the peculiar molecules [malignant cells], find their way into the circulation and "become fresh starting points for the production of the morbid growth?" He favored the latter view because of the remarkable similarity under the microscope of the pathologic specimens taken from different parts of the same person.[18]

These views, expressed in the 1840s, are significant because other authorities were late in accepting the cellular theory of metastasis, clinging long to the old humoral concepts that had dominated all of medicine for more than fifteen centuries. Even Rudolf Virchow, who in 1858 originated the idea of a cellular pathology and the continuous development of cells, was impressed with the frequent appearance of secondary growths in places other than in the direct line of circulation. Consequently, when it came to cancer metastasis, Virchow did not think primarily in terms of cells but of morbid juices.[19]

Revival of Humoralism

Humoralism experienced a revival in the 1830s but in a new and scientific mode—mostly along the lines of blood pathology. The 1840 memoir by Gabriel Andral and Jules Gavarret, *Recherches sur les modifications de proportion de quelques principes de sang*, did much to further this interest. Andral, an eclectic, recognized the existence of symptoms without lesions in the solid organs and turned his investigations to the blood when anatomy revealed no changes. In his book *Essai d'hématologie pathologique* (1843) he examined the blood physically, chemically, and microscopically, and predicted that chemical analyses of body liquids altered by disease would play an increasingly important role in pathogenesis.[20]

Hodgkin kept up with the overseas literature, especially from France. He was acquainted with Andral, whose inspections at the Charité he had observed during his student year in Paris, and was undoubtedly influenced by his work. Hodgkin believed that the new and important information contributed by research in animal chemistry and by microscopic observations was indicative of a gradual return to a new humoral pathology. This would add more importance than before to alterations in the fluids in connection with changes that unquestionably take place in the solids. Inasmuch as exchanges are continually occurring between the solid parts and the blood, "it is in the blood that we must look for many important modifications in connection with disease."[21] Hodgkin believed that disease would one day be explained in terms of "molecular movements," more chemical than mechanical, "by which our bodies . . . are continually changing the elements of which they are composed."[22]

Hodgkin and Andral were correct in their predictions. What has happened in the second half of the twentieth century is that the practice of medicine, whether centered in the doctor's office, the clinic, or the hospital, has become oriented around the analysis of blood and other body fluids.

Diseases of the Skin and Special Hospitals

The nonmedical public did not know or care about molecular movements, or cells, or morbid juices. However, it could be disturbed and alarmed by anything it perceived to be a danger to its health. Residents in the vicinity of a newly established Dispensary for Skin Diseases became very apprehensive about the new facility and petitioned city officials to close it down because it would bring crowds of diseased persons "loathsome to the sight and dangerous to the touch, obstructing the progress of passengers."[23] Apparently, the community cry of "Not in our neighborhood!" is not a new one.

Hodgkin, a staff physician for the dispensary, dismissed the community's allegations as fiction and misrepresentation. In an open letter to the public, published as a pamphlet, he pointed out that the proportion of patients whose disfigured appearance in the street evoked feelings of disgust was, in reality, very small. The probability of two such cases being seen at the same time was not great. He offered reassurance that the disease would not be spread by the existence of the institution. These people were already blended in with the population, passing through the crowded streets and coming more closely into contact with other persons in various shops and businesses than was likely to take place even at the doors of the dispensary.[24]

Hodgkin favored the concept of special institutions (for example, The Eye Infirmary in Moorfields) where specific diseases were ably treated by professional men experienced in the general principles of medicine and surgery and whose perception and judgment were enhanced by practice in a particular line.[25]

Responding to the fears of contagion to adjoining homes, Hodgkin reminded his readers that these skin patients were frequently seen by practitioners in their own homes. "Are their other patients deterred from consulting them on this account? or do their aristocratic neighbours complain of the nuisance? or does any one offer either objection or remonstrance [sic], when the poor, with sickly, pallid countenances, suffering from various diseases, and clothed in filthy rags, are, at times, congregated to receive the superfluous meats which are left from the tables of the great?"[26] Hodgkin's open letter helped allay the community's fears. The facility remained in Blackfriars until 1953.

During the first half of the nineteenth century, specialty hospitals were springing up in London at the rate of one every two years. Similar activity was taking place in the scientific community. Between 1788 and 1838, twelve new societies devoted to science specialties came onto the scene.[27] In 1844 another new scientific specialty made its appearance. It was a spin-off from the Aborigines' Protection Society (APS).

Ethnology, a Questionnaire, and a New Society

When Thomas Hodgkin formed the APS in 1837, it was to serve partly as a political pressure group and partly as an ethnological society. Its dual purpose was to save the aborigines in the British colonies from possible extinction as a result of exploitation by settlers and commercial enterprises and to study these uncivilized peoples on the verge of disappearance for evidence of the early history of the human race. The society became the principal secular group informing public opinion about the character, habits, needs, and problems of indigenous peoples, in or near British colonies, and correcting false allegations that the aborginals were naturally inferior. It wanted to bring a halt to the oppression and violence by providing basic legal and political rights to the natives in their contacts with settlers. Colonization was not condemned; it was considered justified and morally desirable. The APS wanted only to change its character.

The society served as a clearinghouse for information from a worldwide network of missionaries, traders, and civil servants. Their accounts of the horrors, atrocities, and injustices perpetrated under the auspices of British imperialism were collected, abstracted, and printed in the Transactions of the Society, *The Colonial Intelligencer; or Aborigines' Friend*, and passed to the British press. Public meetings were held. Petitions were sent to Parliament, and legislation was proposed to regulate government interaction with the aboriginals in the colonial territories.

With never more than a hundred or two of members, whose small subscriptions and donations provided its only income, the society wielded an influence out of all proportion to its meager resources, an influence attested to by the fear and hatred of it which nineteenth-century settlers often expressed. However, Hodgkin and his associates in the society lacked any lasting influence or power to promote or implement their policies. Part of the problem was that, instead of being more defined or limited, they spread themselves thin and were too comprehensive in their global objectives. At one point, with the society largely in debt and facing curtailment of its publication, Hodgkin asked the members whether their small gains and disappointment meant that the society "has been engaged in a needless work, and been espousing a cause which has no merits to sustain."[28]

Although the APS addressed each successive Secretary of State for the Colonial Department and pleaded for those natives who had been victimized by injustice and oppression, the society was not succeeding in its humanitarian objectives. The problems and pressure points of colonization had continued unabated. The government tried to protect the rights, lands, and social customs of the indigenous peoples but could not control all phases of its colonial program.

Boer migration and border clashes in South Africa; unrestrained settling, land disputes, and armed hostilities in New Zealand; and continuing troubles in other British settlements made it clear to the APS that it had failed to follow through successfully on its general objectives. In addition, the society's financial status took a downward turn in 1841 and 1842, forcing a cutback in publications. Some reorientation was necessary.

The APS decided to broaden its base and give more attention to the collection and analysis of information on the social and physical status of the races. The printed objective of the society was changed from protecting the defenseless to recording their history. It was decided that the best way to help aboriginals was to study them. Despite this change of emphasis, annual reports indicate that ethnology remained subordinate to political and philanthropic objectives.

As a result of continued priority given to humanitarian concerns and in light of the society's political failures and financial setbacks, Richard King, now the secretary of the APS, issued a prospectus for an Ethnological Society on July 20, 1842. Making no reference to colonial and political objectives, he outlined proposals for a new society to study the natural history of man. The response to King's appeal was poor at first. But, early the following year, Hodgkin invited the group to meet in his home. By the start of 1844 the new group was on a firm enough footing to establish itself formally as the Ethnological Society of London. Those who joined had no difficulty in maintaining a dual affiliation.[29]

If the group was looking for an institutional alternative to philanthropy, it didn't have far to look. Across the channel, the Société Ethnologique de Paris, chartered in 1839, served as a scientific model and provided the nomenclature, which was still new to English usage. The French society, the first devoted entirely to scientific ethnology, was the result of a visit to Paris by Hodgkin to generate interest in a companion French humanitarian organization. His friend W. F. Edwards was receptive to the idea, but since the French had no colonial aborigines that needed protecting and were more interested in scientific study of the races of man, a different type of organization was established.

Closer to home a subcommittee of the British Association had been set up in 1839 specifically for the study of the races of man. It was in response to the efforts of James Cowles Prichard, a former Quaker and the leading British ethnologist of the time, who had sharply criticized the European colonial practices that were leading to the extermination of most aboriginal tribes.[30] Many scientific and philosophical problems relative to the development of mankind needed to be studied and would be unsolved, he said, if primitive peoples were destroyed. Consequently, it was of the utmost importance to obtain much more information than was now known about their physical and moral (i.e., social) characteristics. His appeal led to the formation of a subcommittee headed by himself and including Charles Darwin and Thomas Hodgkin. Its assignment was to prepare and circulate a set of questions for distribution to travelers, ships' captains, missionaries, and others to obtain information on the peoples of the world. Hodgkin was not very confident of getting much help from missionaries. He had charged in an earlier essay that in their zeal to do God's work, they often destroyed the relics, traditions, and anything connected with "idolatrous worship" and "superstitions" and encouraged their new converts to do the same.[31]

From 1839 to 1843, leadership of the committee gradually passed into the hands of Hodgkin. He was primarily responsible for the annual reports to the British Association and for an extensive, well-organized set of questions relative to foreign peoples and cultures. Most ethnologists of that time did no work in the field but carried out their research in the library and museum, relying on data and information supplied by others. Hodgkin's questionnaire[32] was an early example of field method in anthropology and reflected his and Prichard's views on the close connection between race and language. Comparative analysis of language (but also of civil and religious manners and customs, works of art, and mythological fables) was expected to build the case for monogenesis by tracing the history of the widely dispersed peoples of the Earth back to a single source.

The list of questions was an expanded version of the instructions and requests for information that he had given to Richard King for the latter's voyage to the Arctic Ocean in 1833–35. There were eighty-nine detailed multipart questions covering ten categories: physical characteristics (especially descriptions and measurements of the head); language; individual and family life; buildings and monuments; works of art; domestic animals; political institutions, government, and laws; geography and statistics; social relations; religion and superstitions, and so on. The British Association wanted this data because it feared the extinction of native populations and the irretrievable loss to science of their psychological, physiological, and philological character as well as their history. Copies of the questionnaire were sent to the remotest regions of the world, including the Americas, Africa, Asia, India, and the islands of the Pacific.

The Ethnological Society of London (ESL) had no intention of getting into political and humanitarian projects. Its purpose, instead, was to investigate the distinguishing characteristics, physical and social, of the varieties of mankind that now inhabit or in the past have inhabited the Earth; to learn the causes of these characteristics; and to see whether the distinguishing characteristics of different groups were simply modifications of one original type, or whether they represented differences in original hereditary make-up. Voyages of exploration had discovered a variety of mankind heretofore unknown and raised serious scientific and theological questions. Are the races of man divisions of a common origin according to biblical account, or were they created separately? Ethnologists viewed the uncivilized peoples as representative of the earliest state of man or the state to which he had degenerated.

Scientific inquiry did not mean an ideological break with the APS. While the ESL actively investigated the question of the unity or plurality of the human species, most of its members accepted as scientific theory the monogenist thesis that for members of the APS was doctrine. After all, the motto of the APS was *ab uno sanguine*—"of one blood." For ethnology the problem was to find the evidence that tied all mankind into a single family tree. The model of explanation emphasized environmental factors, such as geography, climate, and food, as responsible for modifying human physical characteristics. The favored methodology was the comparison of languages to establish similarities between physically different groups.[33]

Ethnology was Hodgkin's favorite study. It combined his philanthropic and humanitarian interests in primitive peoples with an organized scientific approach to collection of data about them. He served on the council of the Ethnological Society from 1844 until his death and at one time was vice-president.

Hodgkin's Comic Relief

Despite the status of a separate society, British ethnology remained in the shadow of traditional humanities and the natural sciences, and its papers to the British Association were presented under Physiology. Hodgkin read three papers to the ethnological subsection of the association at the annual meeting in York in September 1844.[34] Two of the papers, with the exotic titles "On the Tape-Worm as prevalent in Abyssinia" and "On the Stature of the Guanches, the extinct Inhabitants of the Canary Islands," drew no special notice. The third presentation, with the ordinary title "On the Dog as the Associate of Man," caught the attention of the press and rated a mention in *Punch* and the *Illustrated London News* for the moments of comic relief that it provided. To his own great surprise, and no doubt that of everyone else who knew him, this Quaker Englishman, serious at all times and hardly a charming or captivating personality, and with little if any sense of humor, could be funny and entertaining! To illustrate his talk, Hodgkin imitated the growl, snarl, and bark of many different kinds of dogs and accompanied them with facial impressions of the looks of these dogs with the aid of a wig and shaggy eyebrows. *Punch* called his presentation "one of the most successful papers that were read at the meeting." Hodgkin was "particularly felicitous as the old English hound, for which the natural mildness of his countenance admirably adapted him." The *Illustrated London News* printed wood engravings of the heads of the nine different kinds of dogs described. This account added that Hodgkin's paper attracted the most notice.[35]

This was not a lighter side to Hodgkin. Amusing though he was, it must have been unintentional. This was a serious report. The abstract of his paper in the Association's Report makes no mention of the disguises. A full-length report on the subject was published the following year. In it Hodgkin discussed the role played by climate, circumstance, and intermixture of varieties in producing modifications in form, size, and other characteristics of the species of dog. Hodgkin wanted to show by analogy that the variety in the species of dogs and in the different races of man are in like manner accidental and not specific. There were no illustrations.[36]

Hodgkin also followed his presentation on the Guanches with a full-length paper on the origin of these extinct inhabitants of the Canary Islands. From a review of descriptions in the ancient and early modern literature, it appeared to Hodgkin that the early Canary Islanders were tall, athletic, and vigorous. Inasmuch as skeletons of the few fragmented Canarian mummies that he observed were small, Hodgkin suggested that the most plausible explanation was that the Canary Islands had been inhabited at different periods in its history by tribes or nations with different physical characteristics.[37]

Hodgkin's essay on the Canary Islanders came before the science of anthropology had acquired its own identity and professional class, and when most of the research in physical anthropology was carried out by physicians. The founding father of this science was Johann Friedrich Blumenbach,[38] whose research on skull measurements led him to identify five divisions of mankind: Caucasian (white), Mongolian (yellow), Maylayan (brown), Ethiopian (black), and American (red). He and others followed the monogenist view that God had created man in his own image. While allowing all races a place in the pantheon of humanity, some preferred to place the European variety of man at the top of the scheme.

Unity of the Human Species

Hodgkin was a monogenist from religious conviction as well as for scientific reasons. He considered himself an impartial and objective investigator and studied racial variety in order to better understand the origins of man. He could find no significant characteristic differences in human skulls between distinctly and distantly separated groups of the human race, such as the Indians of North and South America. For him this was additional supporting evidence of the unity of the human species—that all men were descended from a single pair—from which diverse races had branched off over time and spread throughout the world—and that any observable differences in the races of man were only those of an environment-induced variety.[39] However, his friend and frequent correspondent from Philadelphia, Dr. Samuel G. Morton,[40] was a polygenist and came to a different conclusion. Morton believed that the races were distinguished by measurements of their skulls as well as by color, and he rejected the idea of the unity of the human species. He believed that the human races were of diverse origin and were adapted from the beginning to their particular geographic locale.

Hodgkin was not disturbed by ethnological data that tried to divide man according to differences in visible physical characteristics, which, if valid, would contradict the biblical account of the single origin (unity) of the human species. He did not shy away from reading the controversial writings of other scientists and frequently referred to them in his own publications.

The Evolution of Evolution

Hodgkin was a religious man with unshakable faith, and as far as he was concerned, religion had nothing to fear from such investigations or from the new revelations of geology.[41] These studies had found rock strata packed with fossils of long-extinct animals and plants that had no apparent link to the completely unique animal and plant forms in previous layers of rock. Geologists saw these fossils as clues to a new and immensely lengthened history of the

Earth that contradicted the biblical teaching of creationism. The increasing number of new biological species being found convinced more and more naturalists of the possibility of an evolution, rather than an independent creation, of related life-forms. Discovery of human artifacts in the same site with the remains of extinct animals implied the existence of prehistoric man and a much greater antiquity than was usually supposed. The publication of Charles Darwin's *On the Origin of Species* (1859) made the nature of man a subject of general intellectual concern and presented new concepts and unexpected challenges. Victorians were excited about developments in science and biology and prayed that there would be no gulf between religion and science.

Hodgkin could reconcile science and religion and was not disturbed by the idea of evolution, but he did try to accommodate the opposing views of science and religion within a religious framework. He observed that structural similarities in all vertebrated animals, and in lower forms of life as well, deduced from a study of comparative anatomy, had led some contemporary anatomists to come up with "the doctrine of analogies, and of an unity of plan pervading the whole animal kingdom. . . . This doctrine, in itself extremely beautiful, and even sublime . . . affords a happy explanation of many remarkable phenomena in the organization of animals."[42] Hodgkin was mixing theology with natural science—and was dealing a hand to the Creator.

By the end of the 1850s, after a decline in membership, interest in the Ethnological Society of London began to pick up. There was renewed interest in the observation and measurement of human physical types. The emphasis on human differences became more physical and often harshly racial. Some writers rejected the idea of human equality and preached a polygenic doctrine, i.e., that the races were different and not derived from a single source and that Negroes were an inferior race. The leading exponent of these racial views was Robert Knox, who had befriended Hodgkin in Edinburgh and later in Paris. Knox's book, *Races of Men*, first published in 1850, argued that the differences between human races meant that they were not members of the same species.[43]

However, racist views on human diversity were unpopular with the dominant Quaker group in the ESL, and relationships among the members became strained. Other differences developed that may have been closely tied to issues of race. What probably precipitated the open split in the organization was a difference of opinion over the choice of illustrations for an article on Sierra Leone. Hodgkin was on the committee that selected the drawings that were eventually published. The committee rejected the minority view that preferred the harsh and almost bestial representations of Negroes that were appearing in some of the racist publications of the time. The dispute led to the formation of a competing organization, the Anthropological Society of London, on January 6, 1863.[44]

The *anthropologicals* wanted to study the whole nature of man, with emphasis on the distinctions between the human races, and to get away from biblical dogma and speculation over the unity or plurality of races. The approach would be empirical—to collect facts and to reject unproven hypotheses. The new society grew with phenomenal speed, despite internal dissension and frequent resignations, and soon exceeded the membership of the Ethnological Society. Differences in scientific orientation, political attitudes, and in organizational and personal style generated recurring attacks, bitterness, and recriminations between the two organizations. After several failed attempts at reconciliation, the two groups were reunited to form the Anthropological Institute of Great Britain and Ireland and held its first meeting on January 31, 1873.[45] The society later received a royal charter and is still in existence.

CHAPTER TWELVE

Public, Profession, and Quackery

Cold, Hunger, and Unemployment

After leaving St. Thomas's in 1843, Hodgkin published on a wide range of interests and activities, both medical and nonmedical. No longer in a hospital setting with access to pathological specimens and interesting cases, he resorted to past medical lectures and records of old case histories. Papers on medical subjects appeared with decreasing frequency during the next twenty years—the final years of his life. There was a collaborative effort in 1846, in which Hodgkin referred to his 1832 paper on the spleen—the section dealing with local injury—by way of introducing a report on disease of the spleen sent to him by a prominent Boston physician.[1] Because long periods of inactivity were alien to Hodgkin, he turned his attention to problems of the poor, unfair practices of the Royal College of Physicians, and free trade in the aftermath of Britain's abolition of slavery.

Problems of unemployment and the needs of the poor do not vanish overnight. And so, in 1847, fifteen years after his pamphlet on the cholera epidemic and the environmental causes contributing to its spread, Hodgkin again addressed many of the same problems facing the poor and unemployed. He proposed that vouchers for bread, coal, and clothing should be distributed in the schools for the children or their needy families. However, employment instead of charity was the key to making the poor "the agents of their own deliverance" and doing away with "that tendency to an abject, slothful disposition, which the receipt of ordinary alms is wont to produce, and which too often becomes the cause of permanent degradation."[2]

Hodgkin recommended snow removal from the public ways as a means of employment and even suggested storing the collected snow for sale as an inferior grade of ice. He urged the unemployed themselves to volunteer suggestions for feasible work projects and proposed rewards of money for the best ideas.[3]

Although he championed the poor and oppressed, Hodgkin had no sympathy for the indolent of the destitute class who had been brought to these circumstances by "their own faults and deficiencies." A very great and serious difficulty in relieving the poor, warned Hodgkin, was to be found in the character of this class. "They have not the dispositions favourable for helping themselves, and are, consequently, not easily helped by others. . . . In the majority of cases, the difficulty to be contended with consists in that lamentable want of spirit and energy which makes all kind of continued useful exertion more irksome than the privations of poverty and the pinchings of hunger. When employment is provided for such persons, they perform it slowly and badly"; and because of chronic loafing on the job, they required additional supervision, which added considerably to the expense of their employment. They also set a bad example to the moderately industrious. If persuasion could not "induce them to change their habits, to stir up their energies, and to feel that, with the wholesome appetite which industry creates, the bread of industry is sweeter than the bread of idleness," then the incorrigible should be marked in some way to relieve society from this class and protect the community from injury by them.[4]

It is surprising that Hodgkin, a medical man, was not more sympathetic and apparently lacked the perception to see that the poor worked badly because they were hungry and sick. His views on public health, poor law reform, and related issues, enlightened as they were, nevertheless reflected some of the biases of his contemporaries. These expressions on the "undeserving" poor and their tendencies toward indolence were a deprecating view of the working class and were fairly typical of the prejudices of the educated middle class.[5] However, this attitude toward the poor was not typical of Hodgkin, and he is most admired because he did so often transcend the prejudices that were common for his times. Hodgkin did not reject the poor and often treated them at no charge. Despite the prevailing reservations within society, private individuals and groups in an outpouring of voluntary labor and money exhibited an almost incredible variety of charitable interests, which in their course worked to relieve tensions in English life.[6]

The "traditional" views of the middle class were still in vogue despite new and unexpected findings of an investigation into the causes of "fever"[7] conducted in 1838 in certain districts in London. The study, suggested to the Poor Law Commission by Edwin Chadwick, contradicted the generally accepted view—apparent in the philosophy of the new poor law—that pauperism was the result of "voluntary" failings of the poor, namely, idleness, improvidence, and alcoholism. On the contrary, the new data pointed to causes beyond the control of the individuals concerned, such as ill health brought about by filthy environmental conditions, especially in housing, street sanitation, and drainage. Illness was the cause, not the result, of destitution. Consequently, new programs did not address poverty but rather the prevention of disease, by clearing the environment of the filthy living conditions that turned the poor into the indigent and thereby increased the burden on the taxpayers[8] (see also chapter 7, note 9).

Free Trade

There were other economic problems at play with far-reaching implications for a changing society. Britain's abolition of slavery and the slave trade set into motion economic forces that required a new look at trade practices. The government's policy of free trade favored the cheaper slave-made products from non-British colonies. This was bad for the planters in the British West Indian colonies, whose labor market was now restricted to paid laborers (i.e., recently freed slaves). During the 1840s, this situation spawned the main issue that confronted and divided British abolitionists—the sugar tariff. West Indian sugar was protected on the British market by high tariffs on foreign producers of sugar, a holdover from the mercantilist era. Since West Indian sugar was more expensive to produce than Cuban or Brazilian sugar and was limited in quantity, this and the tariff made sugar much more expensive in England than on the Continent. The issue divided not only public opinion but also the antislavery party and its large Quaker membership, because in the 1840s, to many reformers, free trade was a more important issue than slavery.[9]

The removal of sugar tariffs meant lower prices for the slave-grown sugar of Cuba and Brazil. This would lead to increased demand for sugar and for slaves to harvest the crop, thereby stimulating the slave trade. Manufacturers opposed the sugar tariffs so that with increased sales foreign exporters of sugar could afford to be importers of English cotton goods. Why surrender the market, they said, for the sake of morality?

The Quakers were also caught up in the debate. Their enthusiasm for free trade made some Quakers sound like apologists for slavery, which was quite at odds with Quaker antislavery traditions of the past.[10] It was all a matter of business. Quakers had an ongoing love affair with making money. Most general accounts of the Society of Friends talk about their "devotedness to the acquisition of money." It was a characteristic considered to be almost inseparable from Quakerism. Accordingly, they pursued riches "with a step as steady as time, and with an appetite as keen as death."[11]

Hodgkin was a foe of slavery, but he was also a committed capitalist. Caught up in the dilemma of the contradictions presented by free trade and its effect on the slave labor market, he took an intermediary position.

Hodgkin was decidedly for free trade, but the misapplication of its principles, he wrote to a member of Parliament, had forced the government into complicity with the African slave trade. He wanted a "temporary continuance of some accustomed indulgence" (i.e., protection) so as not to ruin the economy of the West Indies and surrender the best markets in the world (Africa) to the most oppressive of slave owners. He sought relief for the West Indian planters but would not support the old-line protectionists, who wanted a high duty in order to continue sugar production with their defective processes and abusive financial practices to the great annoyance and expense of the British public. Hodgkin wanted to reconcile the apparent conflict between free trade and the stimulus to the slave trade that it engendered. All he asked, "in the name of justice and humanity, is, merely so much of protection as shall guard the producer, whether proprietor or labourer, against dishonest competition, and save this country from the guilt and disgrace of" becoming "the patron and advocate of the African Slave Trade and of Colonial Slavery in their worst forms."[12]

Hodgkin denied being a protectionist, and he pointed out that he had refused "the flattering and advantageous offer of Fellowship in the College of Physicians" some years earlier because he was "so thoroughly averse to exclusive systems and close [sic] bodies."[13]

Hodgkin's Testimony to Parliament

Hodgkin's reference to the "exclusive systems" of the College of Physicians was no casual observation. He had recently addressed the Harveian Society on Medical Reform and had testified on June 27, 1848 before a Committee of Parliament on Medical Registration considering legislation on the distinctions and inequities within the medical profession. Citing the special privileges and irregularities stemming from the authority of the Royal College of Physicians, Hodgkin pleaded for extension of rights to the University of London equal to those of Oxford and Cambridge universities to grant a full license to practice medicine without having to be reexamined by the Royal College of Physicians.[14]

Hodgkin's testimony came during the period between 1840 and 1858, when bill after bill for the reform of medical education and licensure went down to defeat, because the Royal College of Physicians, and the Royal College of Surgeons, and the Society of Apothecaries always opposed any compromise legislation that adversely affected their status and privileges or provided for uniformity or standardization of medical education or qualifications. The physician and surgeon elites holding hospital positions were indifferent to their lowly competitors in salaried posts, whom they neglected and relegated to inferior status within the hierarchy of the college membership.[15]

The Royal College of Physicians of London long remained a stronghold of resistance to reform of medical curriculum, training, and modernization procedures of medical licensure. The college was more concerned with questions of procedure, precedence, and privilege and with protecting its monopoly of the London practice than it was with promoting scientific advance or educational standards. The highly conservative leadership of the college was content to stand on its dignity, the performance of its rites, and the collection of fees. It was little concerned with the suppression of unqualified practice, which was its original responsibility. However, the college vigorously prosecuted any physician who practiced without its authorization even though his qualifications were of equal value.

But, to survive, change and accommodation are inevitable, and by 1847, all the fellows were being selected in an impartial manner from one comprehensive list of licentiates. However, the college had also begun to admit as licentiate and, by courtesy therefore, to the distinction of the title of Doctor, those who had "no academic degree, and whose education may have been received at one of the merely medical schools." The Royal College of Physicians began this practice because it wanted to compete with the new University of London, and so examined for a license to practice those who had no medical degree, and agreed to call those who passed, doctors of medicine. This new practice, Hodgkin told the Harveian Society, was unjust to those who had received the license prior to this innovation, unfair to the universities, and not strictly honest to the public.[16]

Chaos in the Profession

The new examination and licensing procedure of the Royal College of Physicians drew attention to the chaotic regulatory practices that existed in the medical profession in Great Britain. Educational backgrounds of medical practitioners varied so widely that distinction between the qualified and unqualified was difficult to determine. Even those with legitimate credentials from any one of the numerous bona fide licensing agencies might be only partially qualified. The Royal College of Surgeons of England conferred its diploma—which was not a legal requirement for the practice of surgery—after an hour's oral examination without any clinical test or examination in medicine or materia medica. The license of the Apothecaries' Company did not certify any knowledge of anatomy or surgery, but it was one of the first accrediting bodies to institute a written examination as opposed to the oral question and answer. Eventually the apothecaries' and surgeons' societies required courses in surgery and physic for their respective diplomas.

However, as late as 1832, the apothecaries' exam was oral and a farce. The Latin test could be completed in a few minutes. In materia medica the examiner asked the common name of several galenical medications. For chemistry, one question asked what substance forms both acids and alkalies. The answer was oxygen.[17]

On the whole, the examining bodies were very easily satisfied. The granting of titles was a lucrative source of income. With so many independent, uncontrolled licensing authorities, all competing with one another to attract candidates and fees, it is hardly surprising that standards were often deplorably low. Nevertheless, should an applicant fail to pass his examinations, there were many other "qualifications" available, almost for the asking. He could purchase a German degree in Tottenham Court Road or obtain a Scottish degree from the University of St. Andrews, which was said to give the degree to all who experienced difficulty in securing it elsewhere by examination. St. Andrews required no residence or even attendance for an examination but merely accepted testimonial letters from two practitioners of good standing attesting to the candidate's knowledge and abilities—plus a fee.[18]

Besides the evils of quackery, there was also an inadequacy in the training of many of the so-called qualified. Men could take a degree in Arts, "walk a hospital" from three to six months, and immediately be licensed to practice as physicians. The academic

courses in medicine at Oxford and Cambridge universities provided much leisure time, but degrees in medicine were readily
conferred, nevertheless.[19]

After the establishment of the Royal College of Surgeons in
1800, it became a regular but voluntary practice for many apothecaries to apply for the license (diploma) of the college as an
additional qualification. Licenses from the Royal College of Surgeons and the Society of Apothecaries, held by the same man,
became the best available credentials for the "general practitioner,"[20] a term *The Lancet* castigated as clumsy and vulgar.[21]
The Lancet and the rank and file preferred the term *doctor*, but
this did not take hold until late in the century.

Apothecaries' Act of 1815

By 1815, the new class of "surgeon-apothecary" was the largest
part of the profession in town and country[22] and tended to the
health of over 95 percent of the population of England and Wales.
They prescribed the medicine, performed minor operations, pulled
teeth, dressed wounds, and attended women in childbirth.[23] These
surgeons and apothecaries often served long apprenticeships and
were probably better prepared for their work than the physicians,
especially if they were able to add to their vocational training by a
course at a private medical school.[24] Besides, the poor and the
working class could not afford the high fees charged by the
physicians.

By the 1830s, the stratified system of health services, in place for
centuries and established partly by law and largely by custom, was
beginning to fall apart. The sharp traditional divisions within the
medical profession were disintegrating under the pressures of new
societal needs and structures arising from the growth of industrial
towns, the spirit of free competition, and rugged individualism.
Physician, surgeon, and apothecary, as distinct and separate practitioners, existed in little more than name alone. Their practices
overlapped. It was even becoming difficult to distinguish them
from a new group, the chemists and druggists. Few physicians
could make a living *as physicians* by limiting their practice to

examining patients, diagnosing disease, and prescribing medicines for internal diseases to be compounded and dispensed by the apothecaries. By 1834, many physicians included surgery, mid-wifery, and even pharmacy in their practice.[25]

Hodgkin was aware of this fragmentation when he said, "As respects the public in general, and perhaps even a large proportion of the profession also, these distinctions are very little thought of, and very little understood. The wounds of the public are dressed, their fractures are set, their dislocations are reduced, with little if any reference to them."[26]

Although the Apothecaries' Act of 1815 had finally legalized the practice of medicine by apothecaries, it did so by maintaining the obsolete status quo that its supporters had sought to reform and tended to degrade rather than elevate them. Oxford and Cambridge universities and the Royal Colleges of Physicians and of Surgeons were specifically exempted by the act, as were chemists and druggists, who received no medical education whatever.[27] Apothecaries were placed under the direct control of the Apothe-caries' Company, which, although it issued a license to practice as an apothecary, was largely engaged in the wholesale drug business. As a consequence, apothecaries were tied to a five-year apprentice-ship that was more suited to a trade than to a profession. This became the *sine qua non* of the apothecary's education and helped shape the public's perception of medical practitioners as trades-men.[28] This inferior status was derived in part from the practitioner being engaged in competition and profit, both of which depended on public approval rather than professional authority. These atti-tudes were reflected by novelists, who portrayed doctors during the first half of the century as ignorant, coarse, and grasping.[29]

Hodgkin's Medical Reform

Hodgkin's "Medical Reform" would do away with the profes-sional conflicts and unpleasant feelings generated by the multiple distinctions and designations of diploma, license, and fellowship, including whether the fellowship was acquired by invitation or examination. His plan was a concession to conservatism and presented no violent change to the profession or its regulatory bodies.[30] His intention was to retain "so much of the present forms as to avoid shocking those who would be alarmed at seeing a total overthrow of that which time may seem to them to have consecrated."[31]

Hodgkin proposed the establishment of a third college, on a par with those of the physicians and surgeons, to be composed of general practitioners, pharmacists, and chemists. A common government-sponsored examination for the license to practice would be taken by all, whether they intended to practice medicine, surgery, or both. The pharmacists and chemists would be required to pass only that portion of the examination relating to their field. Hodgkin claimed to be impartial in his scheme. He had begun his professional studies with the chemists and pharmacists, performed research with the surgeons, and practiced medicine according to the scrupulous restrictions of the physicians. Throughout all of this, he said, he had not gotten involved "with the councils and politics of any of the three bodies" and had "but one unbiassed wish for the general prosperity and honourable advancement of the Medical Men of my country."[32]

Hodgkin's proposals were only one of repeated attempts made between 1840 and 1858 to reconcile the divergent interests and claims of the medical and surgical corporations in England, Scotland, and Ireland; the extramural teachers of surgery and medicine; the universities that provided medical education and degrees; and the general practitioners—the rank and file of the medical profession. All sides had their parliamentary spokesmen and engaged in active lobbying. But these opposing forces, competing for government attention at a time notable for other political and social reforms, brought about postponement or defeat of many medical bills.[33]

The first of these reform bills was proposed to Parliament by Thomas Wakley and associates and called for registration of medical practitioners and the formation of a single College of Medicine whose fellows could practice in all branches of medicine. It was an obvious attempt to replace the existing corporations with a new medical body that included general practitioners. Naturally, the entrenched London elites opposed this and any other legislation that weakened their power to select the profession's leadership.

Medical Act of 1858

After seventeen different bills were introduced in Parliament, the Medical Act of 1858 was passed. It was the first attempt by the government to control the profession and protect the public by reorganizing medical education and licensing procedures. The bill regulated the qualifications of practitioners of medicine and surgery by establishing minimum standards for admission to an annual Medical Register. It created a General Council of Medical Education and Registration of the United Kingdom (General Medical Council or GMC), where for the first time representatives of the nine medical corporations and ten universities in England, Scotland, and Ireland were united in a single official body. All medical men who had satisfied the examiners of any one of the representative bodies on the council were listed as "qualified medical practitioner." The GMC could remove the names of those guilty of criminal offences or of serious professional misconduct. In addition, the council was to publish a national pharmacopoeia. Since the council's role in education was advisory, the individual members retained authority to grant licenses, set their own educational requirements, and confer honorary distinctions such as fellowship in the Royal Colleges.[34]

After 1858, the lengthy apprenticeship requirement, subjected to increasing criticism since 1830, was falling into abeyance as the student spent more and more of his time at lectures and in dissecting rooms and hospital wards and less and less time as a private pupil. The growing requirements for course work and hospital experience undercut the importance of apprenticeship, and it ceased to be a significant feature of English medical education.[35]

The Medical Act removed the legal distinctions between physicians, surgeons, and apothecaries, thus recognizing de jure what had already occurred de facto. The act also abolished the antiquated local and regional prohibitions against regularly qualified practitioners from Scotland and Ireland and ended the anomalous authority of the Archbishop of Canterbury to grant medical licenses.[36]

The Medical Act of 1858 was possible because medical knowledge had become more scientific, medical education more systematic, and the medical profession more unified. Between 1830 and 1858 the libraries of Oxford and Cambridge and the daily visit by the apothecary were replaced by the teaching hospital. University education for general practice was available for the first time in England at University College London.[37]

Public, Profession, and Quackery

Although unlicensed practitioners were now barred from government service, the Act of 1858 did not, unfortunately, ban quacks[38] or the activities of the thousands of untrained and irregular "practitioners" who endangered the health and lives of the public, especially in rural areas. This continued well beyond mid-century. Unqualified practice had flourished from the earliest times because the authorities allowed everyone the right to choose his own "doctor" or "surgeon"—qualified or unqualified. Anyone, licensed or not, could practice in England and Wales on any patient who, knowing his lack of qualifications, would allow him to do so. Licensure is only a certification of training. It was, however, always an offense for anyone to claim to have had training that he had not received. Nor could anyone without the appropriate recognized diplomas sue for payment for giving advice, for prescribing drugs, for performing surgery, or for any other treatment. Neither the public nor the government was ready to condemn the unqualified as totally unacceptable. As far as the public was concerned, prohibition of unlicensed practice constituted excessive government interference in the freedom of choice of whatever medical attention one wanted.[39] Limiting legal registration to those who qualified by examination in medicine or surgery was as far as the politicians were prepared to go at this time to enable the public to distinguish the educated and qualified from the uneducated and unqualified practitioner.[40]

Parliament did not grant licensed medical men a monopoly over the practice of medicine because, reflecting the mood of society, it had no confidence in the medical license as evidence of medical expertise. The legislators apparently understood that the motivation of the medical "profession" was not based on the superiority of medical science but on a desire for protection against competition. All levels of society resorted to home remedies or patent medicines and sought the services of unlicensed "practitioners."[41]

The public tolerated the "irregulars" because it was confused by the constant quarreling by the medical leaders and their followers over medical practices and the contention among the numerous licensing bodies over the right to confer professional titles. This fed the public distrust of the medical profession during the late eighteenth and early nineteenth centuries. The public also feared the medical profession because its methods were painful and generally unpleasant and its hospitals were equated with filthy prisons as places of torture and death.[42]

Quackery received public approval because its medication (patent medicine) was easy to take, although it was often useless or dangerous. The growing popularity of patent medicines, spurred by effective advertising in newspapers and other periodicals, did not reflect increased credulity among the masses but merely the age-old search for panaceas.[43]

Hodgkin clearly understood this ambivalence in society.

> With respect to protection against quacks and irregular practitioners. . . . The difficulty of performance arises not so much from any defect in the law, as from the predilection for quackery which pervades a large portion of the public of all classes. . . . The effectual suppression of quackery must, therefore, be brought about by the public mind being enlightened on the subject; and, when this is accomplished, the patient will be as unwilling to trust his life in the hands of an ignorant practitioner, as the sportsman would be to discharge an untried gun-barrel.[44]

CHAPTER THIRTEEN

In Defense of Natives

Marriage

The 1850s began on a joyous note for Thomas Hodgkin. On January 3, 1850, in his fifty-second year, and to the great surprise and amusement of the Quaker community and his friends, he married. The bride was Mrs. Sarah Frances Scaife née Callow (1804–1875), a widow from Nottingham with two grown sons. There was another wedding in the family a few months later, when Hodgkin's brother, John, Jr., married a young Irish Friend whom he had been courting for several months. Six children were born of this marriage, his third.[1] His first two wives had five children.

The Nottingham Friends were not anxious to admit Mrs. Scaife. There were repeated committee interviews and inspections and all sorts of other delaying tactics in handling her application. She had studied Quaker teaching and wanted to observe its practices, but her treatment was distasteful and embarrassing. Hodgkin was angry and resentful. Eventually her membership was approved. The nephews and nieces were pleased by the idea of marriage but were surprised by their uncle's choice. Mrs. Scaife did not measure up to the family's intellectual expectations and her lower-class origin disappointed them. Her late husband, a former patient of Dr. Hodgkin, had been employed as a tailor.[2]

Although an oddly matched pair—she was heavyset, and he below average size—they were genuinely fond of each other and it was a happy marriage. His third Sarah was a gracious hostess for Hodgkin's many friends and cheerfully put up with the wide assortment of visitors that his many interests brought to their new home at 35 Bedford Square (Fig. 8) at almost any hour.[3] Hodgkin's "parlour" became a meeting place for philanthropists, ethnologists, geographers, and all kinds and conditions of men of varying colors and creeds from almost every nation and continent. One notable visitor was David Livingstone (1813–1873), the Scottish medical missionary and explorer, who became a national hero on his return to England on December 9, 1856, after sixteen years in Africa. Barely two months later, on February 4, 1857, he presented an exciting personal travelogue about his adventures and missionary work and discovery of Victoria Falls to Hodgkin and his guests.[4]

In Defense of Natives

Hodgkin worked to save the primitive peoples of the world not only through the political machinery of government but also by collecting and preserving the records of their day-to-day life. His 1840 questionnaire on the human race was updated and a revised and expanded new edition was published in 1852. The sections on physical characteristics and language were enlarged, and there was a new part on grammar, bringing the total number of questions to 103, plus an additional unnumbered multipart question on domestic animals. They were "seeking Facts, and not inferences; what is observed, and not what is thought."[5] Intended for consuls, foreign residents, and travelers, it was a means of obtaining precise observations about the social organization of the tribes facing extinction. The information was to be sent to the British Association.

Following the declining health and death of Thomas F. Buxton in 1845, Hodgkin became the chief spokesman and leading force of the Aborigines' Protection Society. He served for many years as secretary or honorary secretary, as well as on the committee. As

Fig. 8. 35 Bedford Square. (Courtesy of the Greater London Photograph
Library.)

long as the other societies flourished, the APS could devote its principal attention to the Australian aborigines and the American Indians of Upper Canada. After 1847, when it began to publish its own journal, it took an increasing interest in Africa. The society's transactions recorded Hodgkin's petitions, letters, and declarations to foreign secretaries and colonial governors.

In April 1852, Hodgkin expressed the APS's concern over problems in South Africa. Rather than seek a military solution, Hodgkin urged "as the only sure means of preventing disputes and collisions with the native inhabitants of the countries colonized by us, the full recognition of the principle, that they possess an unqualified right to their country and liberty." Furthermore, when surplus lands were obtained from the natives, it should be done only by treaty and with compensation. Instead of deposing and trampling on existing native authorities, the society advocated supporting them "as the administrators of an improved code, gradually assimilated to our own, and, as far as possible, connected with our colonial government in its execution."[6]

A few weeks later, his letter on the New Zealand Bill covered questions of voting, proportional representation, distribution and sale of land, intermarriage, bilingualism, and finances. Changes were suggested that would make the constitution fairer to the natives. When the bill passed in the House of Commons, essentially unaltered, the Aborigines' Protection Society petitioned the Lords, requesting amendment of the bill to secure the political and territorial rights and interests of the New Zealand aborigines.[7]

Hodgkin insisted that although the aborigines were pagan and uncivilized, this should "neither exclude them from the pale of humanity nor justify the crimes of pseudo-Christians."[8] Hodgkin asked that "the feebler races of mankind should be respected in their lives, persons, and property."[9] Disregard of this principle, he added, had led to the needless loss of human life, the vast expenditure of public money, the disaffection of the colonists, and the hostility of the native tribes.

Soon after the Cape Colony received its constitution and right of self-government, with responsibility for the treatment of the natives, Hodgkin pleaded for justice, protection, and equality of rights for the natives without distinction of color. He asked for some degree of indulgence and allowance for the disadvantages resulting from successive generations of barbarism. The natives, continued Hodgkin, were entitled to be helped up from their lowly status by the civilized, the powerful, and the Christian settlers from Europe. A humane policy toward the natives was the best means of preventing "those mutual aggressions which invariably prevail when different races in different degrees of civilization are living in close approximation to each other, and which necessarily bring dishonour to the strong and destruction to the weak." But conflicts continued to occur, and Hodgkin requested a thorough investigation of the records of the Colonial Office for "the causes and circumstances of our collisions with the natives."[10]

Final Medical Papers

While advocating these humanitarian policies for the government, Hodgkin continued to write on medical subjects. But he had to reach back into his past records. One such article was his lecture on the numerical method of Pierre Louis, which he had read to the Physical Society of Guy's Hospital in 1834 (see chapter 8, note 8); another was a report to the British Association in August 1836 on a connection between the lymphatic system and the veins.[11] He also published lectures on diabetes[12] and cachexia,[13] which he had given to the Harveian Society during the 1852–53 and 1853–54 sessions, respectively.

In his talk on diabetes, he commented on how easy it was to miss the diagnosis of this disease but noted that he did not seek out diabetic patients and never took up this incurable disease as a specialty. He also observed that wounds and injuries in diabetic patients did not heal easily and could give way to destructive inflammation, which sometimes resulted in sores and gangrene in the feet. He remarked on the sweet odor of the breath, urine, and perspiration and the loss of sexual power. He believed that the seat of the disorder was in the digestive organs, especially the stomach, and recommended those means that indirectly relieve gastric acidity, such as relief from care, cheerful but not engrossing mental activity, fresh air, care of the skin, and rest. Hodgkin noted that diabetes was associated with Bright's disease.

Here was a man, primarily a physician-pathologist-scientist, operating in two worlds at the same time, pursuing his interests as a member of dozens of professional societies and philanthropic organizations. Well into middle age, Hodgkin would have drawn no criticism had he slowed down and concentrated on one area and made an occasional contribution to the other. But he gave his total effort to both. Hodgkin even had something left for the individual getting a bad deal.

Causes great and small attracted Hodgkin's interest and involvement. It was the injustice itself and not the numbers affected or the remoteness of the locale that set his pen into action. In a letter to the *Association Medical Journal,* Hodgkin took up the complaint of a naval medical officer who, after devoting much of his active life to the naval service, was passed over for promotion. Dr. M'Cormick had served well in many areas of the world, including two Arctic and one Antarctic expeditions, as well as in the tropics, and at times also acted in nonmedical capacities. Hodgkin cited this as a failure of the seniority system. Describing the position in which the young medical officer is placed on entering the naval service as degrading, Hodgkin admitted that he tried to discourage his younger professional associates from entering this service.[14]

Not all of Hodgkin's correspondence for the Committee of the Aborigines' Protection Society was to officials of the British Government or its overseas colonies. In March 1856, Hodgkin wrote to the American ambassador to Britain, James Buchanan, on the eve of his departure from England and soon to campaign for the Presidency of the United States. Hodgkin expressed the committee's appreciation for "every effort which may be made for the preservation & elevation of that interesting race of which our common forefathers commenced the injury & spoliation." He hoped that the American people, so well known for their successful undertakings, would find a means for the "preservation & improvement of a perishing race which preceded them in the occupation of their great country." Hodgkin also called attention to "those Indian tribes in the North West & in the South who have had less advantages from missionary efforts & more deterioration

& exasperation in the lamentable conduct of fur traders, gold diggers, mormons & other classes of white men not remarkable for either the polish of civilization or the benignant exhibition of Christian virtues."[15]

The letter was written midway between two meetings of the Harveian Society at which he gave a two-part lecture on morbid pathology of the heart.[16] His activities were in a constant state of dynamic equilibrium between science and philanthropy, and at any given moment in time it was impossible to know on which side of the equation he was working—he moved so easily between them. But the momentum that maintained the equilibrium had finally run its course. The lecture on the heart was his first full-length publication in two years and his last medical paper. For the remaining ten years of his life, his appearances in print dealt mainly with geographical exploration, social and humanitarian issues, and causes on behalf of the underprivileged and the disadvantaged.

Hodgkin's affinity for the disadvantaged and suffering was well known to his friends. His niece recalled how, one day while in conversation with some friends, a name was mentioned of someone whom Hodgkin disliked—probably for good reason. Upon hearing the man's name, Hodgkin launched into a harsh criticism of this person and denounced him as being unworthy of the company of his friends. As the conversation continued, it was said that the man had recently experienced severe financial losses and was facing hard times. No sooner did Hodgkin hear this than he immediately offered to go to the man's aid, to comfort him and lend him money, in order to help him over his difficulties. But the story was all false! Hodgkin's friends had staged the conversation as a trick for the amusement of observing Hodgkin's turnabout.[17]

Finances

Hodgkin often displayed poor judgment when it came to money. He made bad investments and extended loans to unreliable acquaintances. It appears that Hodgkin was a "soft touch." His niece recalled that the family used to think that he took up all sorts of undesirables and adventurers for whom no one else cared. He supported many of them. Hodgkin's misplaced confidence led him more than once into business speculations that were financially disastrous.

A friend of Hodgkin's admonished him for squandering his flagging energy on a variety of projects that were better suited to inferior minds and were unworthy of him. The friend was saddened to see a great mind like his frittered away because politeness and kind feeling allowed him to be used by foreigners.[18] And foreigners there were many. Hodgkin's house was the setting for hospitality to "representatives of every nationality in Europe [and] . . . men of every hue and of every race from Asia, Africa, America, Australia, and Polynesia." Hodgkin's "recognition of their equality was something more than a genial habit growing out of his natural kindliness and hospitality: it sprang from a religious duty; it was a principle which gave shape and colour to his life, and made him give up his time, ability, and fortune to succour the needy and to defend the oppressed."[19] But the perception that Hodgkin was an "easy mark" outlived him. An obituary stated that "his own guileless and trusting disposition rendered him peculiarly liable to suffer from the attempts of the mercenary to excite his sympathy by spurious tales of distress."[20] Another referred to Hodgkin's hospitality and added that "this was occasionally taken advantage of by men who were unworthy to share his friendship."[21]

His good nature and lack of desire for financial gain from his practice made him hesitant and careless about collecting professional fees even from those who could well afford to pay. Some of his friends and patients stopped consulting him or referring others because he would not take adequate fees. The story is told in *The Lancet*'s obituary and repeated by nearly all his biographers that, having been called to a very wealthy man who was ill, he sat up all night with him. The patient recovered and in gratitude handed Hodgkin a blank check, telling him to fill in any amount he thought suitable. Hodgkin wrote in ten pounds. The patient was offended by such a modest fee and asked why. Hodgkin replied that the patient did not look as if he could afford more. It was said that the patient was so angry that he never again called for Hodgkin. Undoubtedly, other wealthy patients were also offended by small fees for his services and did not consult him again. His practice also suffered from the many extended periods he spent away from London.

His attitude toward charging for his advice and services caused more than a little comment. *The Lancet* in its obituary of Hodgkin said: "Although possessing the entire confidence of those who knew his worth and talent, Dr. Hodgkin never obtained a large share of practice. He had no worldly wisdom, and did himself and, perhaps, others injustice by a disregard of due professional remuneration, which amounted almost to eccentricity."[22]

Not surprisingly, this nonattention to the financial side of medical practice attracted many of the poor. They came in large numbers from the neighborhood whenever Thomas visited his brother, which was nearly every Sunday. Hodgkin would spend the whole afternoon in seeing them, and at no charge.[23] Hodgkin's associates objected to this free advice being given to many who should have paid a fee to him or to someone else.

Could Hodgkin afford to waive fees because he was independently well off? There is little evidence about his financial resources. Hodgkin's ledger for 1837 shows a considerable income of £2,728, 11s. 3d. His expenses for the year were £2,721, 5s. 6½d., leaving a balance of £7, 5s. 6½d. How typical these earnings and expenses were is not apparent from other records,[24] but the earnings, assuming most were from his practice, compared favorably with the reported earnings of other physicians.[25]

When Hodgkin reached age twenty-one, he inherited money, stocks, and property valued at more than £8,700 that had been left in trust by his father's uncle, the Ackworth schoolteacher for whom Thomas had been named. Hodgkin's investments were as varied as his nonmedical interests. They included a costly real estate and brickmaking venture in Paris; horsebreeding closer to home; Pennsylvania coal mines and railroad stock recommended by his American friend Elliott Cresson; bad investments in land and mulberry trees in Syria for cultivation of silkworms, which failed because of unscrupulous partners; and speculation on an invention for the extraction of palm oil. When Cresson died in 1854, he left Hodgkin $2,000 in appreciation of their friendship. Hodgkin also received small bequests from Luke Howard (his brother's first father-in-law), Hudson Gurney (a family friend), and John Barry, who had rejected his apprenticeship at Plough Court. Although hardly a poor man, Hodgkin was always complaining about finances. Some of his money worries were relieved by the inheritance from his father. The bulk of John Hodgkin, Sr.'s considerable estate was divided between his sons. Thomas received some property, two houses in Shipston, and £2,000. John, Jr., also received various parcels of land, the house in Pentonville, and some money. Hodgkin's American investments, some of which were lost in the Civil War, were managed by William Coppinger, Secretary of the American Colonization Society. They never met, but the executors of Hodgkin's estate found embarrassing irregularities in Coppinger's accounts.[26]

Fortunately for Hodgkin, his friend and patient Sir Moses Montefiore was wise in financial matters. Montefiore's financial success was largely due to his connection with Nathan Rothschild, for whom he acted on the London Stock Exchange. Early in their friendship, in 1824, Montefiore arranged for Hodgkin to buy ten shares in one of his newly organized insurance companies, the Alliance British and Foreign Life and Fire Assurance Co., at the original issue price of £10 per share. The shares quickly increased in value, guaranteeing immediate profit. Hodgkin held on to them. Montefiore again extended these stockholder advantages to Hodgkin when other enterprises were organized. One was a company in which Montefiore took special satisfaction, the Imperial Continental Gas Association, which pioneered the introduction of gas lighting to the streets of European cities. In recognition of this practical use of science, The Royal Society elected Montefiore a fellow in June 1836.

Hodgkin served a few years as physician to two Jewish friendly societies (the Society of United Israelites and the Society of United Sisters) that helped Jewish immigrants from eastern Europe adapt to their strange, new, and often unfriendly environment. He gave up these affiliations in July 1831 for reasons of health[27] but continued to treat many poor Jews in London's East End.

Hodgkin's niece recalled, "I think the Aborigines & the Jews took the first place in his heart. He was much beloved by the Jews in the East End of London, & well-known in the poor quarters there, where he continually attended them without any charge."[28]

Hodgkin's interest in money-making ventures did not extend to his practice of medicine. His attitude toward fees was probably influenced by a belief that he should not accept any unless he could achieve some considerable benefit for the patient. He was well aware of the limitations of medical practice and of his specialty in particular. Although he placed great emphasis on clinical and pathological correlations, he knew that pathological anatomy is often unable to suggest the best form of treatment. "We may learn from it where disease is situated, what its unchecked progress must conduct to, and what is the kind and extent of improvement which we may desire to see brought about."[29] Hodgkin's studies and those of others were continually adding to the knowledge of diseases and their diagnosis, but this contributed very little at that time to their cure or relief.

Rejected Testimonial

Neither his appointment at Guy's nor that at St. Thomas's forbade private practice. But like several other distinguished and capable physicians, he was not successful in this endeavor. In Hodgkin's case, the financial side of private practice was distressing and it remained small. Having always treated many patients in his home community and elsewhere for little or no fee, he had limited income from this source. His close friends were concerned over his nonpursuit of money in the marketplace of medicine and decided, as a token means of compensation and recognition, to call attention to his medical achievements and philanthropic and reform activities. Perhaps Hodgkin's frequent complaints about money were an additional—though not acknowledged—reason for their action. Toward the latter part of 1856, and led by Sir James Clark, they initiated a fund-raising campaign as a testimonial to Hodgkin.

The solicitation for Hodgkin produced an anonymous letter to *The Lancet* that questioned whether he merited this distinction.

Sir, — A circular is, I suppose, going the round of the profession, — at any rate I have received one, — soliciting subscriptions for a testimonial to Dr. Hodgkin. The supposed grounds for conferring a distinction on the doctor are thus enumerated: — His researches during the formation of the museum of Guy's Hospital, and its catalogue; his Lectures on Morbid Anatomy; his contributions to the "Medico-Chirurgical Transactions;" his Public Lectures on Preserving and Promoting Health, stated in the circular to be "amongst the first contributions towards Sanitary Reform;" his efforts to obtain an adequate remuneration for the services of Poor-law Medical Officers; his labours for the relief of the sick poor, in behalf of Medical Reform, and for the improvement of Medical Education; his representations to the Government in connexion with the Aborigines Protection Society; and his exertions as one of the Secretaries of the Royal Geographical Society, as a member of the Council of the Statistical Society, and as one of the founders of the Ethnological Society.

Can you or any of your numerous correspondents inform me in what respect Dr. Hodgkin has outstripped any of his contemporaries in the above-named undertakings, and in what special particulars he has enlarged the boundaries of science? Was he really a founder of the Ethnological Society, in conjunction "with his friend Dr. Pritchard [sic], Sir Charles Malcolm, and other eminent men"?—for I had believed (perhaps erroneously) that the original formation of that Society was due to Dr. Richard King and some others. I should be happy to join in contributing to a testimonial to Dr. Hodgkin, if such a memorial be really due to his labours; but really it appears to me that public testimonials will diminish greatly in estimation if they are conferred, as the tendency seems to be now-a-days, for matters less attended with personal risk, or loss, or self-sacrifice of any kind. I am, Sir, yours obediently,
London, November, 1856.   JUSTUS.[30]

Two weeks later there was a response from one of Hodgkin's former students, who warmly defended his teacher's accomplishments and well-deserved recognition (see chapter 9, note 47). More than £280 was raised. However, Hodgkin, although he did not object to recognition from professional associates, still disapproved of public receptions and ceremonies and would not accept the money. A compromise was reached whereby Mrs. Hodgkin was presented with a commemorative piece of plate, and the rest of the collection, £204 10s., was invested in stocks, the interest to fund an educational prize biennially at the Royal Medical Benevolent College (now Epsom College).[31]

Sir Moses Montefiore, Bart.

Shortly after the testimonial affair, Hodgkin embarked on the first of several long journeys with Sir Moses Montefiore, Bart. Montefiore's involvement in London's financial world and social and charitable functions brought him into contact with upper English society. He had been knighted by Queen Victoria in 1837 following election as Sheriff of London. Victoria made him a baronet in 1846 for his humanitarian efforts, after his visit to Czar Nicholas I to seek relief from government restrictions and harassment of Jews in Russia.

Although Hodgkin and Moses Montefiore saw each other frequently after Hodgkin left the employ of Abraham Montefiore, there is no firm evidence as to when Hodgkin became Moses Montefiore's physician. It was probably sometime after 1824, early in their friendship.[32] Montefiore's diaries refer to attendance by an "eminent physician" as early as 1828.[33] In any event, Montefiore asked Hodgkin on several occasions to join him and his wife on travels overseas. In 1857 Hodgkin accompanied the Montefiores as personal physician on their fifth trip to the Holy Land to review the projects sponsored during previous visits and to provide additional financial support where needed. Each new visit was an occasion for financial aid—his own and that collected by others—to ease the general misery and help the neediest cases. Montefiore endowed hospitals, settlements, and charitable institutions. When the sultan granted Montefiore a firman in 1855 allowing him to buy land in Palestine, he founded the first Jewish residential quarter outside the walls of the Old City. This was the beginning of the New City of Jerusalem.[34]

They left England on February 25, 1857. Crossing France into Italy, they traveled via Naples to Malta. They reached Alexandria on May 5 and continued by rail to Cairo, where Hodgkin took a side trip to see the pyramids and the sphinx. Roads were bad, but all along the way Sir Moses and his entourage of escorts were greeted by local officials, dignitaries, and well-wishers. Resembling a procession, they got to Jerusalem May 20.

Hodgkin was very disappointed in Jerusalem, "a poor and miserable place," and in "the deplorable state" of the Jews. He criticized their dependence on charitable funds contributed by Jews in countries worldwide.

> Numbers flock to Jerusalem either in advanced age expressly to die there or still young . . . for the purpose as they term it of 'Serving the Lord' which really means doing nothing but reading the Talmud & going to the Synagogue. . . . Till very lately the children had little or no instruction but schools have lately been established for girls by Sir M. Montefiore & for boys by a fund bequeathed by a German Jew — The language used by Jews of Jerusalem is . . . a mixture of Spanish, Arabic, German, Polish & Hebrew. . . . The Christians of Jerusalem are much divided & those places which are misnamed Holy & have long been the shining attraction to the fanatical & superstitious are in a state of disgraceful dilapidation [&] deplorable in an archeological point of view.[35]

He regretted attempts to convert Jews, in particular activities by the London Society For Promoting Christianity Amongst The Jews. Hodgkin was convinced that missionary organizations specifically to convert Jews were wrong both in principle and practice. There were 8,000 Jews in Jerusalem at that time, almost half the city's population. The remainder were Moslems and Christians in equal number.[36]

Hodgkin assisted Sir Moses on his visits to farms, a girls' school, a dispensary, and a textile shop that the philanthropist had established and answered letters and petitions, drafted proposals for new undertakings, and wrote reports and other documents. These European (i.e., heathen) cultural improvements and those in agriculture and mechanics met opposition and contempt from fanatical rabbinic authorities. Jewish philanthropists from Paris and Vienna experienced similar difficulties in introducing new schools.

The visit to Jerusalem convinced Hodgkin that a mechanics' institute modeled after those in England could promote the welfare and comfort of the people and bring about "cordial cooperation [between the] Jews, Christians, and Turks."[37] He suggested this at a meeting with Europeans in Jerusalem and advocated teaching the principles of simple machines, such as the lever, inclined plane, and wheel, to replace the inefficient and laborious carting by donkey, camel, and man. Public health would be addressed by lectures on personal hygiene and the need for cleanliness of dwellings and streets.

This was not a new interest for Hodgkin. Sewage and waste disposal were major problems in London, where more efficient and orderly removal were needed. In 1847 he had participated in formation of the Metropolitan Sewage Manure Company to promote waste products as agricultural fertilizer. The plan never got off the ground.[38]

After returning to London, Hodgkin appealed to mechanics' institutes in Britain for simple portable apparatus, easily explained diagrams, very elementary lectures, models, books on the sciences, and instructive biographies as examples to encourage study and hard work. Hodgkin had been an advocate of adult education since his Spitalfields lectures on the maintenance of health two decades earlier. However, what may work in a modern society often cannot overcome the cultural barriers of a backward community.

They left Jerusalem on June 7 and, traveling by way of Trieste and across central Europe to Hanover, were back in England in mid-July after an absence of nearly five months. Hodgkin reported his impressions to the British Association for the Advancement of Science about the proposal for a canal across the Isthmus of Suez. He concluded that there would be immense physical difficulties in the construction and maintenance of such a canal. The Mediterranean side was not only shallow and sandy but was of constantly varying depth because of shifting sandbanks. Dredging vessels would have to operate continuously to maintain open passage. Citing the enormous cost, Hodgkin questioned whether the anticipated volume of commercial traffic would justify the investment. Consequently, he advocated a railroad instead of a canal across the isthmus.

His presentation was harshly criticized by *The Railway Times*, which believed the canal to be a very feasible project compatible with a railroad.[39] Sir Moses rejected an 1855 offer from Ferdinand de Lesseps (1805–1894) to invest in construction of the Suez Canal and favored a railway for the region (between Jaffa and Jerusalem). Not surprisingly, Hodgkin had similar views. Montefiore did not think so great an undertaking would be a financial success. Thirty years earlier, in 1825, he had turned down a directorship from de Lesseps in a company planning a Panama Canal.[40] Hodgkin also had an opinion about a Panama Canal, favoring a railroad and canals across the isthmus. He believed that hostility from local Indians could be overcome by placating and civilizing them.[41]

Hodgkin returned from the Middle East sporting a luxuriant beard, which prompted an editorial writer for *Guy's Hospital Gazette* to compose the following *jeu d'esprit*: "Hodgkin went out with Moses [Montefiore] and returned with Aaron (hair-on)."[42] He is shown here (Fig. 9) with a beard and wearing Quaker clothes. The flower pinned to his jacket is an unusual adornment for a plainly dressed Quaker and may have been the suggestion of the photographer to dress up one of the poses.[43]

The Quaker style of dress had become so out of date and eccentric that it attracted attention, which was hardly the original intention. In 1860, dress and speech were made optional and other rules of behavior were also relaxed. It marked the beginning of changes for the Society of Friends that brought Quakerism closer to other Christian denominations in English Society. For Hodgkin and his brother, however, these corporate decisions did not alter the practices of a lifetime. They continued to observe the traditional Quaker practice in dress and speech that they had learned as children.

All of Sir Moses's overseas aid and rescue missions were successful—but one. The exception was a cause célèbre involving a seven-year-old Bolognese Jewish child, Edgar Mortara, forcibly taken from his parents by police of the Papal States on June 24, 1858.[44] Bologna was part of the Papal States. The boy had been secretly baptized by a teen-age Catholic servant girl when he was one year old and dangerously ill. The servant feared for the boy's salvation if he died unbaptized. Consequently, the child belonged to the Church and must be raised as a Catholic, which led to the

Fig. 9. *Two studio photographs of Thomas Hodgkin in the later years of his life. (Courtesy of the Library Committee of the Religious Society of Friends—London Yearly Meeting.)*

abduction. The precedent for the action dated from the seventh century, when the Councils of Toledo ruled that Hebrew children, even if baptized in error, should be separated from their parents lest they follow them in error. These canons were reaffirmed by Pope Benedict XIV in the eighteenth century and were canon law in 1858.[45]

The kidnapping produced a worldwide outcry from Jews and Christians. Protest meetings were held throughout Europe and in the United States.[46] Francis Joseph I and Napoleon III urged the Pope to release the child. The British Foreign Secretary expressed the concern of Her Majesty's government, "as Protestants were as much exposed to such acts of injustice as Jews," and promised to make strong representations to Rome.[47]

The Board of Deputies of British Jews had learned of this incident from Jewish communities in Sardinia and Turin and asked its president, Sir Moses Montefiore, to persuade the Vatican to return the child to his parents. Accompanied by Hodgkin, Sir Moses and Lady Montefiore departed Dover on March 3, 1859. The Foreign Office provided the usual letters of introduction to British embassies along the way and, although it sympathized with the mission, cautioned Sir Moses that there was not the slightest hope of success.

Sir Moses's efforts to gain a hearing were constantly rebuffed by papal authorities, but he persisted and with help from the British embassy was granted an audience with Cardinal Antonelli, the Papal Secretary. It was a cordial meeting, but that was as far as he got. Pope Pius IX refused to see Montefiore or to free the child. Sir Moses renewed his efforts in this case, but the Church would not budge. Edgar Mortara was placed in a monastery, raised as a Catholic, and in 1873 ordained as a priest.

After returning from Rome, Hodgkin was soon involved in meetings with American colonizationists. The American Colonization Society had been sending small groups of blacks to establish the colony of Liberia on land purchased on the West African coast. Hodgkin had been an early supporter of the colonization of Liberia and one of the first to advocate nation status for it. He hoped that a successful Liberia would encourage emigration of emancipated blacks from the United States and be the means of bringing civilization and Christianity to Africa. He later introduced Liber-ia's first president, Joseph Jenkins Roberts (1809–1876), to Lord Palmerston, the British Foreign Secretary, when the new nation was seeking British recognition. When Britain and Liberia exchanged treaties of recognition in 1849, Hodgkin represented the newly independent country.[48] The United States withheld official recognition until 1862.

Much activity on behalf of free blacks was taking place on the other side of the Atlantic. Initially, most black leaders and antislavery whites opposed schemes for emigration and insisted that blacks were entitled to equal rights in the land of their birth. Eventually, however, the continual frustrations of second-class citizenship, even for those freed blacks with ability and achievement, convinced many that they should consider emigration to Africa as an alternative to continued degradation and futile political agitation in the United States.

Delany and African Resettlement

In May 1858, a Wisconsin-based group wrote to Professor Joseph Hobbins of the Wisconsin State University and asked that the letter be forwarded to the Royal Geographical Society of London for advice on an African location to settle freed slaves.[49] The inquiry was answered by Thomas Hodgkin, honorary secretary of the society.[50] The leader of the group was Martin Robison Delany (1812–1885),[51] a black activist and lecturer on the abolitionist circuit. He wanted to establish a new black nation controlled entirely by blacks that would provide economic opportunity and political and social freedom for them. He was convinced that Africa's future must rely on the civilizing influence of America's blacks and that the black man's "elevation must be the result of *self-efforts*, and work of our *own hands*."[52]

In his answer, Hodgkin encouraged their initiative and suggested the Niger area of West Africa. Although climate and navigation might present problems, Hodgkin was confident that they would have a better reception and greater chance for success than earlier white-led expeditions, which failed to establish farms and factories in the territory. Hodgkin also suggested a stopover in Liberia, where they could adjust to the new environment before reaching a final destination.

The result was a two-man Niger Valley Exploring Party consisting of Delany and Robert Campbell, a Jamaica-born science teacher from Philadelphia. The proposed exploration had gained the attention of antislavery supporters in England, as well as manufacturers interested in new sources of raw cotton. Campbell sailed first—but to England, where he intended to raise money for the expedition and to meet with abolitionists and philanthropists. Thomas Hodgkin was one of several who contributed to provide "for his outfit and free passage to the coast of Africa."[53] Delany managed to get some backing for the trip and sailed later directly to Liberia.

While all this was going on, another emigration group, the African Civilization Society, with ties to the American Colonization Society, had been formed (September 1858), and it sent the Rev. Theodore Bourne, a white man, to England to raise money. Bourne met his first English audience of "the Friends of Africa" at Hodgkin's home, on August 18, 1859.[54] The English preferred blacks to white Americans as advocates of the antislavery cause,[55] and when Delany and Campbell returned in May 1860 from their expedition and made the rounds promoting their emigration project, Bourne was shunted to the background. Hodgkin, on the other hand, preferred Bourne and praised his integrity, zeal, and knowledge of the subject. "I think him greatly beyond Delany and in most respects they will not bear comparison, yet Delany is courted for his colour, & I fear that flattered by this [he] may stay to the injury of the cause."[56] It may have been Hodgkin's close ties to the American Colonization Society or simply a clash of personality and temperament. Delany, the outspoken advocate of cultural black nationalism, was the embodiment of black pride. Interaction may not have been easy for the Quaker. Delany's need for independence was likely at odds with the unsolicited advice that Hodgkin always gave.

On May 17, 1860, fresh from their African trip, Delany and Campbell "met a number of noblemen and gentlemen, interested in the progress of African Regeneration, in the parlour of Dr.

Hodgkin, F.R.G.S."[57] On June 11, 1860, Hodgkin introduced Delany and Campbell to the Royal Geographical Society, where Delany read a paper on western Africa.[58]

Hodgkin and many other Englishmen believed that cotton and other products produced by free labor in Africa would make slave labor in the United States and elsewhere unprofitable. Competition and legitimate trade would be a means to end the slave trade. Fear of a cotton shortage should war break out in the United States and the potential of trade for English business interests were factors in harmony with plans for an Afro-American settlement. The booming British textile industry, which employed over three million people, wanted new sources of cotton. Whereas, cotton was "King" in America, it was "Bread" in England, and a shortage of American cotton, for whatever cause, would spell economic disaster for Britain. The cultivation and export of African cotton was an important part of the overall plan for colonization.[59] At the same time, resettlement would promote Christian civilization of the African races and English commercial interests. Trade and religion, they believed, would end the slave trade. Hodgkin believed that "the most effectual Christian missionaries for native Africans are exemplary and zealous Christian negroes."[60]

British Syrian Relief

With the steadily deteriorating political situation in the United States threatening an outbreak of civil war, the attention of England was suddenly shifted in the opposite direction, to the eastern end of the Mediterranean. In July 1860, reports reached London of massacres in Syria. Several thousand Christians had been killed by the Druze, and very many villages were destroyed. Some 20,000 Christians, including women and children, fleeing the massacres, were wandering and starving on the mountains of Syria. When Sir Moses Montefiore learned of these events, he addressed, and personally delivered, a letter to *The Times* suggesting formation of a committee to raise money for the relief of the persecuted Syrian Christians and enclosed his own check for £200. There was quick response from the financial community and from influential government officials, resulting in formation of the British Syrian Relief Fund with Sir Moses as chairman of the executive committee.[61]

Hodgkin lent his help to the new relief effort and drew up lists of necessary medicines for the emergency. This was not a new kind of involvement for him. There already was in existence a Syrian Medical Aid Association, which he helped to set up in 1842. It sponsored European doctors and free dispensaries in Beirut and Damascus and served all religious sects. In addition to sending medical men, the association hoped to gain converts to Christianity.[62]

The relief fund organized in 1860 sent large sums of money for distribution by British consuls in Beirut and Damascus. Montefiore also asked the Foreign Office to use its influence to protect and save the Jews of Damascus—who were not attacked in the outbreaks—against unfounded accusations by the Christians that they had participated in the massacres.[63] Eventually, order was restored by intervention of France and England, and a French peacekeeping force was sent to Beirut. An investigation of the atrocities indicated that "however criminal may have been the excesses into which the Druzes were subsequently betrayed, the original provocation came from the Christians, & that they are themselves in a great measure responsible for the torrents of blood which have been shed."[64]

The focus of European attention soon returned to the United States. With the start of the American Civil War, factional differences between abolitionists and colonizationists came to an end, and Hodgkin gave his entire sympathy to the North. He didn't believe the often-made claims of the American Colonization Society that many Northerners favored the continuation of slavery. But he was concerned that anti-American feelings in England were aggravated by the war's effect on the textile workers. Hodgkin and other Quakers, fearing this might result in British recognition of the Confederacy, contributed to relief funds for the workers.[65] He also encouraged native Africans and descendants of Africans who visited England to meet periodically and to consider how they might contribute to the welfare of their countrymen. One such meeting was held in his home at 35 Bedford Square on November 7, 1861.[66]

With the outbreak of the war, Hodgkin had a new cause of anxiety for the North American Indians. Only recently had he warned the Royal Geographical Society[67] and the Colonial Secretary about the continuing deterioration of the Indians. In an effort to reverse the rapid decrease in Indian population in North America, a proposal was made by Capt. William Kennedy, son of an Indian woman and an agent of the Hudson's Bay Company, for a new Indian settlement in Canada near the Red River. At a meeting, held in his home on November 12, 1859, Hodgkin offered suggestions on selection of the site, town planning, distribution of land, and financial support. Always sensitive to protecting the Indians' cultural identity, he suggested that the settlement be given a well-sounding Indian name, connected with the locality.[68]

Nothing came of the plans for the settlement. To the Colonial Secretary, Hodgkin complained that despite sympathy for the Indians expressed in high quarters, the prevailing policy was decidedly hostile to their well-being. Because of the unfairly low prices paid by the Hudson's Bay Company for furs, the Indians, dependent for their subsistence on the fur trade, were kept in a state of miserable dependence on the company. Hodgkin asked for an investigation of the legality of the Hudson's Bay Company's charter, but the impact of the petition was diffused by his citing, also, continuing problems of misgovernment and maladministration of justice in Sierra Leone and the Cape of Good Hope.[69]

Letter to an American Indian

Now there were new concerns, and in a letter to John Ross (1790–1866), leader of the Cherokee Nation,—a letter that, if it was sent, may never have been delivered due to disruption of mail services—Hodgkin urged the Indians to refrain from joining in the war.

> For a long time previously down to the present day I have been deeply interested in whatever concerns the North American Indians & I have endeavoured in various ways but with too little success to

promote their welfare. It is with this object at my heart that I now address thee. . . .

I have but lately learnt that thou with many hundreds of thy countrymen art joining the army of the United States Government for the purpose of maintaining the integrity of that great Union which from its first instance has attracted the attention & received the admiration of the civilized World—the people of England as I believe very generally deplore the events that have brought discord and fratricidal bloodshed amongst their American relatives, & whilst as a people we keep aloof from the quarrel the side of the North has on various accounts our unanimous sympathy. . . .

As a friend of Peace, as a Quaker & most especially as the friend of the Indians I deplore your taking any share whatever in the fighting part. Let the past melancholy history of thy deeply injured & fast perishing race suffice to convince thee & thy people & your Indian brethren that taking part in the quarrels of your neighbours no less than the wars which you have waged amongst yourselves has contributed largely to your misfortunes—Let me tell thee that remotely as you are situated & little as we hear from you there are those in England who regard your far off settled tribes with much interest & hope—[70]

Following Lincoln's Emancipation Proclamation on January 1, 1863, inactive antislavery organizations reappeared as freedmen's aid groups, usually representing particular religious denominations. Substantial sums of money were contributed to local groups and directly to freedmen's aid societies in America. Clothing and agricultural equipment were also sent. As usual, most of the principal donors were Quakers.[71] Hodgkin also became active in these societies, and the earliest meetings of the London branch were held in his home.[72]

CHAPTER FOURTEEN

The Final Journey

Evils of Tobacco

Thomas Hodgkin had a broad agenda of scientific and social interests and activities whose objective was the betterment of the quality of life. There was one activity, however, that he detested and vigorously condemned. He went further in this respect than the Society of Friends, which merely disapproved of it, namely, smoking. As a result, Hodgkin was an active participant in the midcentury anti-tobacco movement and served on the committee of still another organization, the British Anti-Tobacco Society.

The major activity of the society was concentrated almost entirely in its secretary, Thomas Reynolds, who, having some private means, worked full-time lecturing, writing, distributing pamphlets, and editing the *Anti-Tobacco Journal*. A former smoker himself, he extravagantly blamed all kinds of physical, mental, and moral ailments and even social shortcomings on smoking. The literature of the society was moralistic, and it urged smokers to give up this bad habit by moral effort.[1]

Hodgkin wrote the preface for an anti-tobacco pamphlet, in which he said: "I would strongly urge any one, who is attached to the employment of Tobacco, to read and weigh my friend Thomas Reynolds's 'Fifty-four Objections to Tobacco,' since each of them is truly *argumentum ad hominem*—a personal appeal to every man, and applies to his bodily and mental well-being—to his happiness in his children—to the interests of his property—to his social comfort, and even, in some degree, to his eternal hopes."[2]

In a paper to a Social Science Congress in 1859, Hodgkin painted an even more ominous picture.

> Self-denial, the virtue which Christians are enjoined to practice daily *with humility*, and which philosophers and heroes have exhibited with pride, takes flight before the fumes of Tobacco, like the Devil Asmodeus from the cookery of Tobias. And how, in the absence of self-denial, can any of the Christian virtues be truly exercised?
>
> The vice, for vice I must call it, is often commenced at an early age, and then disobedience to parents, carelessness, idleness, low company, extravagance, intemperance, and even dishonesty, may be the miserable consequences. I knew a once amiable and promising young man who was unhappily brought to a suicidal death by the evil courses into which he was beguiled, and I cannot forget the remarkable declaration of his distressed but excellent father, when he said on the occasion, "I should not have been surprised at the sad act had I known that my son had become a smoker."[3]

Thomas Hodgkin attributed the sickly condition and chronic indigestion of many of his patients to their use of tobacco. As medical examiner for life insurance, he frequently rejected applicants because of "general depression of the system, feeble circulation, and nervous irritability," due to the use of tobacco. He maintained that the British had degenerated physically because of the growing consumption of tobacco. "The dirty pipes or cigars in their mouths and the filthy smell proclaim the fact, and . . . the cause of the degeneracy." He added that "the injurious effects of tobacco . . . are not merely lasting in the confirmed smoker himself, but are transmitted to his posterity."[4] But neither the medical profession nor the public generally accepted these unverified theories of impotence and degeneracy. On the whole, Victorian doctors tolerated or approved of "moderate" smoking, and neither the churches nor the temperance movement on the whole condemned the moderate use of tobacco. It seems that Anglican clergy and Protestant ministers smoked privately and discreetly.[5]

Metric System

A new issue drew Hodgkin's attention during the summer of 1862. The British Medical Association was considering the adoption of a new system of weights for use in the preparation and dispensing of medicines. However, the plan intended to retain the old names for the new weights. Rather than change the system of weights and measures, he appealed to the association to replace it with the metric system,[6] "that beautiful and practically convenient system of weights and measures." Though devised by the French, said Hodgkin, this should arouse no national jealousy, since the system belonged to all nations, and its continued rejection in England would place the country in a position of backward isolation.[7] The president of the British Medical Association offered no comment other than to note that the subject was being considered by the General Medical Council. Nothing came of its review. Government bureaucrats, still attached to the traditional ways, were reluctant to change, and there remained a hostility to things French.[8]

Lady Montefiore's Death

Before her death on September 24, 1862, Lady Montefiore had asked her husband to obtain additional concessions from the Turkish government to facilitate the proper working and expansion of the institutions they had set up for the Jewish poor during a previous visit to the Holy Land. Although still in mourning and weak in health, Sir Moses was determined to carry out his wife's request. Lady Montefiore had also asked Hodgkin to accompany her husband on his future travels, and this he had promised to do. Sir Moses's plan for a trip to Constantinople included a brief stay in the south of France to help him regain his health.[9] Hodgkin accompanied him. While in Marseilles Hodgkin wrote a short article on his personal experiences with nightmares and the action of anesthetics,[10] both of which he related to the status of his stomach.

The journey was timely. A new sultan was on the throne, and there was some question whether this would signal a change in the benevolent attitude of the Turkish government toward its Jewish subjects. Reaching Constantinople in May, during the three weeks' wait for an audience, Sir Moses made many charitable donations in memory of his wife, while Hodgkin offered advice on roads, sanitation, housing, and plans for a maternity facility for poor women and training of midwives to combat the high mortality from childbirth.[11] When the interview was eventually granted, the new sultan, Abdul-Aziz, reaffirmed privileges granted to Jews in the Holy Land by his late brother's firmans in 1840, including the right to purchase land and to build homes in Jerusalem. The grand vizier gave Sir Moses an official letter to the governor of Jerusalem, advising of the sultan's confirmation of the firmans. However, because of Hodgkin's concern for the grieving widower's health, Sir Moses was persuaded to return home. They arrived in London early in July after an absence of more than six months.[12] In only a few months, and before the year's end, they were to set out again, this time to Morocco.

Journey to Morocco

During October 1863 came an urgent appeal for help from the Jewish congregation on Gibraltar on behalf of the Jews of Tangier.[13] It seems that a Spanish national employed by the Spanish vice-consul at Saffi, a seaport on the west coast of Morocco, had died suddenly, and poisoning was suspected. The police arrested a fourteen-year-old Jewish boy who had lived with the family of the deceased. There followed the usual sequence of arrest, torture, confession, and implication of numerous other Jews "suggested" to the boy by the police. The boy was condemned and executed, and three of those named were sent to Tangier, where one was publicly executed, probably to impress foreign diplomats with the extent of Spanish influence in the court of the Sultan of Morocco. The Jews of Tangier were alarmed and, fearing the same fate for the other imprisoned Jews in Saffi and Tangier, communicated with Gibraltar.

Sir Moses contacted the Foreign Office, which telegraphed the British ambassador in Tangier, who gained a temporary halt of further executions. Sir Moses was determined to go to Morocco to seek release of the imprisoned Jews. But he had another purpose in mind. Realizing that a repetition of these events was inevitable in a country where Jews had no legal rights, Sir Moses decided to seek an audience with the Sultan of Morocco, to obtain a definite legal status for the 500,000 Jews[14] in that country—and to obtain the same protection and privileges for Jews and Christians as were enjoyed by Moorish citizens.[15]

Sir Moses departed from Dover for Calais on the morning of November 17, 1863. In the party were Sampson Samuel, solicitor and secretary to the Board of Deputies of British Jews, Haim Guedalla (1815–1904), husband of Sir Moses's niece, whose father was a native of Morocco, two trusted and reliable servants, and an experienced courier familiar with the territory and the language. Hodgkin went along "as an old and attached fellow-traveller and friend.[16]

Montefiore's financial position provided authority abroad. His personal standing with the Foreign Office was extremely valuable on these missions of personal diplomacy, especially since they were also in the interests of British foreign policy. His journeys were carefully planned, and he was well supplied with letters of credit from the Rothschilds and documents of introduction to British ambassadors, consuls, and all necessary local authorities.

Sir Moses went first to Madrid, where he was received by Queen Isabella and the King Consort. In Madrid and Seville he obtained letters to the Spanish minister in Tangier. The letters resulted in the release of Jewish prisoners in Tangier and Saffi. In Tangier he also won the release of a Moslem imprisoned for two-and-a-half years without trial on suspicion of having murdered two Jews.

Throughout the journey Hodgkin recorded impressions of everything he saw. In Tangier he described the inhabitants: "The Jewesses are far more personable than the other women of the country, whom we had the opportunity of seeing, and many of them are really beautiful." He even described their eye make-up, nail polish, and clothing. He also noted that despite "the evidence of careful attention paid to the education of Jewish youth, it seemed not improbable that the Moorish custom of neglecting the education of females might, in some degree, affect the Israelite girls of the poorer class."[17]

From Tangier, Sir Moses and his party crossed to Gibraltar, where a British naval frigate transported them to the Atlantic coast of Morocco. The overland journey to the capital, with an escort of the sultan's troops, took eight days, including a day of rest on the Sabbath. Sir Moses made the difficult journey in a portable chair. Upon reaching Marrakesh on January 25, 1864, they waited in a small palace reserved for them until the sultan was ready to see them. However, Hodgkin, at the request of the prime minister, slipped out on three evenings to provide medical services for him and some of his friends.[18]

Hodgkin wrote an entertaining account of the journey and described the approach lane along the walled road lined on both sides by rather an odd-looking assortment of troops. They resembled

> a sort of degraded European army. In the first place the men were of various ages, sizes, and colour—some old, others only lads; some quite diminutive, others tall; some as fair as almost any German, others the darkest Negroes, with every intermediate shade. . . . Many of the heads are shaven, but even then some hair is left which shows its character. Few, if any, of the men had shoes or stockings, but some I believe had slippers. I do not know whether they had shirts or not, but their old cloth jackets were indiscriminately of red, blue, or green. The garments worn for trousers did not cover the legs. These troops had very much the appearance of prisoners clothed in left off soldiers' garments. Each held a musket in due form by his side, but some had bayonets, others not. Even the officers were but little better clad.[19]

Sir Moses, wearing the uniform of the City Lieutenancy, presented his message, translated into Arabic, to the sultan, who handed the sealed document to his vice-chamberlain. Their interview was not long, but as Hodgkin later learned, it was one of the grandest the emperor had given and was marked by symbols of his complete satisfaction. This was especially shown in his riding a white horse of a special pure-bred stock that had been kept by the family for many generations (Fig. 10).

Fig. 10. The quadrangle of the palace at Morocco where the Sultan received Sir Moses Montefiore, Bart. Lithograph by F. Jones from a drawing by Thomas Hodgkin in Narrative of a Journey to Morocco, in 1863 and 1864. (Courtesy of the National Library of Medicine, Bethesda, Maryland.)

Hodgkin's account of the trip included the diplomatic exchange between Sir Moses and the sultan. In his edict (*dahir*) dated February 5, 1864, the sultan commanded that

> all Jews residing within our dominions . . . shall be treated by our Governors, Administrators, and all other subjects, in manner conformable with the evenly balanced scales of justice, and that in the administration of the Courts of Law, they (the Jews) shall occupy a position of perfect equality with all other people . . . and if any person should wrong or injure one of them (the Jews), we will, with the help of God, punish him.[20]

The language of the *dahir* was very high-sounding, but the key terms did not necessarily mean the same thing in Morocco as in Europe. Jews did not receive the same rights as foreign Christians living in the ports.[21]

After receiving the imperial edict (Fig. 11) they paid a farewell visit to the sultan, who greeted them in a kiosk in the palace gardens. They were given an extensive tour of the palace grounds, but from a location where the imperial residence could not be seen. In addition to irrigation canals, there were two large ornamental quadrangular pools or lakes, on one of which was the working model of a steamboat with paddles turned like a grindstone by a single operator on board. Finally, they visited the Jewish quarter, where it seemed the entire population came out to honor their famous friend. Because of the crowding in the narrow lanes, it was extremely difficult for Sir Moses's sedan chair to be carried through the mass of people.

> Sir Moses, as usual, first visited the synagogue, or rather one of the synagogues. It was a small, rudely decorated room, with evident indications of antiquity; but had the raised reading desk, and other requisites of Jewish worship. The crowd was so dense that it was with difficulty we entered. This was the only occasion of my visiting it, and I regret my inability more completely to examine and describe it. We did not enter any of the other synagogues, having visits to pay.[22]

Fig. 11. Sir Moses Montefiore, Bart. with the Imperial Edict. Lithograph by J. A. Vinter in Narrative of a Journey to Morocco, in 1863 and 1864. *(Courtesy of the National Library of Medicine, Bethesda, Maryland.)*

The homeward trip by way of Gibraltar and Tangier brought them again for a stopover in Madrid, where Sir Moses presented a copy of the sultan's edict, with a Spanish translation, to Queen Isabella. The next stop was Paris, where on March 31, in the company of Hodgkin, he presented a copy of the edict, with a French translation, to Emperor Napoleon III. They were back in England early in April after an absence of twenty weeks. On June 20 Sir Moses was received at Windsor Castle and reported on his trip to Queen Victoria.

The exchange with the sultan reaffirmed Hodgkin's trust in personal diplomacy and moral persuasion to achieve peaceful resolution of disputes between men or nations. Of course, arriving on a British naval vessel was helpful, as was the involvement of the consuls and the Foreign Office. But Hodgkin attributed the success of the mission to British prestige, not to gunboat diplomacy; he and Montefiore trusted in the long-term permanence of the mission's positive results.

For Hodgkin, the journey to Morocco was both a pleasure trip and a geologic excursion. In addition to describing the time spent in France, Spain, Gibraltar, and North Africa, he took notes on the ethnology and geography of these regions and described the flora and fauna, the antiquities, water systems, buildings, and agricultural methods encountered during the nearly five-month trip. In his published account of the journey, Hodgkin included geologic and geographic descriptions of the terrain of northwestern Morocco;[23] notes and observations of Morocco by others; a copy of a letter from Sir Moses to the Jews of Morocco, urging them to be loyal subjects of their sovereign and to obey the laws of the land; and an address by Hodgkin himself to the citizens of Tangier (December 12, 1863) urging them to build educational institutions for the youth of the city and vicinity. In stressing education he used catchphrases such as "Knowledge is Power" and "Virtue is Happiness."[24]

Hodgkin's impressions provided an account of the journey, illustrated with four lithographs prepared from his own original drawings. The monograph of the trip was published after his death in 1866 by subscription as a memorial to him (Fig. 12) and was dedicated to Sir Moses Montefiore, Bart.

Fig. 12. Thomas Hodgkin. Lithograph by J. A. Vinter from a photograph. Used as a frontispiece to Narrative of a Journey to Morocco, *in 1863 and 1864. (Courtesy of the National Library of Medicine, Bethesda, Maryland.)*

Unusual Friendship

The Montefiore diaries mention Hodgkin more than thirty times. What initially drew these two men together very probably was their individuality and independence, each distinctly different in his own environment. Their long-lasting friendship endured despite some interesting and unusual contrasts in their backgrounds and personalities. One was a Sephardic Jew who followed the orthodox path of Judaism and actively opposed inroads by the reform movement to alter congregational observances and practices. The other was a dedicated member of a radical Christian sect that distrusted formal doctrine and dismissed established dogma. Montefiore, with limited formal education, was a Fellow of The Royal Society, whereas Hodgkin, an educated linguist, scientist, and physician, rejected fellowship in the Royal College of Physicians. Even their appearances were a sharp contrast. Montefiore looked every bit the dignified broker—successful, influential, and rich—his friend was unimposing in appearance, financially inexperienced, and naive. The tall, six-foot-three-inch one-time captain in the Surrey local militia enjoyed the drill and ceremony and once faced down a howling mob in Bucharest. He met with kings, queens, sultans, pashas, czars, emperor, and shah, and socialized with Britain's ruling class. His friend for over forty years was a short, wiry, plainly dressed pacifist, always serious, who enjoyed the company of scientists, physicians, and humanitarians.

Despite their differences, they had much in common. Each belonged to a small religious minority and understood the difficulty of maintaining their observances in the midst of an alien majority. They participated in public efforts to end the remaining religious discriminations in British life in civil rights[25] and higher education. Both believed in self-help projects for the disadvantaged and less fortunate. But there must have been more than mutual respect and understanding, or similar commitments to philanthropy and oppressed minorities, or that in a country with a national church, they both belonged to discriminated-against minorities, which sustained their long friendship. They genuinely liked one another.

The Final Journey

It wasn't long before Hodgkin and Montefiore were off on another trip, this time to the Middle East. For Montefiore, who was then eighty-two years old, it was his sixth journey to the Holy Land and the second with Hodgkin. The purpose was to distribute money collected by Jewish congregations in the British Empire for the relief of the very severe suffering caused by the previous year's drought, locusts, and cholera. Moses Montefiore added his own contribution for "the widow and the orphan, the blind, the sick, and disabled."[26]

Nor was Hodgkin forgetful of his own "constituency" at home before embarking for the Middle East. On the evening before his departure, he addressed a long letter on housing for the poor[27] and sent it to *The Morning Star* newspaper. It appeared, by coincidence, on Wednesday, April 4, 1866, the day of his death.

Hodgkin drew a disturbingly familiar picture of the problems arising from urban renewal and suburban development. He pointed to the large increase of comfortable suburban dwellings that was not matched by any increase of housing units for the working class. New and wider streets were formed and traffic greatly improved when some of the most crowded and unhealthy dwellings of the poor were torn down, but no alternate housing was provided for the former occupants. The remaining buildings became more crowded than before as money-making landlords rented the same living space to more than one family, to the serious detriment of health, decency, and morals.

"The landlord who seeks an income from thus providing steps to degradation for his poorer neighbours may justly be regarded as an enemy to his country, and the public in quietly tolerating the evil cannot be regarded as wholly blameless," wrote Hodgkin.

Hodgkin understood how fashionable neighborhoods undergo decay as a wealthier class of inhabitants moves out and is replaced by a lower class. These, in turn, make way for those who, though still inferior, have also given up residences that they found to be unsatisfactory. Hodgkin recommended that neighborhoods undergoing decline and transition from the fashionable and genteel to the poor and unattractive be renovated or reconstructed. Looking out for the health of the poor, he added that renewal locations should not be on artificial landfills, but on natural ground, because of their improved sanitary drainage and diminished threat from epidemics.

Death and Burial in Jaffa

They left England on Tuesday morning, February 27, 1866, and traveled via Paris and Marseilles to Alexandria. Others in the group were Captain Henry Moore, brother of the British consul in Jerusalem, Dr. Louis Loewe (1809–1888), Sir Moses's secretary and frequent traveling companion, who was an oriental scholar and a master of Eastern languages, and Montefiore's nephew, Joseph Sebag, and his wife. They left Alexandria on Sunday, March 18, and arrived at Jaffa on the next day. Sir Moses had intended to continue to Jerusalem after a one-day stopover at Jaffa, but the plan had to be delayed when Hodgkin became ill. Hodgkin had not been in the best of health prior to departure from England and was not too keen about making the trip. But he undertook the journey "in the hope and belief that the voyage and change of air would prove beneficial to him." There was also his promise to Lady Montefiore.

"Being most reluctant to leave him, I remained with him up to the latest moment, until it became absolutely necessary to depart for Jerusalem, in order to arrive there in time for the Passover holidays," Montefiore wrote in his diary.[28] At this time, reports reaching Sir Moses of the suffering and fearful loss of life due to a recent outbreak of cholera were accompanied by news of the appearance of the new and still green locusts, the much dreaded forerunners of another bad season. Many mornings before sunrise, the townspeople of Jaffa were roused by the rattling of the drum to send them out into the streets to destroy the threatening enemy of locusts before daybreak.

Travel was not in Hodgkin's interest at that time. The best course was for him to remain in the house of Habib Kayat, the British consular agent, where he had been staying since arriving in Jaffa. Before reluctantly leaving for Jerusalem on Sunday, March

25, Sir Moses engaged Dr. Sozzi, the physician of the Lazaretto (a quarantine station), and left his own English servant, along with another he engaged to be constantly in attendance on his esteemed friend. Expecting to be rejoined soon by a recovered Dr. Hodgkin, he left for his use the sedan chair that the Governor of Jerusalem had sent to Jaffa for Montefiore's convenience.

After leaving Jaffa, Sir Moses was kept informed by telegram about the state of Hodgkin's health. When he learned that his condition had worsened, he asked Captain Moore to return to Jaffa with Dr. Chaplin,[29] the physician of Jerusalem. This they did and remained with Hodgkin until his death. Montefiore received the sad news during the night of April 5. This sad event

> overwhelmed me with sorrow and cast a gloom over me which I vainly sought to dispel.
>
> It has pleased the Almighty to take him from us, and that he should not again behold his loving consort and beloved relatives; he breathed his last in a land endeared to him by hallowed reminiscences. To one so guileless, so pious, so amiable in private life, so respected in his public career, and so desirous to assist with all his heart in the amelioration of the condition of the human race, death could not have had any terror.
>
> I trust I may be pardoned for this heartfelt but inadequate tribute to the memory of my late friend. His long and intimate association with me, and with my late dearly beloved wife, his companionship in our travels, and the vivid recollection of his many virtues, make me anxious to blend his name, and the record of his virtues, with the narrative of these events.

The first notification of the sad event was sent by Captain Moore to Thomas's brother, John Hodgkin, Jr., of Lewes. The letter was dated Jerusalem, April 10, 1866 and told that Dr. Hodgkin complained of feeling ill the morning they left Alexandria and that the voyage to Jaffa seemed to have done him no good. By the morning of the fourth day, Hodgkin was in a dangerous state. Inflammation had set in, and his illness had taken the form of acute dysentery. Continuing, Captain Moore wrote:

> I myself cannot find words to express my profound admiration at the calm attitude of this most excellent man and Christian in the

hour of trial and suffering. . . . His last thoughts were of his Maker and the eternity opening before him. He prayed to be allowed a few hours' respite from pain before the final struggle, a request which I have every reason to believe was granted. He passed away calmly.

Dr. Hodgkin expired at a quarter past five in the evening of the 4th of April, and was buried in the English cemetery, near the city walls, outside the new gate, and nearly opposite the British Consul's house. The funeral was attended by the few Protestants residing at Jaffa, the officiating Consul, and the people attached to his office, with the two doctors and myself, and two European attendants left with him by Sir Moses.[30]

In a letter to Mrs. Hodgkin, H. A. Kayat expressed his feelings of deep grief. The doctors "did all they possibly could, and there was no lack of anything for his comfort in my house. But alas! the malady was so virulent that it prostrated and carried him off."[31]

In his last letter to his wife, dictated three days before his death, Hodgkin said:

My kind friend Habib Kayat in whose house I have been nearly a fortnight writes a few lines for me as I cannot hold the pen. I wish in the shortest terms to say all that is loving, grateful & affectionate to thee: to thank thee for thy great kindness, and to excuse all my deficiencies.

Thou knowest how intensely I love my brother and his family but I must only send love, & say how much I have thought upon them.

My dear love to all my friends. I lament the little service I have done and I entreat all to [love] and serve their Lord and Master.

The two last days at Alexandria knocked me up; the weather was oppressive; I have been in almost ceaseless agony, delerium, tenesmus, gasping have worn me down. Dear Sir Moses was obliged to leave me to go to Jerusalem, but he has been boundless in his kindness, and spared nothing for my relief.

I don't say there is no chance of some improvement before this is posted, but I would not leave thee without a letter; God bless thee.[32]

Obelisk Monument

On Monday, April 16, a deeply saddened Sir Moses returned to Jaffa, where he "visited the place which enclosed the mortal remains of my dear friend, Dr. Hodgkin. That spot is at present surrounded by a strong railing, but will, I trust, soon be covered by a granite column, for which I gave orders on my return to England, as a mark of my respect and esteem." On July 24 he purchased a monument (Figures 13 and 14) for the tomb of his lamented friend and sent it on to Jaffa.[33] The inscription on the brownish-red polished Aberdeen granite obelisk is as follows:

HERE RESTS THE BODY

OF

THOMAS HODGKIN M.D.

OF BEDFORD SQUARE, LONDON,

A MAN DISTINGUISHED ALIKE

FOR SCIENTIFIC ATTAINMENTS,

MEDICAL SKILL,

AND SELF SACRIFICING

PHILANTHROPY.

HE DIED AT JAFFA

THE 4TH OF APRIL 1866,

IN THE 68TH YEAR OF HIS AGE.

IN THE FAITH & HOPE OF THE GOSPEL.

"HUMANI NIHIL A SE ALIENUM PUTABAT."

THE EPITAPH IS INSCRIBED BY HIS

DEEPLY SORROWING WIDOW & BROTHER,

TO RECORD THEIR IRREPARABLE LOSS.

On the reverse side is the following:

THIS TOMB IS ERECTED BY

SIR MOSES MONTEFIORE

BART

IN COMMEMORATION OF

A FRIENDSHIP OF

MORE THAN 40 YEARS

& OF MANY JOURNEYS

TAKEN TOGETHER IN EUROPE,

ASIA & AFRICA.

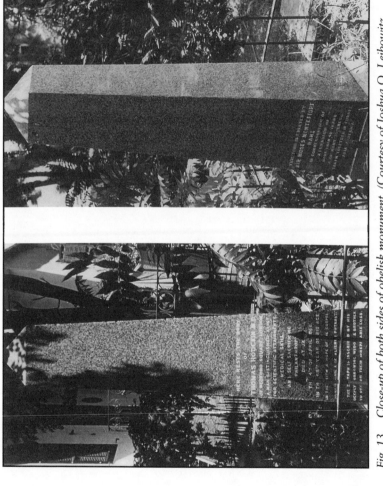

Fig. 13. Close-up of both sides of obelisk monument. (Courtesy of Joshua O. Leibowitz, Jerusalem, Israel.)

Fig. 14.   Unobstructed view of Thomas Hodgkin's gravesite. (Courtesy of Joshua O. Leibowitz, Jerusalem, Israel.)

The Latin motto on the gravestone was provided by John Hodg-kin, Jr., and was adapted from the well-known line by the Roman slave Terence (c.195–c.159 B.C.E.) in *Heauton Timoroumenos* (The Self-Tormentor). *Homo sum: humani nihil a me alienum puto* translates to "I am a man: nothing human is alien to me." The line was also quoted by Cicero in *De Officiis*, I, 30. It was used in slightly altered form in Thomas Hodgkin's dedication of his Edinburgh thesis to Alexander Humboldt.

No details are known about the symptoms of Hodgkin's illness, but his state deteriorated rapidly and he died of an infectious intestinal disease believed by all to be dysentery. According to Montefiore's diary, cholera was raging at that time. It is quite possible that Hodgkin was a victim of cholera, for which his weakened state of health may have predisposed him. Hodgkin may have foreseen the cause of his own death. He was a long-term sufferer from intestinal ailments, and for years he maintained that the sigmoid flexure of his colon was diseased.[34]

In 1875, Sir Moses Montefiore, at the age of ninety, made his seventh and final journey to the Holy Land. In his narrative of the visit he refers three times to Thomas Hodgkin and describes two visits to the tomb: "I went to see again the tomb of my much-lamented friend, Dr. Hodgkin, and arranged that, for the better preservation of the ground, a suitable railing should be made round the monument. It was a melancholy occasion, and made me remember all those virtues by which the departed was so pre-eminently distinguished during his life."[35]

Rediscovered Gravesite

Jaffa is just south of Tel Aviv and is now continuous with it. It is an ancient port city of the Phoenicians and the early Israelites. With the passage of the years, Hodgkin's burial place was lost track of and was neglected. In 1927 it was discovered by Dr. Emanuel Libman of New York and on May 5, 1927, in a memorial ceremony, Libman placed a wreath on the grave. A small but distinguished group of Christian, Moslem, and Jewish notables were present.[36]

During the next two decades, the region was marked by civil disorder, riots, and wars. It often was unsafe to visit Jaffa. Hodgkin's grave was once again forgotten. In 1950, Dr. Hyman Morrison of Boston traveled to Israel and learned the location of Hodgkin's grave. It was in the small Protestant cemetery hidden behind an abandoned English mission house, now a school for girls. The account[37] of his visit renewed interest and, in the years following, numerous visits were made by participants in international congresses, both medical and historical, convening in Israel. In December 1966, a symposium on Hodgkin's disease was held in Israel. Before the official opening a memorial ceremony was held at the graveside to mark the 100th anniversary of his death. The service was attended by the Israeli Minister of Health, the ambassador of Great Britain, and those attending the conference.[38]

Visits to Hodgkin's grave have been organized by the Israel Medical Association and by the Israel Society of the History of Medicine and Science. Individual tourists also visit the burial place. The gate of the cemetery is locked, but visitors may obtain the key at the adjacent Church of Scotland Tabeetha School for Girls.

However, the small graveyard is left untended and becomes so overgrown with foliage that even the tall obelisk erected to Thomas Hodgkin is hidden. On Wednesday June 20, 1984, a visitor to the gravesite observed the scene shown in Figure 15. Although the foliage has been cleared from time to time,[39] it grows back to reproduce this greatly obstructed view. With no relatives or fraternal society to arrange for the care of the grave, in a cemetery no longer in use, in a land far away, the overgrowth of vegetation in the subtropical climate not only makes access and viewing extremely difficult but threatens to obliterate all indications that this is a burial ground.[40]

Fig. 15. *Jaffa Cemetery. (Courtesy of Joel Dana Stern, New York, N.Y.)*

CHAPTER FIFTEEN

Integrity and Justice

Contributions to English Medicine

Thomas Hodgkin's eponymic fame for discovery of a lymph gland disorder is merely one event in an extraordinary life of unusually varied public activities. He was a Victorian man of his times, interested in everything around him. Hodgkin was not alone in trying to change the social and intellectual standards of his day, but he was unique in the wide range of issues of enduring value to which he gave his time, energy, commitment, and money. From a consideration of these interests it is very likely that had he achieved his ambition of appointment to the staff of Guy's Hospital he would have continued to participate in humanitarian, philanthropic, and ethnological activities. The failure to obtain the staff position or to relocate elsewhere merely shifted the emphasis and distribution of his time.

The Victorian age was a remarkable period when the practice of medicine was beginning to rest on scientific foundations and when moral idealism encouraged religious men of wealth to address the social injustices of the time—hardships of the poor, mistreatment of the insane, and exploitation of children, to name but a few. It was a time of less specialized pursuits, when a single individual with ability and a sense of responsibility could use social position to enlist community and government to effect real improvement in a variety of inequitable social and moral conditions.

Thomas Hodgkin's medical contributions were significant. He brought the new pathology of Bichat and Laennec to his research and his teaching at Guy's. It was the French emphasis on accurate observation and the correlation of physical signs observed in life with pathological findings after death that was the great medical advance of the early nineteenth century. Once back in England, Hodgkin and others began to shape the study of morbid anatomy into a modern scientific discipline and medical specialty. The ideas and techniques learned from their French experience, including Laennec's teaching of the use of the stethoscope, contributed to changing English medicine. It was during this period that the medical profession liberated itself from the hodgepodge of theories and systems and transferred its attention to clinical observation and postmortem examination.

Hodgkin affected the activities of English medicine in many ways. He systematized the teaching of morbid anatomy and did as much as anyone in England to show the importance of the study of pathology. He organized the museum at Guy's Hospital, added greatly to it, and prepared its first catalogue, an achievement that made Guy's Medical School one of the leading teaching centers in London. He recognized the value of the improved compound microscope and used it in his teaching. Hodgkin came to be regarded as the foremost morbid anatomist of his day and one of the pioneers of pathology in Great Britain.

With his expertise in microscopy and his understanding of the emerging new clinico-pathologic correlations, Hodgkin had the makings of one of the great clinicians of the mid-nineteenth century. But the opportunity to fulfill this promise was denied him. He was motivated by a deep religious sense, and his high moral standards and idealism were obstacles to advancement of his career. He cared nothing for social manners beyond simple kindness and had no instinct for politics or diplomacy in the competitive workplace. On top of all this, Hodgkin was not an attractive-looking man and, unfortunately, was unable to compensate, as many successful people do, with charm and warmth. Righteous, difficult, and stiff, he must have seemed grim and gloomy to new acquaintances. And his militant approach to improving mankind may have been a bit hard for some to take.

Hodgkin's medical career was obviously hampered by his independence and his penchant for the disadvantaged and underprivileged. He was different in many ways, and he had radical and progressive views. To the conservative governors of Guy's Hospital, this probably meant he was unpredictable and therefore unreliable. On the contrary, if Hodgkin was anything, he was consistent and therefore predictable. He was an "activist" and a "whistleblower" before anyone ever used those terms. His integrity and consistency, especially when it came to human rights, ran contrary to the conventional wisdom and morality of his day and kept him from recognition and advancement.

Had the appointment of assistant physician been made by his professional colleagues, he would have gotten the post without any difficulty. But the selection was made by a highly political syndicate. Hodgkin's medical credentials were impressive, but his failure must be understood in terms of his social and political activities and not in terms of Babington's professional accomplishments. Had Benjamin Harrison, Jr., been engaged in exclusively domestic enterprises, he would have been less likely to have rejected Hodgkin.

But Thomas Hodgkin was neither as lucky nor as flexible as Astley Cooper had been in 1800. At age thirty-two, Cooper almost missed out on his bid for appointment as surgeon at Guy's Hospital on account of the strong republican sympathies that he had picked up from his teacher, Henry Cline, Sr. These sentiments were very unpopular at that time. Fortunately for Cooper, he realized in time that his democratic views might keep him from professional advancement, success in practice, and the good things of life. Ambition triumphed over idealism. Preferring success to politics, he made a timely and convincing recantation.[1]

Hodgkin's early scientific promise could not outweigh his unpopular political radicalism. Although he thought of himself as gentle and conciliatory, he was often quarrelsome and rigid. His unwillingness to compromise or follow a path of expediency in matters of principle[2] worked to his disadvantage in the highly politicized environment of Guy's Hospital. In addition to all this, Harrison, the treasurer, didn't like him.

It has been suggested by various biographers that some perverse spirit always placed Hodgkin in opposition;[3] that his sympathy with the underdog stemmed from his being outside the Establishment and hence also an underdog destined to disappointment;[4] that his strict Quaker upbringing gave him a proper but narrow and idealistic view of life, which, in this imperfect world, led to an inability to get along with some of his associates; and that his lack of a sense of humor was an added social disadvantage.[5] He has even been painted as "the definitive Curator of the Dead, for the people of a world which was being superseded."[6] Even Hodgkin himself, on his deathbed, perpetuated this negative assessment when he lamented the little service that he had done.[7] But these critical and somber analyses are too steeped in unwarranted psychological overtones. He was touched by frustration and failure—who isn't? He also suffered frequent illness and was troubled by occasional bouts of depression and pessimism. But Hodgkin bounced back every time and deserves a less complicated explanation.

Hodgkin's Quaker upbringing in a family atmosphere of intellectualism and religious piety generated a lifelong commitment to philanthropy, social justice, and cultural improvement. His contacts with reform-minded activists, such as William Allen, Thomas Clarkson, Joseph John Gurney, Samuel Tuke, Alexander Humboldt, William Pulteney Alison, and Moses Montefiore, exerted a stimulating and molding influence on his sense of social responsibility. With reverence for truth and justice, and undaunted by personal defeats and unhappiness, he could not stay on the sidelines while his fellow man was being mistreated.

A tireless organizer and member of many philanthropic and scientific societies, Hodgkin was a "do-gooder." His nephew wrote that his uncle had, at an early age, settled on a "combination of generosity to others with something like meanness in personal expenditure" and a total lack of understanding of the meaning of comfort for himself.[8] But Hodgkin's sensitivity to the poor, consistent throughout his life, was expressed within the framework of the educated middle-class Victorian bias against the "undeserving" poor.

Descriptive characterizations based on specific situations have been applied with a broad brush by twentieth-century writers of biographical sketches. Eccentric and unorthodox,[9] rebellious and anti-authoritarian,[10] maverick,[11] and iconoclast[12] are not justified. An eccentric is not offered fellowship in the Royal College of Physicians. Nor would an eccentric be appointed secretary to the Royal Geographical Society, or to the council of the British Association for the Advancement of Science, or as chairman of the Convention of Poor Law Medical Officers and to other committees and delegations, or be invited to testify before Parliament. Anyone with such a reputation would certainly not be invited on journeys to foreign rulers and potentates. An anti-authoritarian Quaker would have defied the elders and married the woman of his choice. Many Quakers did just that—and were expelled from the Society of Friends. A rebellious son would not ask his father's permission to pursue a courtship.

Hodgkin was different and probably more visible, certainly in his later years, because of his Quaker clothes and because of his large number of society memberships and activities. An early biographer described his "remarkably simple and truthful nature."[13] He certainly was without guile, deceit, or ostentation, but there were many moving parts to Hodgkin's machinery—a little naive and too trusting no doubt; uncomplicated perhaps, but not "remarkably simple."

Victorian Man of His Times—and More

Hodgkin was no solitary maverick espousing new or unusual programs or ideas but was in the mainstream of reform thinking. However, compared to another Victorian reformer such as Edwin Chadwick, Hodgkin made very little actual impact. He is rarely mentioned by historians of the social and health reform movements of the nineteenth century and then only in footnotes or in passing as an "also-ran." Undoubtedly, he spread himself too thin by giving his time, efforts, and writing to so many causes and activities. He even neglected his own medical practice by his frequent traveling, much of which was out of the country for long periods of time. Although he was also restricted in movement by frequent bouts with illness during his adult life, it had little if any effect on his voluminous letter writing or dictation to an amanuensis, which he was in the habit of doing in the early morning hours while still in bed.

Hodgkin's epitaph is appropriate—nothing human was alien to him. He had something to say on everything that interested him. For the most part, his pamphlets were one-time efforts and were not followed up with additional publications. Except for his work with the Aborigines' Protection Society, his proposals for affecting policy changes were usually conducted outside the established channels of government.

It would be easy to characterize Hodgkin's writings on the numerical method, trade unions, metric system, medical education, public health, work relief, food supplements, and social attitudes as being farseeing and ahead of his time—as some biographical sketches have maintained.[14] However, there was nothing unique in these positions, and he certainly was not alone in his time in taking them. These issues and others, like tobacco, boxing, and urban renewal, have remained controversial because they inherently involve opposing social, political, and economic forces that have become enmeshed in the fabric of society. Even Hodgkin's favorite cause, the Aborigines, have their twentieth-century counterparts in the third world of underdeveloped nations and in the efforts on their behalf by the organization descended from the Aborigines' Protection Society.

Although Hodgkin's philanthropic activities had little impact, and the social and economic problems of his time are still with us, he was not tilting at windmills. Hodgkin's life exemplifies the advice of the ancient adage, namely, that although one cannot solve all the problems of the world, neither is one free to take no part in the effort. Hodgkin took part in the effort.

Personally and professionally, he touched on many of the social issues and the intellectual fabric of medical life of a century and a half ago. If he seemed to stand out against the current it was only because of his participation on so many fronts. Because of his wide-ranging involvements, historians with a newfound interest in mid-nineteenth-century English medicine have discovered one of the most interesting personalities of the period.

In 1966, after a prolonged period of benign neglect of Hodgkin's memory at Guy's Hospital, a symposium and commemorative issue of *Guy's Hospital Reports* marked the centennial of his death. The absence of visible recognition at the hospital was finally corrected in November 1980 by the naming of a seminar room in his honor. In July 1985 a commemorative plaque was placed at his last residence, 35 Bedford Square (see chapter 13, note 3). Nearly two centuries after his birth, the many careers of Thomas Hodgkin have been discovered and he has emerged a fascinating and inspiring figure. His undeserved obscurity is coming to an end.

Appendix: Excerpts from Obituary Notices

"In the world of science, Dr. Hodgkin will be remembered as one of the pioneers of pathology in Great Britain; and as an accomplished and observant physician. Among men of all nations and all callings, wherever his name becomes known, it will be received and treasured in remembrance as the name of 'one who loved his fellow-men.' " *British Medical Journal,* 1866, 1: 447.

"His medical brethren will feel his loss as that of a physician of rare talent; as one who was a fine scholar, an accomplished linguist, and a large-minded philanthropist. To his more immediate friends his loss is irreparable. Few men were more beloved than Dr. Hodgkin: his truly Christian charity, his unostentatious piety, his utter self-negation, won and kept the love and esteem of all who knew him." *The Lancet,* 1866, 1: 445–446.

"Sincere, unselfish, freely giving up his money, his time and his energies to the service of the poor and the oppressed throughout the world. . . . It was not his habit to follow in the wake of popularity. The forlorn and the outcast appeared to have a special claim upon his sympathies, and often found in him their best earthly friend. . . . His early devotion to the good of others did not slacken in later life.

His love of justice to all, his courageous championship of any who had causelessly suffered wrong, or were the objects of popular odium, formed a striking feature in his character. . . . His uniform charity ever disposed him to put the most favourable construction upon the conduct of others. . . . Very sweet and instructive is the impression left amongst his fellow-members, and . . . of his simple, unaffected piety." *The Friend*, 1866, 6: 81–82.

"He delighted in doing good. The unity of the human family was with him not a mere theory. He rejoiced to treat as brethren men of all races and of every clime. His ear was open to the cry of the oppressed. . . . His interest in the coloured races commenced in his childhood; and his name will long be identified with the various efforts which have been made to protect and free them from oppression and wrong." *Minutes and Proceedings of the Yearly Meeting of Friends*, London, 1867, xv–xviii.

"Dr. Hodgkin knew nothing of one law for the white man and another for the black; or of a graduated scale of morality . . . determined by the varying shades of their complexion." *Aborigines' Friend, and Colonial Intelligencer*, 1859–66, new series, 2: 519–522.

"His . . . strong sympathies with fellow-men of all climes and colours, rendered Dr. Thomas Hodgkin's name familiar to high and low; and his hand was ever held out to aid those who were the least capable of returning his generosity.

Those who had the fewest friends found an unwearied one in him. . . . In the best sense of the words he was a cosmopolite and a philanthropist." *Social Science Review, Sanitary Review, and Journal of the Sciences*, 1866, new series, 5: 534–539.

Notes

CHAPTER ONE

1. Obituaries in *Lancet* (1866, 1: 445–446) and the *British Medical Journal* (1866, 1: 447) mistakenly give January 16 as the day of birth. (They also give the wrong day of death.) *The Dictionary of National Biography* (DNB), Leslie Stephen and Sidney Lee, eds. (London: Oxford University Press, 1968) erroneously gives Thomas Hodgkin's birthplace as Tottenham, a village a few miles farther distant from London than Pentonville (vol. 9, pp. 957–958).

2. *Hodgkin Pedigree Book (1644–1906)*. Compiled by Thomas Hodgkin, D.C.L., Litt.D., &c., 33 pages, 1907. Printed for Private Circulation.

3. Michael Rose, *Curator of the Dead. Thomas Hodgkin (1798–1866)* (London: Peter Owen, 1981), pp. 21, 26, 119. This observation is that of Hodgkin's nephew and namesake (1831–1913), a banker and prolific writer on history, archaeology, and religion. He was a Fellow of University College and received a D.C.L. degree from Oxford in 1886 and an honorary D.Litt. from Trinity College, Dublin, in 1891. His unpublished autobiography and those of his father, John Hodgkin, Jr., and grandfather, John Hodgkin, Sr., provide personal glimpses into the life of Thomas Hodgkin, M.D.

4. William Gibson, *Rambles In Europe in 1839 with Sketches of Prominent Surgeons, Physicians, Medical Schools, Hospitals, Literary Personages, Scenery, Etc.* (Philadelphia: Lea and Blanchard, 1841), pp. 279–280. See also the reminiscences of Hodgkin's niece Mariabella, from the microfilm collection of the letters and papers of Thomas Hodgkin, M.D., MSS #187 (reel 10) at the Friends' House Library, London, England. See also unpublished biographical sketch by R.

Hingston Fox (1919) in MSS #191 (reel 14). According to Fox, Hodgkin's temperament alternated between bright and cheerful while engaged in conversation, and depression at other times.

5. P. E. Thompson Hancock, "Thomas Hodgkin," The FitzPatrick Lecture, *Journal of the Royal College of Physicians of London*, 1968, 2: 404–421, p. 404.

6. From the unpublished biography of Thomas Hodgkin's nephew, Thomas Hodgkin, Jr., quoted by Louise Creighton, *Life and Letters of Thomas Hodgkin* [1831–1913] (London: Longmans, Green, and Co., 1917), p. 2.

7. "The Late Dr. Hodgkin," *The Friend*, 1866 (May), 6: 81–82, p. 82.

8. Amalie M. Kass and Edward H. Kass, *Perfecting the World. The Life and Times of Dr. Thomas Hodgkin 1798–1866* (Boston: Harcourt Brace Jovanovich, Publishers, 1988), pp. 17–18.

9. Ernest C. Cripps, *Plough Court. The Story of a Notable Pharmacy. 1715–1927* (London: Allen & Hanburys Ltd., 1927), p. 30.

10. Ibid., p. 28.

11. *Life of William Allen, with Selections from His Correspondence*, 3 vols. (London: Charles Gilpin, 1846), vol. 1, p. 64.

12. Cripps (1927), p. 34.

13. Ibid., pp. 36–37.

14. Kass and Kass (1988), pp. 22–24.

15. Microfilm collection, MSS #190 (reel 13); also in Kass and Kass (1988), p. 38.

16. Cripps (1927), p. 44; Rose (1981), p. 29; Kass and Kass (1988), p. 26.

17. Kass and Kass (1988), p. 27; see also G. E. H. Foxon, "Thomas Hodgkin, 1798–1866. A Biographical Note," *Guy's Hospital Reports*, 1966, 115: 243–254.

18. William Hale-White, "Thomas Hodgkin," *Guy's Hospital Reports*, 1924, 74: 117–136, p. 120; also see Kass and Kass (1988), pp. 30, 31, 34.

19. Microfilm collection, MSS #188 (reel 11); also in Kass and Kass (1988), p. 39.

20. Kass and Kass (1988), p. 40.

21. Ibid., pp. 41, 43–44; Rose (1981), pp. 35–36.

22. W. D. Conybeare and William Phillips, *Outlines of the Geology of England and Wales, with an Introductory Compendium of the General Principles of that Science, and Comparative Views of the Structure of Foreign Countries* (London: William Phillips, 1822), p. 106 (footnote).

23. Charles Coulston Gillispie, *Genesis and Geology. A Study in the Relations of Scientific Thought, Natural Theology, and Social Opinion in Great Britain, 1790–1850* (Cambridge, Mass.: Harvard University Press, 1951), p. 187.

24. *Biographical Catalogue* (London: Society of Friends, 1888), pp. 355–361.

25. Elizabeth Isichei, *Victorian Quakers* (London: Oxford University Press, 1970), pp. 2–4.

26. Foxon (1966), p. 244; Kass and Kass (1988), pp. 59–60.

27. "The Steele Diaries," Part I, Part II, Part III, *Guy's Hospital Gazette*, 1948, 62: 276–278, 345–346; 1949, 63: 96–99.

28. F. B. Smith, *The People's Health 1830–1910* (New York: Holmes & Meier Publishers, 1979), p. 264; Letter to the editor, *Lancet*, 1830–31, 1: 286, 317–318.

29. M. Jeanne Peterson, *The Medical Profession in Mid-Victorian London* (Berkeley: University of California Press, 1978), p. 40.

30. H. C. Cameron, *Mr. Guy's Hospital 1726–1948* (London: Longmans, Green and Co.), 1954, p. 168.

31. Ibid., p. 125.

32. Ibid., pp. 168–169.

33. "Introductory Clinical Lecture by Dr. Billing," *Lancet*, 1831–32, 1: 233–236, pp. 234, 236.

34. Letter to the editor, *Lancet*, 1825–26, 1: 198–199.

35. "Clinical Lecture on Ague, by Dr. Elliotson," *Lancet*, 1827–28, 1: 139–141, p. 140.

36. Abstract of Evidence Relating to the London Apothecaries' Company, Taken Before the Parliamentary Medical Committee in 1834. Published in June 1836. *Lancet*, 1835–36, 2: 486–490, p. 489 (paragraph 133).

37. Letter to the editor, *Lancet*, 1841–42, 1: 266–267, p. 266.

38. James P. Babington, Introduction, *Guy's Hospital Reports*, 1837, 2: i–vii (the author is listed in the table of contents).

39. Kass and Kass (1988), pp. 65, 67–68.

40. For a brief history, see Douglas Guthrie, *The Medical School of Edinburgh*, published for the British Medical Association Meeting in Edinburgh, 1959, 32 pages.

41. From the Special Collections, Edinburgh University Library.

42. Thomas Hodgkin, "On the Uses of the Spleen," *Edinburgh Medical and Surgical Journal*, 1822, 18: 83–91; Kass and Kass (1988), p. 72.

43. John D. Comrie, *History of Scottish Medicine*, 2 vols., 2nd ed., published for The Wellcome Historical Medical Museum (London: Baillière, Tindall & Cox, 1932), vol. 2, pp. 503–504; D. B. Horn, *A Short History of the University of Edinburgh 1556–1889* (Edinburgh: The University Press, 1967), p. 57; J. B. Morrell, "Medicine and Science in the Eighteenth Century," in *Four Centuries. Edinburgh Life. 1583–1983*, Gordon Donaldson, ed. (Edinburgh: The University Press, 1983), pp. 42–43.

44. Comrie (1932), vol. 2, p. 493; *The Life of Sir Robert Christison, Bart.*, edited by his sons, 2 vols. (Edinburgh and London: William Blackwood and Sons, 1885), vol. 1, p. 68.

45. Horn (1967), p. 109.

46. Comrie (1932), vol. 2, p. 493.

47. Kass and Kass (1988), p. 70.

48. Comrie (1932), vol. 2, p. 473; Morrell (1983), pp. 40–42.

49. Comrie (1932), vol. 1, p. 311.

50. Rose (1981), pp. 40–41; also in Kass and Kass (1988), p. 69.

51. Christison (1885), vol. 1, p. 79; also in S. W. F. Holloway, "Medical Education in England, 1830–1858: A Sociological Analysis," *History*, 1964, 49: 299–324, p. 300.

52. Horn (1967), p. 108.

53. J. R. Wall, "The Guy's Hospital Physical Society (1771–1852)," *Guy's Hospital Reports*, 1974, 123: 159–170, pp. 167–168.

54. Thomas Hodgkin, *An Essay on Medical Education, read before the Physical Society of Guy's Hospital, at The First Meeting of the Session 1827–8* (London: William Phillips, 1828), 24 pages, p. 23. See chapter 3 for Hodgkin's courtroom experience.

55. Comrie (1932), vol. 2, p. 482.

56. *The Autobiography of Charles Darwin 1809–1882*, Nora Barlow, ed. (New York: Harcourt, Brace and Company, 1958), p. 47; also in Comrie (1932), vol. 2, p. 493, and in J. H. Ashworth, "Charles Darwin as a Student in Edinburgh, 1825–1827," *Proceedings of the Royal Society of Edinburgh*, 1935, 55: 97–113, p. 98.

57. Horn (1967), p. 138.

58. Alexander Grant, *The Story of the University of Edinburgh During Its First Three Hundred Years*, 2 vols. (London: Longmans, Green, and Co., 1884), vol. 2, pp. 484–487; Horn (1967), p. 92.

59. Kass and Kass (1988), pp. 71–72, 74–76.

60. Horn (1967), pp. 91–92.

61. Ibid., p. 61; Rose (1981), p. 40.

62. Horn (1967), pp. 136–137, 143.

63. Ibid., pp. 137, 141.

64. Isichei (1970), pp. 152–155; Thomas Clarkson, *A Portraiture of Quakerism. Taken From a View of the Education and Discipline, Social Manners, Civil and Political Economy, Religious Principles and Character, of the Society of Friends*, 3 vols. (New York: Samuel Stansbury, 1806), vol. 1, pp. 39–148.

65. Dr. Hodgkin's Letter (May 12, 1821), *Friends' Quarterly Examiner*, 1912, 46: 162–170, p. 170; see also Kass and Kass (1988), pp. 77–78.

66. Rose (1981), p. 42; see also Kass and Kass (1988), pp. 81–82, 116.

67. Rose (1981), pp. 93, 122.

68. Charles Singer and S. W. F. Holloway, "Early Medical Education in England in Relation to the Pre-History of London University," *Medical History*, 1960, 4: 1–17, pp. 1–2; also see Russell C. Maulitz, "Channel Crossing: The

Lure of French Pathology for English Medical Students, 1816–36," *Bulletin of the History of Medicine*, 1981, 55: 475–496, pp. 482–484, 475–478.

69. Erwin H. Ackerknecht, *Medicine at the Paris Hospital 1794–1848* (Baltimore, Md.: The Johns Hopkins Press, 1967), pp. xi–xii. For an account of the evolution of pathological anatomy in France and the transport of this new science to Great Britain, see Russell C. Maulitz, *Morbid Appearances. The Anatomy of Pathology in the Early Nineteenth Century* (New York: Cambridge University Press, 1987).

70. Maulitz (1981), pp. 479–480, 482–483.

71. G. Canby Robinson, "The Development of Grave Robbing in England," *Johns Hopkins Hospital Bulletin*, 1905, 16: 42–45.

72. *Lancet*, 1827–28, 2: 659–663, pp. 659, 660.

73. Maulitz (1981), pp. 479–480.

74. William Hale-White, *Translation of Selected Passages from De l'Auscultation Médiate, (first edition) by R. Théophile H. Laennec* (New York: William Wood & Co., 1923), preface, p. vi.

75. Ackerknecht (1967), p. 91; Rose (1981), p. 42; for Hodgkin's routine as a student in Paris, see Maulitz (1987), pp. 201–202; also see Kass and Kass (1988), pp. 85–103.

76. Kass and Kass (1988), pp. 91–92; Maulitz (1981), pp. 492, 493; *Dictionary of Scientific Biography*, Charles Coulston Gillispie, ed. (New York: Charles Scribner's Sons, 1973), vol. 7, pp. 414–416.

77. Ackerknecht (1967), pp. 40, 90–91; Maulitz (1981), pp. 489–490; Kass and Kass (1988), pp. 91, 97.

78. Kass and Kass (1988), pp. 105–108.

79. Hale-White (1924), p. 118; E. H. Kass, "Thomas Hodgkin, Physician and Social Scientist," *Guy's Hospital Reports*, 1966, 115: 269–280; Joshua O. Leibowitz, "Thomas Hodgkin (1798–1866)," *Clio Medica*, 1967, 2: 97–101; Hancock (1968), pp. 404–421; Edward H. Kass, Anne B. Carey, and Amalie M. Kass, "Thomas Hodgkin and Benjamin Harrison: Crisis and Promotion in Academia," *Medical History*, 1980, 24: 197–208.

80. *The Quarterly Journal of Foreign Medicine and Surgery*, 1819–20, 2: 51–68, p. 68; *London Medical and Physical Journal*, 1820 (Feb.), 43: 164–170, p. 170 (footnote); *Medico-Chirurgical Journal; or, London Medical and Surgical Review*, 1820 (Jan.), 2: 461–494, p. 494 (footnote).

81. Neither the *DNB* nor the numerous other biographical sketches or obituaries of Hodgkin make any mention of the stethoscope. Samuel Wilks, a biographer of Hodgkin, makes no association either, in a review of the history of the stethoscope. Samuel Wilks, "On the Evolution of the Stethoscope," *Lancet*, 1882, 2: 882–883. Cameron (1954) makes no mention of it, but Rose (1981), p. 43, does.

82. Dr. Stroud, "On Mediate Auscultation," *London Medical Gazette*, 1841–42, new series, 1: 6–9; for description of a jointed, partially flexible stethoscope, also see Nicholas P. Comins (letter), *Lancet*, 1828–29, 2: 685–687.

83. Pierre Louis, "Lecture on the Auscultation of the Chest," *London Medical Gazette*, 1837, 20: 711–717.

84. Stanley Joel Reiser, *Medicine and the Reign of Technology* (New York: Cambridge University Press, 1978), pp. 30–33, 37, 38. Also see R. A. Young, "The Stethoscope: Past and Present," *Transactions of the Medical Society of London*, 1931, 54: 1–22; P. J. Bishop, "Evolution of the Stethoscope," *Journal of the Royal Society of Medicine*, 1980, 73: 448–456; Holloway (1964), p. 317; Peterson (1978), pp. 281–282, 286.

CHAPTER TWO

1. Alexander Grant, *The Story of the University of Edinburgh During Its First Three Hundred Years*, 2 vols. (London: Longmans, Green, and Co., 1884), vol. 1, p. 331.

2. D. B. Horn, *A Short History of the University of Edinburgh 1556–1889* (Edinburgh: The University Press, 1967), pp. 44, 102; Amalie M. Kass and Edward H. Kass, *Perfecting the World. The Life and Times of Dr. Thomas Hodgkin 1798–1866* (Boston: Harcourt Brace Jovanovich Publishers, 1988), p. 117.

3. Horn (1967), p. 44.

4. John D. Comrie, *History of Scottish Medicine*, 2 vols., 2nd ed., published for The Wellcome Historical Medical Museum (London: Baillière, Tindall & Cox, 1932), vol. 2, pp. 477–478; Horn (1967), p. 106. For a personal recollection of final exams, see *The Life of Sir Robert Christison, Bart.*, edited by his sons, 2 vols. (Edinburgh and London: William Blackwood and Sons, 1885), vol. 1, pp. 159–160.

5. Kass and Kass (1988), p. 112.

6. Grant (1884), vol. 1, p. 329; vol. 2, p. 492; Kass and Kass (1988), p. 68.

7. Horn (1967), pp. 44, 46; Anand C. Chitnis, "Medical Education in Edinburgh, 1790–1826, and Some Victorian Social Consequences," *Medical History*, 1973, 17: 173–185, p. 179.

8. For the shared experiences of Hodgkin and Montefiore, see chapters 13 and 14. For a modern analysis of Montefiore's remarkable life, see *The Century of Moses Montefiore*, Sonia and V. D. Lipman, eds. Published for The Littman Library of Jewish Civilization in Association with The Jewish Historical Society of England (New York: Oxford University Press, 1985).

9. M. Jeanne Peterson, *The Medical Profession in Mid-Victorian London* (Berkeley: University of California Press, 1978), pp. 120–121, 163.

10. Amalie M. Kass, "Friends and Philanthropists: Montefiore and Dr. Hodgkin," in *The Century of Moses Montefiore*, Sonia and V. D. Lipman, eds. (1985), pp. 75–76; see also Kass and Kass (1988), pp. 101–103, 117.

11. Kass and Kass (1988), pp. 119–121.

12. Letter from Thomas Hodgkin to John Hodgkin, Jr., dated November 12, 1823, Microfilm collection, MSS #179 (reel 2).

13. Letter from Thomas Hodgkin to John Hodgkin, Sr., dated November 12, 1823, Microfilm collection, MSS #179 (reel 2).

14. Kass (1985), p. 77; Kass and Kass (1988), p. 122.

15. Letter from Thomas Hodgkin to John Hodgkin, Sr., dated January 11, 1824, Microfilm collection, MSS #179 (reel 2).

16. Kass and Kass (1988), pp. 123–127.

17. Kass (1985), p. 79.

18. *DNB*, vol. 19, pp. 795–796.

19. Letter from Thomas Hodgkin to Captain John Norton, Grand River Lake Ontario, Viâ New York, dated December 17, 1824. From the files of the American Philosophical Society Library, Philadelphia.

20. Alexander Hamilton Hume, *The Life of Edward John Eyre, Late Governor of Jamaica* (London: Richard Bentley, 1867), pp. 94–95; also see Michael Rose, *Curator of the Dead. Thomas Hodgkin (1798–1866)* (London: Peter Owen, 1981), p. 38; for a drawing of the boy and a report of the palace visit, see the *Illustrated London News*, 1846 (February 14), 8 (#198): 108; Tenth Annual Report of the Aborigines' Protection Society, May 17, 1847, p. 24; also see Geoffrey Dutton, *Edward John Eyre. The Hero as Murderer* (New York: Penguin Books, 1977), pp. 164, 168.

21. *Illustrated London News* (see note 20).

22. Kass and Kass (1988), p. 93.

23. Rose (1981), p. 46; see also Kass and Kass (1988), p. 129.

24. Rose (1981), pp. 46–47; also in Kass and Kass (1988), pp. 128–129.

25. *DNB*, vol. 11, p. 820.

26. For a contemporary biography, see Thomas Joseph Pettigrew, "Sir Astley Paston Cooper, Bart.," in *Medical Portrait Gallery. Biographical Memoirs of the most celebrated Physicians, Surgeons, etc. etc. who have contributed to The Advancement of Medical Science*, 4 vols., vol. 1, (London: Fisher, Son, & Co., 1838); for an obituary, see "Brief Memoir of Sir Astley Paston Cooper, Bart.," *Lancet*, 1840–41, 1: 764–767. Other biographical sketches are Geoffrey Keynes, "The Life and Works of Sir Astley Cooper, Bart.," *St. Bartholomew's Hospital Reports*, 1922, 55: 9–36; Charters J. Symonds, "Astley Paston Cooper," *Guy's Hospital Reports*, 1940–41, 90: 73–103; R. C. Brock, "Astley Cooper and Arterial Surgery," *Guy's Hospital Reports*, 1940–41, 90: 104–122.

27. Nepotism was a prominent feature of hospital and medical school appointments in Paris also. Erwin H. Ackerknecht, *Medicine at the Paris Hospital 1794–1848* (Baltimore, Md.: The Johns Hopkins Press, 1967), pp. 126–127; also see Peterson (1978), pp. 90–91, 122, 134, 146.

28. *Lancet*, 1862, 1: 605.

29. M. A. Crowther, "Paupers or Patients? Obstacles to Professionalization in the Poor Law Medical Service Before 1914," *Journal of the History of Medicine and Allied Sciences*, 1984, 39: 33–54, p. 40.

30. Frederick G. Parsons, *The History of St. Thomas's Hospital*, 3 vols. (London: Methuen & Co. Ltd., 1936); vol. 3, *From 1800 to 1900*, p. 56.

31. For a running exchange of charge and countercharge, see *Lancet*, 1825–26, 1: 182–184, 224–228, 287, 296–300, 552–556, 587–588, 617–619.

32. H. C. Cameron, *Mr. Guy's Hospital 1726–1948* (London: Longmans, Green and Co., 1954), p. 170.

33. Ibid., pp. 162–166, 169–171; also in Parsons (1936), vol. 3, pp. 51–59.

34. *RCP Annals*, vol. 21, pp. 2–5. From the archives of the Royal College of Physicians (RCP).

35. Rose (1981), p. 54; according to Kass and Kass (1988), p. 139, Hodgkin spent 10–12 hours at the dispensary two times a week.

36. Rose (1981), p. 55.

37. Kass and Kass (1988), p. 151.

CHAPTER THREE

1. For early developments of the microscope and applications to the detection of disease during the second half of the nineteenth century, see Stanley Joel Reiser, *Medicine and the Reign of Technology* (New York: Cambridge University Press, 1978), pp. 69–90. Also see S. Bradbury, *The Evolution of the Microscope* (Oxford: Pergamon Press, 1967), pp. 183–187, 190–197, 200–203; and pp. 200–255 for a discussion of the microscope in Victorian times.

2. Joseph Jackson Lister, "On the Improvement of Achromatic Compound Microscopes," *Philosophical Transactions of the Royal Society*, 1830, 120: 187–200. Also see *Dictionary of Scientific Biography*, Charles Coulston Gillispie, ed. (New York: Charles Scribner's Sons, 1973), vol. 8, pp. 413–415.

3. Thomas Hodgkin and Joseph Jackson Lister, "Notice of some Microscopic Observations of the Blood and Animal Tissues," *Philosophical Magazine*, 1827, new series, 2(8): 130–138, pp. 131–132. This article was enlarged and reprinted as "On the Microscopic Characters of Some of the Animal Fluids and Tissues," by J. J. Lister and Dr. Hodgkin, in the Appendix (pp. 424–447) of *On the*

Influence of Physical Agents on Life, by W. F. Edwards, translated from the French by Dr. Hodgkin and Dr. Fisher (London: S. Highley, 1832).

4. *Lancet*, 1825–26, 1:24.

5. Obituary. Sir Samuel Wilks, Bart., M.D., F.R.S. *British Medical Journal*, 1911, 2: 1384–1390, p. 1385.

6. Thomas Hodgkin, *A Catalogue of the Preparations in the Anatomical Museum of Guy's Hospital. Arranged and Edited by Desire of the Treasurer of the Hospital, and of the Teachers of the Medical and Surgical School* (London: S. Highley, 1829), 581 pages (unpaginated) plus Introduction (iii–xvi), p. iv.

7. Thomas Hodgkin, *Lectures on The Morbid Anatomy of the Serous and Mucous Membranes*, 2 vols.; vol. 1, *On The Serous Membranes; and, as appended subjects, Parasitical Animals, Malignant Adventitious Structures, and the Indications Afforded by Colour* (London: Sherwood, Gilbert, and Piper, 1836), preface, pp. v–vi.

8. Hodgkin (1829), pp. iv–vi.

9. Thomas Hodgkin, "On the Object of Post Mortem Examinations, Being an Address delivered to the Pupils of Guy's Hospital, on the Opening of the Theatre of Morbid Anatomy, Jan. 1828," *London Medical Gazette*, 1828a, 2: 423–431, p. 431.

10. Thomas Hodgkin, *An Essay on Medical Education, read before the Physical Society of Guy's Hospital, at The First Meeting of the Session 1827–8* (London: William Phillips, 1828b), 24 pages, p. 6.

11. "Apothecaries' Act of 1815, and Declaratory Act of 1825," *Lancet*, 1825–26, 1: 4–17.

12. Hodgkin (1828b), p. 6; "Amendment of the Apothecaries' Act," *Companion to the Newspaper*, 1833 (August), 119–121, p. 120.

13. Hodgkin (1828b), pp. 6–7.

14. Ibid., pp. 17–18.

15. Ibid., pp. 14–15.

16. Ibid., p. 19.

17. Ibid., pp. 19–20.

18. *Lancet*, 1827–28, 1:60–61, 91–93.

19. Charles Singer and S.W.F. Holloway, "Early Medical Education in England in Relation to the Pre-History of London University," *Medical History*, 1960, 4: 1–17, pp. 10, 16–17; Russell C. Maulitz, "Channel Crossing: The Lure of French Pathology for English Medical Students, 1816–36," *Bulletin of the History of Medicine*, 1981, 55: 475–496, pp. 488–489; Erwin H. Ackerknecht, *Medicine at the Paris Hospital 1794–1848* (Baltimore, Md.: The Johns Hopkins Press, 1967), pp. 191–194. See also, Adolph Muehry, *Observations on the Comparative State of Medicine in France, England, and Germany, During a Journey into these Countries in the Year 1835*, translated from the German by E. G. Davis (Philadelphia: A. Waldie, 1838), p. 66.

20. *Lancet*, 1827–28, 1: 959–960 (March 29, 1828); 2:20–22 (April 5, 1828).

21. *Morning Chronicle* (newspaper), December 13, 1828, p. 4; December 15, 1828, pp. 3–4; "Cooper *v.* Wakley," *Lancet*, 1828–29, 1: 353–373 (December 20, 1828).

22. For a review of Wakley's life and the activities of the *Lancet*, see "The Century of The Lancet," *Lancet*, 1923 (vol. 205) 2: 687ff; also see Obituary, pp. 605–606, and "Memoir of Thomas Wakley, Esq.," *Lancet*, 1862, 1: 609–612. For a biography of Wakley, see S. Squire Sprigge, *The Life and Times of Thomas Wakley* (Introduction by Charles G. Roland), facsimile of 1899 edition (Melbourne, Fla.: Robert E. Krieger Publishing Co., 1974).

23. *Lancet*, 1825–26, 1:1.

24. *Lancet*, 1828–29, 1: 362.

25. Herbert L. Eason, "Specimen 1864 in the Gordon Museum, Guy's Hospital–Cooper *v.* Wakley, 1828," *Guy's Hospital Gazette*, 1932, 46: 381–395, p. 385. For the same report with editorial emphasis, see *Lancet*, 1828–29, 1: 662.

26. *Lancet*, 1828–29, 1: 371.

27. Ibid., p. 369.

28. Ibid., 2: 95–96.

29. H. C. Cameron, *Mr. Guy's Hospital. 1726–1948* (London: Longmans, Green and Co., 1954), p. 154.

30. *Lancet*, 1832–33, 2: 186–187.

31. F. B. Smith, *The People's Health 1830–1910* (New York: Holmes & Meier Publishers, 1979), pp. 263–264.

32. M. Dorothy George, *Catalogue of Prints and Drawings in the British Museum: Department of Political and Personal Satires* (London: British Museum, 1954), vol. 11 (1828–1832), Print #16428, pp. 406–408.

33. "Memoir of Thomas Wakley, Esq.," *Lancet*, 1862, 1: 609–612, p. 609.

34. Eason (1932), p. 387.

35. Hodgkin (1828b), p. 23.

36. Ackerknecht (1967), p. 180.

37. Hodgkin (1836), p. 4.

38. Thomas Hodgkin, "Case of Willis," *London Medical Gazette*, 1829, 4: 318.

39. Thomas Hodgkin, "On the Anatomical Characters of Some Adventitious Structures," *Medico-Chirurgical Transactions*, 1829, 15 (part 2): 265–338.

40. M. D. Oxon (letter), "Dr. Baron *v.* Dr. Hodgkin," *London Medical Gazette*, 1829, 3: 668–670.

41. M. D. (letter), *London Medical Gazette*, 1828, 2: 459–463.

42. "Guy's Hospital. Tumor in the Neck (Dissection by Dr. Hodgkin)," *London Medical Gazette*, 1828, 2: 380–382.

43. M. D. Oxon, see note 40.

44. Thomas Hodgkin (letter), "Dr. Hodgkin *v.* Dr. Baron," *London Medical Gazette*, 1829, 3: 804–805.

CHAPTER FOUR

1. Thomas Kelly, *George Birkbeck. Pioneer of Adult Education, 1776–1841* (Liverpool: University Press, 1957).

2. Thomas Hodgkin, *The Means of Promoting and Preserving Health*, 2d ed., with additions (London: Simpkin, Marshall & Co., 1841), preface to 2d ed., p. v.

3. Ibid., Introduction, p. 1.

4. Letter to Dr. S. G. Morton, dated May 12, 1830. From the files of the American Philosophical Society Library, Philadelphia.

5. Hodgkin (1841), p. 81.

6. Book Review. *Edinburgh Medical and Surgical Journal*, 1835, 44: 231–234.

7. Elizabeth Isichei, *Victorian Quakers* (London: Oxford University Press, 1970), pp. 156, 238, 240. For the changing Quaker role in the temperance movement after 1830, see pp. 235–243.

8. Hodgkin (1841), p. 279.

9. Ibid., pp. 358–359.

10. A. S. Turberville, *The House of Lords in the Age of Reform 1784–1837* (London: Faber and Faber, 1958), p. 177.

11. Hodgkin (1841), p. 360.

12. Book Review, 1835 (note 6 above), p. 233.

13. Hodgkin (1841), pp. 473–474.

14. Ibid., pp. 384–385.

15. Book Review, 1835 (note 6 above), p. 234.

16. Book Review. *London Medical Gazette*, 1835, 15: 839.

17. Hodgkin (1841), pp. 391–392.

18. Microfilm collection, MSS #187 (reel 10).

19. Hodgkin (1841), pp. 175–176. Hodgkin also warns of the risk of fire due to smoking (pp. 233–234).

20. Book Review, 1835 (note 6 above), p. 231. Andrew Combe, *The Principles of Physiology applied to the Preservation of Health, and to the Improvement of Physical and Mental Education*, 2d ed. (Edinburgh: 1834 and 1835).

21. Erwin H. Ackerknecht, *Medicine at the Paris Hospital 1794–1848* (Baltimore, Md.: The Johns Hopkins Press, 1967), pp. 149–153.

22. Thomas Hodgkin, "Lectures on the Principles and Classification of Dis-

ease, Delivered at St. Thomas's Hospital," *London Medical Gazette*, 1843, new series 1, 31: 360–365, 385–388, 497–503, p. 364.

23. Thomas Hodgkin, *A Catalogue of the Preparations in the Anatomical Museum of Guy's Hospital. Arranged and Edited by Desire of the Treasurer of the Hospital, and of the Teachers of the Medical and Surgical School* (London: S. Highley, 1829), 581 pages (unpaginated) plus Introduction (iii–xvi), p. xvi.

24. R. Knox, "Xavier Bichat: His Life and Labours. A Biographical and Philosophical Study," *Lancet*, 1854, 2: 393–396, p. 393.

25. Thomas Hodgkin, *Lectures on The Morbid Anatomy of the Serous and Mucous Membranes*, 2 vols.; vol. 1, *On The Serous Membranes; and, as appended subjects, Parasitical Animals, Malignant Adventitious Structures, and the Indications Afforded by Colour* (London: Sherwood, Gilbert, and Piper, 1836), pp. 2–3.

26. Thomas Hodgkin, "On the Object of Post Mortem Examinations, Being an Address delivered to the Pupils of Guy's Hospital, on the Opening of the Theatre of Morbid Anatomy, Jan. 1828," *London Medical Gazette*, 1828, 2: 423–431, p. 427.

27. Hodgkin (1836), p. 2.

28. Ibid., p. 3.

29. Ibid., p. 6.

30. Ibid., p. 23.

31. Ibid., pp. 22–23.

32. For a warm and affectionate portrayal of his friend, written shortly after his death, see Thomas Hodgkin, *Biographical Sketch of Dr. William Stroud, M.D.* (London: Judd & Glass and A. W. Bennett, 1858), 23 pages.

33. Thomas Hodgkin, *Lectures on The Morbid Anatomy of the Serous and Mucous Membranes*, 2 vols.; vol. 2, part 1, *On The Mucous Membranes* (London: Simpkin, Marshall, and Co., 1840), preface, pp. v–vi. The *DNB* wrongly states that both volumes were published in 1836.

34. *Edinburgh Medical and Surgical Journal*, 1843, 59: 155–169. For a modern analysis of Hodgkin's *Lectures*, see Russell C. Maulitz, *Morbid Appearances. The Anatomy of Pathology in the Early Nineteenth Century* (New York: Cambridge University Press, 1987), pp. 205–209.

35. Matthew Baillie, *The Morbid Anatomy of Some of The Most Important Parts of the Human Body*, 1st ed. (London: J. Johnson and G. Nicol, 1793); Matthew Baillie, *A Series of Engravings, accompanied with Explanations, which are intended to illustrate The Morbid Anatomy of Some of The Most Important Parts of the Human Body; divided into ten fasciculi* (London: W. Bulmer and Co., 1799).

36. Giovanni Battista Morgagni, *De Sedibus et Causis Morborum per anatomen indagatis, libri quinqui* (On the Seats and Causes of Disease Investigated by Anatomy, five books) (Venice: 1761).

37. Hodgkin (1836), p. 9.

38. Stanley Joel Reiser, *Medicine and the Reign of Technology* (New York: Cambridge University Press, 1978), p. 18.

39. Hodgkin (1836), p. 12.

40. William Hale-White, "Thomas Hodgkin," *Guy's Hospital Reports*, 1924, 74: 117–136, p. 130.

41. S. W. F. Holloway, "Medical Education in England, 1830–1858: A Sociological Analysis," *History*, 1964, 49: 299–324, p. 305.

CHAPTER FIVE

1. Personal communication from D. W. C. Stewart, Librarian of The Royal Society of Medicine, London.

2. Thomas Hodgkin, "On Some Morbid Appearances of The Absorbent Glands and Spleen," *Medico-Chirurgical Society, Transactions*, 1832, 17: 68–114, p. 68.

3. Ibid., pp. 85–86.

4. Thomas Hodgkin, *Lectures on The Morbid Anatomy of the Serous and Mucous Membranes*, vol. 1, *On The Serous Membranes* (London: Sherwood, Gilbert, and Piper, 1836), lecture 11, p. 322; vol. 2, part 1, *On The Mucous Membranes* (London: Simpkin, Marshall, and Co., 1840), lecture 16, pp. 149–150.

5. Hodgkin (1832), p. 96.

6. Ibid., p. 98.

7. Ibid., pp. 89–90.

8. Robert Carswell, *An Atlas of Illustrations of Pathology Compiled (Chiefly from Original Sources) for the New Sydenham Society*, fasciculus XII, "Infective Disease of the Lymphatic System: Lymphadenoma or Hodgkin's Malady" (London: New Sydenham Society, 1898).

9. Peter J. Dawson, "The Original Illustrations of Hodgkin's Disease," *Archives of Internal Medicine*, 1968, 121: 288–290.

10. Richard Bright, "Observations on Abdominal Tumors and Intumescence: Illustrated by Cases of Disease of the Spleen. With Remarks on the General Pathology of that Viscus," *Guy's Hospital Reports*, 1838, series 1, 3: 401–461, pp. 405, 436–438.

11. Samuel Wilks, "Cases of Lardaceous Disease and Some Allied Affections. With Remarks," *Guy's Hospital Reports*, 1856, 3rd series, 2: 103–132, p. 114.

12. Ibid., p. 104.

13. Ibid., pp. 131–132.

14. Samuel Wilks, "Diseases, Etc., Of the Ductless Glands. I. The Spleen," *Transactions of the Pathological Society of London*, 1859, 10: 259–263, p. 260.

15. Samuel Wilks, "Cases of Enlargement of the Lymphatic Glands and Spleen, (or, Hodgkin's Disease,) with Remarks," *Guy's Hospital Reports*, 1865, 3rd series, 11: 56–67, p. 56.

16. Ibid., p. 57.

17. Ibid., p. 67.

18. Samuel Wilks, "Historical Notes on Bright's Disease, Addison's Disease, and Hodgkin's Disease," *Guy's Hospital Reports*, 1877, 3rd series, 22: 259–274, p. 272.

19. Samuel Wilks, "A Short Account of the Life and Works of Thomas Hodgkin, M.D.," *Guy's Hospital Gazette*, 1909, 23: 528–532, p. 530.

20. For a critical assessment of Wilks's "altruistic role," see Sherwin B. Nuland, "The Lymphatic Contiguity of Hodgkin's Disease: A Historical Study," *Bulletin of the New York Academy of Medicine*, 1981, 57: 776–786, pp. 780–781.

21. William Hale-White, "Thomas Hodgkin," *Guy's Hospital Reports*, 1924, 74: 117–136, p. 127.

22. Andrew Wallhauser, "Hodgkin's Disease," *Archives of Pathology*, 1933, 16: 522–562, 672–712.

23. C. A. Wunderlich, "Pseudoleukämie, Hodgkin's Krankheit oder multiple Lymphadenome ohne Leukämie," *Archiv der Heilkunde*, 1866, 7: 531–552.

24. W. S. Greenfield, "Specimens illustrative of the pathology of lymphadenoma and leucocythaemia," *Transactions of the Pathological Society of London*, 1878, 29: 272–304.

25. This section is based on the following sources: Lester S. King, *The Growth of Medical Thought* (Chicago: The University of Chicago Press, 1963), pp. 187–188; Hans G. Schlumberger, "Origins of the Cell Concept in Pathology," *Archives of Pathology*, 1944, 37: 396–407; John R. Baker, "The Discovery of the Uses of Colouring Agents in Biological Micro-technique," *Journal of the Quekett Microscopical Club* (London), 1938–1943, 4th series, 1: 256–275.

26. For a short contemporary history of the construction and uses of the microscope, see *Edinburgh Medical and Surgical Journal*, 1850, 73: 161–186.

27. L. J. Rather, "Who Discovered the Pathognomonic Giant Cell of Hodgkin's Disease?," *Bulletin of the New York Academy of Medicine*, 1972, 48: 943–950, pp. 948–949.

28. Greenfield (1878), see note 24 above.

29. Rather (1972), p. 944.

30. C. Sternberg, "Über eine eigenartige unter dem Bilde der Pseudoleukämie verlaufende Tuberculose des lymphatischen apparates," *Zeitschrift für Heilkunde*, 1898, 19: 21–91.

31. Dorothy M. Reed, "On the Pathological Changes in Hodgkin's Disease, with Especial Reference to its Relation to Tuberculosis," *Johns Hopkins Hospital Report*, 1902, 10: 133–196.

32. William B. Ober, "Hodgkin's Disease. Historical Notes," *New York State Journal of Medicine*, 1977, 77: 126–133, p. 129; Henry S. Kaplan, "Historical Aspects," in *Hodgkin's Disease* 2d ed. (Cambridge, Mass.: Harvard University Press, 1980), pp. 1–15, p. 8; see also, George W. Jones, "An Historical Review of Hodgkin's Disease with Special Reference to Its Histology and Characteristic Cells," *Annals of Medical History*, 1940, 3rd series, 2: 471–481.

33. Henry S. Kaplan, "Hodgkin's Disease and Other Human Malignant Lymphomas: Advances and Prospects—G. H. A. Clowes Memorial Lecture," *Cancer Research*, 1976, 36: 3863–3878, p. 3864.

34. Kaplan (1980), p. 12.

35. King (1963), pp. 220–221.

36. Reed (1902), p. 135.

37. Ibid, p. 156.

38. N. Senn, "The Therapeutical Value of the Röntgen Ray in the Treatment of Pseudoleucaemia," *The New York Medical Journal*, 1903, 77: 665–668, p. 665.

39. Ober (1977), pp. 128, 130. See also, J. B. Cavanagh, "The Occurrence of Low Virulence Virus Infection in Hodgkin's Disease and Other Disorders," *Guy's Hospital Reports*, 1966, 115: 331–339; S. Leibowitz, "Immunity in Hodgkin's Disease," *Guy's Hospital Reports*, 1966, 115: 341–357; I. A. Baker, "The Aetiology of Hodgkin's Disease," *Guy's Hospital Reports*, 1966, 115: 307–317. For more recent discussions of viral etiology, see "Clustering in Hodgkin's Disease," *Lancet*, 1972, 2: 907–908, and Kaplan (1980), pp. 12, 16–28, 47–51.

40. Herbert Fox, "Remarks on the Presentation of Microscopical Preparations made from Some of the Original Tissue Described by Thomas Hodgkin, 1832," *Annals of Medical History*, 1926, 8: 370–374; reprinted (with alterations) in *Guy's Hospital Reports*, 1936, 86: 11–16.

41. Kaplan (1980), p. 10.

42. Rudolf Virchow, "Weisses blut," *Froriep's Neue Notizen aus dem Gebiete der Natur-und Heilkunde* (Weimar), 1845, 36: 151–156.

43. Schlumberger (1944), pp. 397–398.

44. Greenfield (1878), p. 297.

45. Reed (1902), p. 143.

46. Nuland (1981), p. 783.

47. Kaplan (1980), p. 15.

48. Kaplan (1976), p. 3863.

49. Leonard G. Wilson, "Internal Secretions in Disease; The Historical Relations of Clinical Medicine and Scientific Physiology," *Journal of the History of Medicine and Allied Sciences*, 1984, 39: 263–302.

50. D. J. Corrigan, "On Permanent Patency of the Mouth of the Aorta, or Inadequacy of the Aortic Valves," *Edinburgh Medical and Surgical Journal*, 1832, 37: 225–245.

51. Report of Discussion at Hunterian Society following Reading by Secretary of paper by Thomas Hodgkin, "On Retroversion of the Valves of the Aorta," *London Medical Gazette*, 1828–29, 3: 429–430, 489–490.

52. Thomas Hodgkin, "On Retroversion of the Valves of the Aorta," *London Medical Gazette*, 1828–29, 3: 433–443, p. 433.

53. Ralph H. Major, *Classic Descriptions of Disease. With Biographical Sketches of the Authors*, 3rd ed. (Springfield, Ill.: Charles C. Thomas, 1945), pp. 339–343, 344–346.

54. Hale-White (1924), p. 128.

55. Samuel Wilks, "Note on the History of Valvular Diseases of the Heart," *Guy's Hospital Reports*, 1871, 3rd series, 16: 209–216, p. 211.

56. Samuel Wilks, "An Account of Some Unpublished Papers of the Late Dr. Hodgkin," *Guy's Hospital Reports*, 1878, 3rd series, 23; 55–127, pp. 65–68.

CHAPTER SIX

1. John Simon, *English Sanitary Institutions, Reviewed in Their Course of Development, and in Some of Their Political and Social Relations* (London: Cassell & Company, Limited, 1890). Reprint. New York: Johnson Reprint Corp., 1970, pp. 253–254. For an account of the deplorable environmental conditions in urban England during the nineteenth century, see, Anthony S. Wohl, *Endangered Lives. Public Health in Victorian Britain* (London: J.M. Dent & Sons Ltd, 1983).

2. S.W.F. Holloway, "Medical Education in England, 1830–1858: A Sociological Analysis," *History*, 1964, 49: 299–324, p. 319.

3. Richard Harrison Shryock, *The Development of Modern Medicine. An Interpretation of the Social and Scientific Factors Involved* (Philadelphia: University of Pennsylvania Press, 1936), pp. 105, 106, 216.

4. Ibid., p. 212; Fielding H. Garrison, *An Introduction to the History of Medicine*, 4th ed. (Philadelphia: W. B. Saunders Company, 1929), p. 774; R. E. McGrew, "The First Cholera Epidemic and Social History," *Bulletin of the History of Medicine*, 1960, 34: 61–73, p. 62.

5. Charles Rosenberg, "The Cause of Cholera: Aspects of Etiological Thought in Nineteenth Century America," *Bulletin of the History of Medicine*, 1960, 34: 331–354, p. 331.

6. For a contemporary discussion of cholera's transcontinental origin, pro-

gress, physiological effects, treatment, and sanitary precautions, see *Lancet*, 1831–32, 1: 241–284.

7. M. Dorothy George, *Hogarth to Cruikshank: Social Change in Graphic Satire* (New York: Walker and Company, 1967), p. 193. See also McGrew (1960), p. 67; Rosenberg (1960), p. 333; Shryock (1936), p. 214.

8. Charles Singer and E. Ashworth Underwood, *A Short History of Medicine*, 2d ed. (New York: Oxford University Press, 1962), pp. 214–215, 729. For a discussion of the ups and downs of these competing theories, see Erwin H. Ackerknecht, "Anticontagionism Between 1821 and 1867," *Bulletin of the History of Medicine*, 1948, 22: 562–593.

9. R. J. Morris, *Cholera 1832. The Social Response to an Epidemic* (London: Croom Helm, 1976), pp. 172–173, 180–183.

10. F. B. Smith, *The People's Health 1830–1910* (New York: Holmes & Meier Publishers, 1979), pp. 233–234; Rosenberg (1960), pp. 333–334. The moralism of predisposing causes and sin is discussed by Charles E. Rosenberg, "The Cholera Epidemic of 1832 in New York City," *Bulletin of the History of Medicine*, 1959, 33: 37–49. See also R. J. Morris (1976), pp. 129–158.

11. R. J. Morris (1976), pp. 143–149.

12. Charles-Edward Amory Winslow, *The Conquest of Epidemic Disease. A Chapter in the History of Ideas* (Princeton, N.J.: Princeton University Press, 1944), pp. xi, 182.

13. R. J. Morris (1976), pp. 176–178, 184–186, 200.

14. Ibid., pp. 79–94; McGrew (1960), pp. 64–66.

15. McGrew (1960), pp. 66–67. For reaction to cholera according to class relationships, see R. J. Morris (1976), pp. 95–128.

16. R. J. Morris (1976), pp. 101, 103–106, 108ff. See also McGrew (1960), pp. 64ff for examples of social and political disturbances accompanying cholera on the continent.

17. R. J. Morris (1976), pp. 96, 98; McGrew (1960), p. 67; *Lancet*, 1831–32, 1: 377–378.

18. Thomas Hodgkin, *Hints relating to the Cholera in London: Addressed to the Public in General, but especially to those who possess influence in their Parishes and Districts. And a Letter to a Member of the Board of Health* (London: S. Highley; J. & A. Arch; Harvey & Darton, 1832a), 24 pages, p. 16.

19. Ibid., pp. 16–20.

20. Ibid., pp. 17–19, 22; R. J. Morris (1976), pp. 118–119.

21. Ackerknecht (1948), p. 590.

22. Hodgkin (1832a), pp. 5–8.

23. Ibid., pp. 8, 12.

24. Ibid., pp. 14–15.

25. Ibid., pp. 23–24.

26. Margaret Pelling, *Cholera, Fever and English Medicine 1825–1865* (London: Oxford University Press, 1978), p. 5. For a contemporary review, see "History of the Origin, Progress, and Mortality of the Cholera Morbus," *London Medical Gazette,* 1849, new series, 9: 507–511, 556–559, 600–602; see also pp. 719–728 for a list of 17 contemporary publications on cholera, and critical comments.

27. John Snow, *On the Mode of Communication of Cholera,* 2nd ed., much enlarged (London: John Churchill, 1855). Reprint. New York: Commonwealth Fund, 1936.

28. Pelling (1978), p. 3.

29. *Lancet,* 1849, 2: 493. For the *Lancet*'s doubts, see pp. 406–407. For a detailed account of the cholera controversy and Snow's contribution, see Pelling (1978), pp. 146–249.

30. Howard Temperley, *British Antislavery 1833–1870* (Columbia, S.C.: University of South Carolina Press, 1972), p. 46.

31. Brian Gardner, *The African Dream* (London: Cassell, 1970), pp. 20–21; E. H. Kass, "Thomas Hodgkin, Physician and Social Scientist," *Guy's Hospital Reports,* 1966, 115: 269–280, pp. 273–274.

32. Thomas Hodgkin, *On Negro Emancipation and American Colonization* (London: Richard Watts, 1832b), 24 pages, pp. 3–4.

33. Ibid., p. 10.

34. C. D. Haagensen and Wyndham E. B. Lloyd, *A Hundred Years of Medicine* (New York: Sheridan House, 1943), p. 34.

35. Thomas Hodgkin, *Society for the Improvement of the Condition of Factory Children,* [1832] one page.

36. Elizabeth Isichei, *Victorian Quakers* (London: Oxford University Press, 1970), pp. 246–248. For a contemporary critical assessment of Quaker involvement, see *The Times* (London), August 30, 1838, p. 4, column 4.

37. James A. Williamson, *A Short History of British Expansion. The Modern Empire and Commonwealth,* 4th ed. (London: MacMillan and Co., Limited, 1953), p. 21; Isichei (1970), p. 228. See also Philip D. Curtin, *The Image of Africa. British Ideas and Action, 1780–1850* (Madison: The University of Wisconsin Press, 1964), p. 289; Temperley, (1972), p. xi.

38. Thomas Hodgkin, *An Inquiry into The Merits of the American Colonization Society: and A Reply to the Charges Brought Against It. With an Account of the British African Colonization Society* (London: J. & A. Arch; Harvey & Darton; Edmund Fry; and S. Highley, 1833), 62 pages & map, pp. 8–10.

39. Ibid., p. 5.

40. Ibid., pp. 56–58.

41. James Morris, *Heaven's Command. An Imperial Progress* (New York: A. Helen and Kurt Wolff Book, Harcourt Brace Jovanovich, 1973), p. 39.

42. Hodgkin (1833), pp. 59–60.

43. Ibid., p. 32.

44. Ibid., pp. 53–54; Amalie M. Kass, "Dr. Thomas Hodgkin, Dr. Martin Delany, and the 'Return to Africa,'" *Medical History*, 1983, 27: 373–393, pp. 378–379.

45. Temperley (1972), p. 267.

46. Hodgkin (1833), p. 55.

47. Thomas Hodgkin, *On the British African Colonization Society. To Which are Added, Some Particulars Respecting the American Colonization Society; and a Letter from Jeremiah Hubbard, Addressed to a Friend in England, on the Same Subject* (London: Richard Watts, 1834), 32 pages.

48. Hodgkin (1834), p. 13. For the problems confronting the settlers, see Temperley (1972), p. 51; also see Gardner (1970), pp. 20–21.

49. Hodgkin (1834), p. 15.

CHAPTER SEVEN

1. Gertrude Himmelfarb, *The Idea of Poverty. England in the Early Industrial Age*, chapter 6, The New Poor Law: Pauper Versus Poor (pp. 147–176) (New York: Alfred A. Knopf, 1984), p. 153. For the evolution of decentralized control before 1834, see George Rosen, "Economic and Social Policy in the Development of Public Health. As Essay in Interpretation," *Journal of the History of Medicine and Allied Sciences*, 1953, 8: 406–430, pp. 413–414.

2. Thomas Hodgkin, *On the Mode of Selecting and Remunerating Medical Men for Professional Attendance on the Poor of a Parish or District: Read before the Hunterian Society* (Lindfield: printed by W. Eade, at the Schools of Industry, 1836), 16 pages. The new poor law and the development of its medical services has been described by Himmelfarb (1984), pp. 147–176; M. A. Crowther, *The Workhouse System 1834–1929* (London: Batsford, 1981), pp. 156–190; M. W. Flinn, "Medical Services Under the New Poor Law" in *The New Poor Law in the Nineteenth Century*, Derek Fraser, ed. (London: Macmillan, 1976), pp. 45–66; F. B. Smith, *The People's Health 1830–1910* (New York: Holmes & Meier Publishers, 1979), pp. 346–362; Ruth G. Hodgkinson, *The Origins of the National Health Service. The Medical Services of the New Poor Law, 1834–1871* (Berkeley: University of California Press, 1967). Also see Ruth G. Hodgkinson, "Poor Law Medical Officers of England 1834–1871," *Journal of the History of Medicine and Allied Sciences*, 1956, 11: 299–338.

3. Crowther (1981), pp. 12, 11.

4. Himmelfarb (1984), pp. 154, 159–161; Crowther (1981), pp. 12, 21.

5. Himmelfarb (1984), p. 162; Crowther (1981), p. 18; Hodgkinson (1967),

p. 1. For criticism of the commission's research methods and goals, see F. B. Smith (1979), pp. 350–351ff.

6. Himmelfarb (1984), pp. 163–165; Rosen (1953), pp. 419, 422.

7. For an account of the harsh conditions and cruelty in the workhouses, see Hodgkinson (1967), pp. 147–175; also see Crowther (1981), pp. 24–29.

8. Smith (1979), p. 350.

9. Flinn (1976), p. 48; Rosen (1953), pp. 424, 425–427; Charles Singer and E. Ashworth Underwood, *A Short History of Medicine*, 2nd ed. (New York: Oxford University Press, 1962), pp. 212–214.

10. Hodgkinson (1967), p. 5.

11. Flinn (1976), p. 49; M. Jeanne Peterson, *The Medical Profession in Mid-Victorian London* (Berkeley: University of California Press, 1978), pp. 111, 113; Hodgkinson (1967), p. 21. For the hardships to the poor resulting from the actions of the Relieving Officer in the delivery of health care, see Hodgkinson (1967), pp. 19–25.

12. Peterson (1978), pp. 112, 130; Crowther (1981), pp. 158, 162; also see chapter 8.

13. Hodgkinson (1967), p. 62; Flinn (1976), p. 46.

14. Hodgkinson (1956), pp. 301–302; M. A. Crowther, "Paupers or Patients? Obstacles to Professionalization in the Poor Law Medical Service Before 1914," *Journal of the History of Medicine and Allied Sciences*, 1984, 39: 33–54, pp. 35, 37.

15. Hodgkin (1836), pp. 3–5.

16. S. W. F. Holloway, "Medical Education in England, 1830–1858: A Sociological Analysis," *History*, 1964, 49: 299–324, p. 313.

17. Peter Dunkley, "The 'Hungry Forties' and the New Poor Law: A Case Study," *The Historical Journal*, 1974, 17(2): 329–346, p. 341.

18. Ibid., pp. 341, 344–345.

19. Crowther (1981), p. 158; Peterson (1978), pp. 111, 113; Smith (1979), p. 357; Hodgkinson (1967), pp. 284–285; (1956), p. 307.

20. Dunkley (1974), pp. 342–343; Crowther (1984), pp. 40–41; Hodgkinson (1956), p. 331. For the medical profession's entanglement with the poor law, numerous examples of abuse of poor law medical officers by the Guardians and Relieving Officers, and meanness in authorizing payment, see Smith (1979), pp. 346ff.

21. Crowther (1981), pp. 120–121. For duties and onerous working conditions of the workhouse lay employees, see pp. 113–134.

22. *Lancet*, 1846, 2: 332.

23. Smith (1979), pp. 24–37, 43–44; also see *Lancet*, 1871, 1: 454. For the judicial system's handling of charges of medical manslaughter, see *Lancet*, 1845, 1: 341–342, 451–452; 1846, 1: 393.

24. Hodgkinson (1967), p. 245; Flinn (1976), p. 45.

25. Hodgkinson (1967), p. 8; (1956), p. 311; Flinn (1976), p. 53.

26. Flinn (1976), p. 51.

27. Hodgkin (1836), pp. 5–7.

28. Ibid., p. 14.

29. Ibid., p. 7.

30. Ibid., pp. 8–9. For the many prominent French scientists who did not advance through this system, see Erwin H. Ackerknecht, *Medicine at the Paris Hospital 1794–1848* (Baltimore, Md.: The Johns Hopkins Press, 1967), p. 126; also see "Medical Education in 19th Century France," *Journal of Medical Education*, 1957, 32: part 1, 148–152.

31. Hodgkinson (1967), p. 680; Rosen (1953), p. 423.

32. I. S. L. Loudon, "The Origins and Growth of the Dispensary Movement in England," *Bulletin of the History of Medicine*, 1981, 55: 322–342, pp. 330, 334, 340–341.

33. Ibid., pp. 326, 328, 330, 334–336.

34. Hodgkin (1836), pp. 11–13.

35. Ibid., pp. 11–14.

36. Hodgkinson (1967), pp. 429–430; Peterson (1978), pp. 23–24, 27, 29.

37. Hodgkinson (1967), p. 431; Peterson (1978), pp. 111, 113, 116; Crowther (1981), p. 158; Smith (1979), p. 355. Also see *Lancet*, 1850, 1: 739.

38. "Convention of Poor-Law Medical Officers," *Lancet*, 1850, 1: 188–189.

39. "The Poor-Law Commission and the Poor-Law Medical Officers," *Lancet*, 1850, 1: 739.

40. Crowther (1984), pp. 42–44; Hodgkinson (1967), p. 432.

41. Thomas Hodgkin (letter to the editor), "Poor-Law Medical Reform," *British Medical Journal*, 1857 (January), pp. 96–97.

42. Hodgkinson (1967), pp. 433–450.

43. Ibid., p. 450.

CHAPTER EIGHT

1. James H. Cassedy, *American Medicine and Statistical Thinking, 1800–1860* (Cambridge, Mass.: Harvard University Press, 1984), p. 61; Richard H. Shryock, "The History of Quantification in Medical Science," *Isis*, 1961, 52: 215–237, p. 230.

2. George Rosen, "Problems in the Application of Statistical Analysis to Questions of Health: 1700–1880," *Bulletin of the History of Medicine*, 1955, 29:27-45, pp. 37–38; Shryock (1961), p. 231.

3. William Osler, "Influence of Louis on American Medicine," *Bulletin of*

the *Johns Hopkins Hospital,* 1897, 8: 161–167; Walter R. Steiner, "Dr. Pierre-Charles-Alexander Louis, A Distinguished Parisian Teacher of American Medical Students," *Annals of Medical History,* 3rd series, 1940, 2: 451–460.

4. Cassedy (1984), pp. 60–61; Erwin H. Ackerknecht, *Medicine at the Paris Hospital 1794–1848* (Baltimore, Md.: The Johns Hopkins Press, 1967), pp. 9–10, 102–104.

5. Ibid., p. 74.

6. Thomas Hodgkin, *Lectures on The Morbid Anatomy of the Serous and Mucous Membranes,* 2 vols.; vol. 1, *On The Serous Membranes; and, as appended subjects, Parasitical Animals, Malignant Adventitious Structures, and the Indications Afforded by Colour* (London: Sherwood, Gilbert, and Piper, 1836), pp. 13–15.

7. Richard Harrison Shryock, *The Development of Modern Medicine. An Interpretation of the Social and Scientific Factors Involved* (Philadelphia: University of Pennsylvania Press, 1936), p. 163.

8. Thomas Hodgkin, "Numerical Method of Conducting Medical Inquiries," *Association Medical Journal,* 1854 (December), 1090–1094. This essay was read to the Physical Society of Guy's Hospital in 1834.

9. Ibid., p. 1093.

10. Idem., p. 1093. For a similar conclusion and a less than enthusiastic appraisal of the numerical system, see Austin Flint, "Remarks on the Numerical System of Louis," *New York Journal of Medicine and Surgery,* 1841, 4: 283–303.

11. Shryock (1961), p. 233. For a discussion of some of the controversy and confusion at the time, see J. Philip Goldberg, "The Numerical Method; How It Struck a Contemporary," *Isis,* 1963, 54: 133–135.

12. Thomas Hodgkin, "On the Effects of Acrid Poisons," *Report of the British Association for the Advancement of Science,* 1835, 5: 211–233, pp. 219–220. For a brief preliminary report by Dr. Hodgkin and Dr. Rüppell, see *Report of the BAAS,* 1834, 4: 681.

13. Thomas Hodgkin, in Samuel Wilks, "An Account of Some Unpublished Papers of the Late Dr. Hodgkin," *Guy's Hospital Reports,* 1878, 23: 55–127, p. 64.

14. James P. Babington, Introduction, *Guy's Hospital Reports,* 1837, 2: i–vii, p. i.

15. *Lancet,* 1835–36, 1:596–597. For a history of the *Reports* see R. C. Brock, "The Guy's Hospital Reports," *Guy's Hospital Gazette,* 1952, 66: 252–261. Because of steadily increasing costs, publication ended with volume 123 in 1974.

16. Thomas Hodgkin, "The History of an Unusually-Formed Placenta, and Imperfect Foetus, and of Similar Examples of Monstrous Productions. With an

Account of the Structure of the Placenta and Foetus, by Sir Astley Cooper, Bart.," *Guy's Hospital Reports*, 1836, 1: 218–240.

17. Bransby Cooper, "Cases of Compound Fracture, Wound of the Knee-Joint, Retention of Urine, and Hernia. With Observations," *Guy's Hospital Reports*, 1836, 1: 189–217; Dr. Ashwell, "Observations of the Propriety of Inducing Premature Labour in Pregnancy Complicated with Tumour," *Guy's Hospital Reports*, 1836, 1: 300–337.

18. Thomas Hodgkin (comments), "Case of A Large Bony Tumor in the Face completely Removed by Spontaneous Separation. To Which are added, Observations Upon Some of the Functions of the Soft Palate and Pharynx, by Mr. Hilton," *Guy's Hospital Reports*, 1836, 1: 493–506, pp. 495–498.

19. Thomas Hodgkin, "Provisional Report on the Communication between the Arteries and Absorbents on the part of the London Committee," *Report of the BAAS*, 1836, 6: 289–290. For a summary, see *London Medical Gazette*, 1836, 18:885–886. The full report was not published until 1854. See chapter 13, note 11.

20. Thomas Hodgkin, "Description of a Remarkable Specimen of Urinary Calculus: to which are added, Some Remarks on the Structure and Form of Urinary Calculi," *Guy's Hospital Reports*, 1837, 2: 268–278.

21. The origins of the Royal Colleges of Physicians and of Surgeons, and of the Society of Apothecaries, are reviewed in the following citations and are derived from "Report from the Select Committee of the House of Commons on Medical Education; with the Minutes of Evidence, and Appendix (1834)," *The Edinburgh Review, or Critical Journal*, 1845, 81: 235–272. Also in W. J. Bishop, "The Evolution of the General Practitioner in England," in vol. 2 of *Science Medicine and History. Essays on the Evolution of Scientific Thought and Medical Practice*, 2 vols., E. Ashworth Underwood, ed. (London: Geoffrey Cumberlege, Oxford University Press, 1953), pp. 351–357; F.N.L. Poynter, "Medical Education in England Since 1600," in *The History of Medical Education*, C. D. O'Malley, ed. (Berkeley: University of California Press, 1970), pp. 235–249; George Clark, *A History of The Royal College of Physicians of London*, 2 vols. (Oxford: Clarendon Press, 1964, 1966), vol. 1, pp. 1–67.

22. Shryock (1936), pp. 50–51.

23. Z. Cope, "Influence of the Society of Apothecaries Upon Medical Education," *British Medical Journal*, 1956, 1: 1–6, p. 1; Poynter (1970), p. 237.

24. *Edinburgh Review* (1845), p. 240.

25. Thomas Hodgkin, *Medical Reform. An Address read to The Harveian Society, at the Opening of its Seventeenth Session, October 2, 1847* (London: John Churchill, 1847), 18 pages, p. 4.

26. M. Jeanne Peterson, *The Medical Profession in Mid-Victorian London* (Berkeley: University of California Press, 1978), pp. 153–154.

27. Ibid., p. 194; also see Poynter (1970), p. 242.

28. "The Petition from the Committee of Associated Licentiates of the Royal College of Physicians," *Lancet*, 1834–35, 2: 678–679.

29. Clark, vol. 2 (1966), p. 691; P. E. Thompson Hancock, "Thomas Hodgkin. The FitzPatrick Lecture," *Journal of the Royal College of Physicians of London*, 1968, 2: 404–421, p. 412.

30. Charles Singer and S.W.F. Holloway, "Early Medical Education in England in Relation to the Pre-History of London University," *Medical History*, 1960, 4: 1–17, pp. 10, 12, 16, 17. For the middle class's growing awareness of the role of education in maintaining social position and providing better-quality medical care, see S.W.F. Holloway, "Medical Education in England, 1830–1858: A Sociological Analysis," *History*, 1964, 49: 299–324, pp. 314–320.

31. For initial steps and obstacles to this project, see G. T. Garratt, *Lord Brougham* (London: MacMillan and Co. Ltd., 1935), pp. 185, 187; Thomas Kelly, *George Birkbeck. Pioneer of Adult Education 1776–1841* (Liverpool: University Press, 1957), p. 153; also see Poynter (1970), p. 243.

32. Singer and Holloway (1960), p. 13.

33. Holloway (1964) p. 323.

34. H. C. Cameron, *Mr. Guy's Hospital 1726–1948* (London: Longmans, Green and Co., 1954), p. 182.

CHAPTER NINE

1. First Annual Report, Aborigines' Protection Society, 1838 (May 16), 1: 10–11; see also "The Late Dr. Hodgkin," *The Aborigines' Friend, and Colonial Intelligencer*, 1859–66, new series, 2: 519–522.

2. For a discussion of the events and motivation leading to the formation of the APS, and its objectives and methods, see George W. Stocking, Jr., "What's In a Name? The Origins of The Royal Anthropological Institute (1837–71)," *Man*, 1971, 6: 369–390, pp. 369–371; Ronald Rainger, "Philanthropy and Science in the 1830's: The British and Foreign Aborigines' Protection Society," *Man*, 1980, 15: 702–717, pp. 702–710.

3. For a descriptive sketch of Harrison, see "Obituary. Sir Samuel Wilks, Bart., M.D., F.R.S.," *British Medical Journal*, 1911, 2: 1384–1390, p. 1384. See Cruikshank caricature (chapter 3, Fig. 1).

4. Howard Temperley, *British Antislavery 1833–1870* (Columbia, S.C.: Univeristy of South Carolina Press, 1972), pp. 70–73.

5. James A. Williamson, *A Short History of British Expansion. The Modern Empire and Commonwealth*, 4th ed. (London: MacMillan and Co., Limited, 1953), p. 20.

6. R. J. Morris, *Cholera 1832. The Social Response to an Epidemic* (London: Croom Helm, 1976), p. 131. See also R. de M. Rudolf, *Clapham and the Clapham Sect* (Clapham: published for The Clapham Antiquarian Society by Edmund Baldwin, 1927), pp. 89–91.

7. E. E. Rich, *The History of the Hudson's Bay Company*, 2 vols.; vol. 2, *1763–1870* (London: The Hudson's Bay Record Society, 1959), pp. 345, 422; Eugene Stock, *The History of the Church Missionary Society, Its Environment, Its Men and Its Work*, 3 vols. (London: Church Missionary Society, 1899), vol. 1, p. 246.

8. Parliamentary Paper on the Report of the Commissioners for Inquiring Concerning Charities, 1840, p. 750.

9. Microfilm collection of the papers of Thomas Hodgkin, MSS #188 (reel 11) at the Friends House Library, London, England.

10. Letter from R. King to T. Hodgkin, April 25, 1833. Microfilm collection, MSS #185 (reel 8).

11. Richard King, *Narrative of a Journey to the Shores of the Arctic Ocean, in 1833, 1834, and 1835; Under the Command of Capt. Back, R.N.*, 2 vols. (London: Richard Bentley, 1836), vol. 2, pp. 52, 50.

12. King (1836), vol. 1, pp. 78–79.

13. King (1836), vol. 2, pp. 49–50, 54.

14. Christopher Hill, *The World Turned Upside Down. Radical Ideas during the English Revolution* (London: Temple Smith, 1972), pp. 271–272.

15. Michael Rose, *Curator of the Dead. Thomas Hodgkin (1798–1866)* (London: Peter Owen, 1981), pp. 88–89.

16. King (1836), vol. 2, pp. 292–301 (from a letter by Thomas Hodgkin to the Royal Geographical Society).

17. Letter from T. Hodgkin to B. Harrison, December 1836. Microfilm collection, MSS #189 (reel 12); also see Amalie M. Kass and Edward H. Kass, *Perfecting the World. The Life and Times of Dr. Thomas Hodgkin 1798–1866* (Boston: Harcourt Brace Jovanovich Publishers, 1988), pp. 277–278; also in Rose (1981), pp. 89–91.

18. Letter from B. Harrison to T. Hodgkin, January 5, 1837. Microfilm collection, MSS #185 (reel 8).

19. Ibid., MSS #185 (reel 8).

20. Samuel Wilks and G. T. Bettany, *A Biographical History of Guy's Hospital* (London: Ward, Lock, Bowden & Co., 1892), p. 384.

21. Kass and Kass (1988), pp. 262–263.

22. Samuel Wilks, "A Short Account of the Life and Works of Thomas Hodgkin, M.D.," *Guy's Hospital Gazette*, 1909, 23: 528–532.

23. Rose (1981), p. 61.

24. C. Hardwick, "Thomas Hodgkin 1798–1866," *Guy's Hospital Reports*,

1966, 115: 255–261, p. 259; see also unpublished biographical sketch by R. Hingston Fox (1919) in microfilm collection, MSS #191 (reel 14).

25. Microfilm collection, MSS #185 (reel 8).

26. Kass and Kass (1988), pp. 273–274.

27. Ibid., pp. 275–276.

28. Microfilm collection, MSS #185 (reel 8).

29. Ibid., MSS #185 (reel 8).

30. Idem.

31. Ibid., MSS #179 (reel 2); also see Kass and Kass (1988), p. 285.

32. Microfilm collection, MSS #181 (reel 4).

33. Ibid., MSS #183 (reel 6).

34. Ibid., MSS #181 (reel 4).

35. Letter from T. Hodgkin to B. Harrison, August 7, 1837. Microfilm collection, MSS #185 (reel 8).

36. Microfilm collection, MSS #185 (reel 8).

37. Microfilm collection, MSS #186 (reel 9).

38. Microfilm collection, MSS #185 (reel 8).

39. Rose (1981), p. 96.

40. Letter from T. Hodgkin to J. Hodgkin, Jr. Microfilm collection, MSS #185 (reel 8).

41. In a lengthy memoir written several months after the election, Hodgkin described his acrimonious encounters with Harrison when he declared his candidacy and was confronted by the treasurer's specific objections, and the aftermath when he was offered an empty title. Kass and Kass (1988), pp. 279–284, 294–296.

42. Minutes of the General Court of Guy's Hospital, H9/GY/A1/2/1, pp. 86–88. From the Greater London Record Office and History Library.

43. Letter from T. Hodgkin to B. Harrison, September 7, 1837. Microfilm collection, MSS #185 (reel 8).

44. Obituary, *British Medical Journal*, 1866, 1: 446–447.

45. For a review of some of the biochemical research at Guy's, see Louis Rosenfeld, "George Owen Rees (1813–1889): An Early Clinical Biochemist," *Clinical Chemistry*, 1985, 31: 1068–1070; Noel G. Coley, "George Owen Rees, MD, FRS (1813–89): Pioneer of Medical Chemistry," *Medical History*, 1986, 30: 173–190.

46. Letter to the editor, *Lancet*, 1836–37 (September 16, 1837), 2: 904.

47. Testimonial to Dr. Hodgkin (by Alfred Aspland), *Lancet*, 1856, 2: 611.

48. William Hale-White, "Thomas Hodgkin," *Guy's Hospital Reports*, 1924, 74: 117–136, p. 119.

49. Thomas Hodgkin, Presidential Address to the Physical Society at Guy's Hospital, 1834, in "Hodgkin and the Physical Society," *Guy's Hospital Gazette*, 1932, 46: 110–113, p. 113.

50. Richard Bright, "Character of The Late Dr. Babington," *London Medical Gazette*, 1833, 12: 264–265; *DNB*, vol. 1, pp. 787–788. For contrary opinion, see *Lancet*, 1832–33, 2: 186, 349, 350.

51. Wilks and Bettany (1892), p. 237; also see *DNB*, vol. 1, pp. 783–784.

52. *London Medical Gazette*, 1829, 3: 555.

53. Samuel Wilks, "An Account of Some Unpublished Papers of the Late Dr. Hodgkin," *Guy's Hospital Reports*, 1878, 3rd series, 23: 55–127, p. 68.

54. G. D. Gibb, "Illustrations of the Practical Application of the Laryngoscope," *Lancet*, 1863 (March), 194–197, p. 196.

55. Manuel Garcia, "Observations on the Human Voice," *Proceedings of the Royal Society of London*, 1854–55, 7: 399–410.

56. Morell Mackenzie, "A Description of the First Laryngoscope, as Invented and Employed by Dr. B. G. Babington, F.R.S., in the Year 1829," *Lancet*, 1864, 1: 546–547; George Johnson, "The Laryngoscope," *Lancet*, 1864, 1: 573–575. See also Walter A. Wells, "Benjamin Guy Babington—Inventor of the Laryngoscope," *Laryngoscope*, 1946, 56: 443–454; T. G. Wilson, "Benjamin Guy Babington, M.D., F.R.C.P., F.R.S. (1794–1866)," *Journal of Laryngology and Otology*, 1953, 67: 90–97; William H. Woglom, "The Laryngeal Mirror," in *Discoverers for Medicine* (New Haven, Conn.: Yale University Press, 1949), pp. 84–99.

57. B. G. Babington, "Hereditary Epistaxis," *Lancet*, 1865, 2: 362–363.

58. Henri Rendu, "Épistaxis répétées chez un sujet porteur de petits angiomes cutanés et muqueux," *Gazette des hôpitaux* (Paris), 1896, 69: 1322–1323; William Osler, "On a Family Form of Recurring Epistaxis, Associated with Multiple Telangiectases of the Skin and Mucous Membranes," *Johns Hopkins Hospital Bulletin*, 1901, 12: 333–337; F. Parkes Weber, "Multiple Hereditary Developmental Angiomata (Telangiectases) of the Skin and Mucous Membranes Associated with Recurring Haemorrhages," *Lancet*, 1907, 2: 160–162.

59. *Lancet*, 1854, 1: 433. The obituaries in *Lancet* and the *British Medical Journal* mistakenly give the year of resignation as 1855.

60. *Lancet*, 1866, 1: 445–446.

61. James P. Babington, Introduction, *Guy's Hospital Reports*, 1837, 2: i–vii, pp. v–vi. James was the younger brother of Benjamin.

62. Thomas Hodgkin, "Numerical Method of Conducting Medical Inquiries," *Association Medical Journal*, 1854 (December), 1090–1094.

63. Kass and Kass (1988), pp. 304–305.

CHAPTER TEN

1. Amalie M. Kass and Edward H. Kass, *Perfecting the World. The Life and Times of Dr. Thomas Hodgkin 1798–1866* (Boston: Harcourt Brace Jovanovich

Publishers, 1988), pp. 303, 306; also in Michael Rose, *Curator of the Dead. Thomas Hodgkin (1798–1866)* (London: Peter Owen, 1981), p. 122.

2. Kass and Kass (1988), pp. 305, 309.

3. Thomas Hodgkin, "On the Practicability of Civilising Aboriginal Populations," *Monthly Chronicle*, 1839 October, 4: 309–321, p. 319.

4. Under a provision of Thomas Guy's will, the hospital was to care for up to 20 incurable lunatics. H. C. Cameron, *"Mr. Guy's Hospital. 1726–1948"* (London: Longmans, Green and Co., 1954), p. 47.

5. Richard Hunter and Ida Macalpine, *Three Hundred Years of Psychiatry 1535–1860* (London: Oxford University Press, 1963), pp. 684–690.

6. R. Hunter, "Thomas Hodgkin, Samuel Tuke and John Conolly," *Guy's Hospital Reports*, 1966, 115: 263–267, p. 265.

7. Charles L. Cherry, "The Southern Retreat, Thomas Hodgkin, and Achille-Louis Foville," *Medical History*, 1979, 23: 314–324, pp. 316, 323.

8. Thomas Hodgkin, *Lectures on The Morbid Anatomy of the Serous and Mucous Membranes*, 2 vols.; vol. 1, *On The Serous Membranes; and, as appended subjects, Parasitical Animals, Malignant Adventitious Structures, and the Indications Afforded by Colour* (London: Sherwood, Gilbert, and Piper, 1836), pp. 2–3.

9. Cherry (1979), p. 316.

10. Ibid., p. 320.

11. Ibid., p. 319.

12. In 1817, Esquirol introduced what was probably the first formal course anywhere of clinical instruction in mental disease. A great many students trained with him. For some of Esquirol's work, see Hunter and Macalpine (1963), pp. 731–738.

13. Erwin H. Ackerknecht, *Medicine at the Paris Hospital 1794–1848* (Baltimore, Md.: The Johns Hopkins Press, 1967), pp. 168–169. For some of Pinel's work, see Hunter and Macalpine (1963), pp. 602–610.

14. Thomas Hodgkin, "A lecture on the past and present medical theories and their bearing on practice," (pp. 96–127), in Samuel Wilks, "An Account of Some Unpublished Papers of the late Dr. Hodgkin," *Guy's Hospital Reports*, 1878, 23: 55–127, pp. 96, 102, 116, 118, 124.

15. The details of Oxford's crime and the ensuing courtroom events are derived from the following: William C. Townsend, "The Trial of Edward Oxford for Shooting at the Queen," in *Modern State Trials With Essays and Notes*, 2 vols. (London: Longman, Brown, Green, and Longmans, 1850), vol. 1, pp. 102–150; J. F. Clarke, "A Medico-Legal Trial," in *Autobiographical Recollections of the Medical Profession* (London: J. & A. Churchill, 1874), pp. 195–213.

16. Hunter (1966) believes that the introduction did take place even though the evidence is circumstantial. Kass and Kass (1988), pp. 539–540, found no

record in any letters or papers of Hodgkin, Tuke, or Conolly to support such a meeting. For Conolly's work in the treatment of mental illness, see Hunter and Macalpine (1963), pp. 805–809, 1030–1038; see also Anand C. Chitnis, "Medical Education in Edinburgh, 1790–1826, and Some Victorian Social Consequences," *Medical History*, 1973, 17: 173–185, p. 181.

17. Townsend (1850), pp. 135–136. Hodgkin was quoting from the two-volume medico-legal work of C.C.H. Marc (1771–1841), which had been published in Paris earlier that year.

18. Thomas Hodgkin, *Biographical Sketch of James Cowles Prichard, M.D. F.R.S. &c. Late President of the Ethnological Society. Read at the Meeting of the Society on the 28. 2mo. (February) 1849* (London: William Watts, 1849), 28 pages. This obituary includes many of Hodgkin's thoughts on medicine, philology, and ethnology.

19. Hunter and Macalpine (1963), pp. 836–842.

20. Thomas Hodgkin, "On Oxford's Trial" (pp. 87–88), in Samuel Wilks, "An Account of Some Unpublished Papers of the Late Dr. Hodgkin," *Guy's Hospital Reports*, 1878, 23: 55–127.

21. Hunter and Macalpine (1963), pp. 837–838.

22. Ibid., pp. 840, 838.

23. Ibid., pp. 567–572.

24. Clarke (1874), p. 212.

25. Jacques M. Quen, "An Historical View of the M'Naghten Trial," *Bulletin of the History of Medicine*, 1968, 42: 43–51, p. 45; Jacques M. Quen, "James Hadfield and Medical Jurisprudence of Insanity," *New York State Journal of Medicine*, 1969, 69: 1221–1226, p. 1224.

26. Hunter and Macalpine (1963), p. 919.

27. Ibid., pp. 919–922, p. 921; also in Quen (1968), p. 48, and Jacques M. Quen, "A History of the Anglo-American Legal Psychiatry of Violence and Responsibility," in *Violence and Responsibility. The Individual, the Family and Society*, Robert L. Sadoff, ed., (New York: SP Medical & Scientific Books: distributed by Halsted Press, 1978), pp. 17–32, p. 24.

28. Quen (1969), p. 1225. For an interesting account of the prosecution's successful use of the McNaughton rule in countering a defense of moral insanity in the trial of the assassin of President James A. Garfield in 1881, see Charles E. Rosenberg, *The Trial of the Assassin Guiteau. Psychiatry and Law in the Gilded Age* (Chicago: The University of Chicago Press, 1968), chapters 3 and 4 (pp. 43–110, 173, 175, 193, 197–199, 252, 254).

29. Quen (1968), pp. 49–50; (1978), p. 24.

30. Letter from Thomas Hodgkin to Dr. Samuel G. Morton of Philadelphia, November 12, 1839. From the archives of the American Philosophical Society Library, Philadelphia.

31. Thomas Hodgkin, *On The Rule of the Society of Friends Which Forbids the Marriage of Fisrt [sic]-Cousins* (privately circulated), London [1840?], 12 pages, p. 1.

32. Ibid., preface. For membership trends in the Society of Friends because of this rule, see Elizabeth Isichei, *Victorian Quakers* (London: Oxford University Press, 1970), pp. 115, 135–136, 147, 163. For additional discussion of Hodgkin's struggle against the rule, see also Kass and Kass (1988), pp. 307, 308, 310, 313–318.

33. Isichei (1970), pp. 136, 159, 115, 164.

34. Frederick G. Parsons, *The History of St. Thomas's Hospital*, 3 vols.; vol. 3, *From 1800 to 1900* (London: Methuen & Co. Ltd., 1936), pp. 89–93; also in Kass and Kass (1988), p. 332.

35. Kass and Kass (1988), pp. 332–334; *Lancet*, 1842–43, 1: 109, 473–475.

36. Thomas Hodgkin, *A Lecture Introductory to the Course on the Practice of Medicine. Delivered at St. Thomas's Hospital, at the Commencement of the Session 1842–3* (London: Richard Watts, 1842), 22 pages, pp. 13–14.

37. Ibid., pp. 4–5.

38. Ibid., pp. 14–15.

39. Parsons (1936), p. 94; also in Kass and Kass (1988), pp. 334–335.

40. Letter from Thomas Hodgkin to Thomas Nunneley of Leeds, August 2, 1843. From the files of the Royal College of Physicians of London.

41. Rose (1981), p. 126; also in Kass and Kass (1988), p. 335.

42. Edward H. Kass and Anne H. Bartlett, "Thomas Hodgkin, M.D. (1798–1866): An Annotated Bibliography," *Bulletin of the History of Medicine*, 1969, 43: 138–175.

CHAPTER ELEVEN

1. S. W. F. Holloway, "Medical Education in England, 1830–1858: A Sociological Analysis," *History*, 1964, 49: 299–324, pp. 300, 302.

2. Richard Harrison Shryock, *The Development of Modern Medicine. An Interpretation of the Social and Scientific Factors Involved* (Philadelphia: University of Pennsylvania Press, 1936), p. 12; Stanley Joel Reiser, *Medicine and the Reign of Technology* (New York: Cambridge University Press, 1978), p. 8.

3. Richard Harrison Shryock, *Medicine in America. Historical Essays* (Baltimore, Md.: The Johns Hopkins Press, 1966), p. 168; Lewis Thomas, *The Medusa and the Snail. More Notes of a Biology Watcher* (New York: The Viking Press, 1979), pp. 159–160.

4. Thomas Hodgkin, "A lecture on the past and present medical theories and their bearing on practice," (pp. 96–127), in Samuel Wilks, "An Account of Some

Unpublished Papers of the Late Dr. Hodgkin," *Guy's Hospital Reports*, 1878, 23: 55–127, pp. 96, 97–98, 101.

5. Ibid., p. 102.

6. Ibid., pp. 125, 127.

7. Ibid., p. 120.

8. Thomas Hodgkin, "Lectures on the Principles and Classification of Disease, Delivered at St. Thomas's Hospital," *London Medical Gazette*, 1842–43, 31: new series 1, 360–365, 385–388, 497–503, p. 360.

9. Thomas Hodgkin, "On the Anatomical Characters of some Adventitious Structures, being an attempt to point out the relation between the microscopic characters and those which are discernible by the naked eye," *Medico-Chirurgical Transactions*, 1843a, 26: 242–285, p. 246. For a short review, see Thomas Hodgkin, "On the Characters and Structural Peculiarities of a group of Morbid Growths in which cancerous affections are included," *London Medical Gazette*, 1843b, 32: new series 2, 475–476.

10. Hodgkin (1843a), p. 245. Theodor Schwann (1810–1882) followed up on the work of the botanist Jacob Mathias Schleiden (1804–1881) of Hamburg, who showed that every part of a plant was made of groups of cells and that each cell had a controlling nucleus. Schwann showed that all vegetable and animal tissues are composed of and developed from cells.

11. Hodgkin (1843a), p. 246.

12. Ibid., p. 284.

13. Ibid., pp. 282, 285.

14. Thomas Hodgkin, *Lectures on The Morbid Anatomy of the Serous and Mucous Membranes*, 2 vols.; vol. 1, *On The Serous Membranes; and, as appended subjects, Parasitical Animals, Malignant Adventitious Structures, and the Indications Afforded by Colour* (London: Sherwood, Gilbert, and Piper, 1836), p. 276.

15. Thomas Hodgkin, "On the Uses of the Spleen," *Edinburgh Medical and Surgical Journal*, 1822, 18: 83–91.

16. Thomas Hodgkin, "Description of an ovarian tumor," in "Case of The Successful Removal of a Large Ovarian Tumor, by Dr. Frederic Bird," *London Medical Gazette*, 1843–44, new series, 1: 832–837, pp. 835–837.

17. Thomas Hodgkin, "Cases Illustrative of Some Consequences of Local Injury," *Medico-Chirurgical Transactions*, 1848, 31: 253–283, p. 282.

18. Ibid., pp. 282–283; Hodgkin (1843a), p. 270.

19. Wilson I. B. Onuigbo, "The Paradox of Virchow's Views on Cancer Metastasis" *Bulletin of the History of Medicine*, 1962, 36: 444–449, p. 444.

20. Erwin H. Ackerknecht, *Medicine at the Paris Hospital 1794–1848* (Baltimore, Md.: The Johns Hopkins Press, 1967), pp. 105–107.

21. Hodgkin (Wilks, 1878), p. 112.

22. Ibid., p. 113.

23. Thomas Hodgkin, *A Letter Addressed to the Inhabitants of Bridge Street, Blackfriars, and its Vicinity, Respecting the Establishment of a Dispensary for Diseases of the Skin* (London: William Watts, 1844a), 11 pages, p. 7.

24. Ibid., pp. 7–8.

25. Ibid., p. 4.

26. Ibid., p. 9.

27. These were Linnean Society (1788), Mineralogical Society (1799), Royal Horticultural Society (1804), Geological Society of London (1807), Chemical Society (1809), Astronomical Society (1820), Royal Geographical Society (1830), Entomological Society of London (1833), Royal Statistical Society (1834), Botanical Society of London (1836), Ornithological Society (1837), and Royal Microscopical Society (1839). Everett Mendelsohn, "The Emergence of Science as a Profession in Nineteenth-Century Europe," (pp. 3–48), in *The Management of Scientists*, Karl Hill, ed. (Boston: Beacon Press, 1964), pp. 27, 47. Numerous medical societies were also formed during these and following years.

28. Thomas Hodgkin, "Address in Support of the Cause from the Secretary of the Society," *The Colonial Intelligencer; or, Aborigines' Friend*, 1852–54, 4: 186–187. In 1909, short on finances, and faced with constantly increasing numbers of uncivilized peoples coming under British rule, the APS merged with the British and Foreign Anti-Slavery Society, formed in 1839, to become the Anti-Slavery and Aborigines' Protection Society. In 1947 the name was shortened to the Anti-Slavery Society, and in 1956 it was changed again to The Anti-Slavery Society, for the Protection of Human Rights.

29. The discussion of the causes and events leading to the formation of the Ethnological Society by members of the APS is derived from George W. Stocking, Jr., "What's In a Name? The Origins of the Royal Anthropological Institute (1837–71)," *Man*, 1971, 6: 369–390, pp. 371–372; Ronald Rainger, "Philanthropy and Science in the 1830's: The British and Foreign Aborigines' Protection Society," *Man*, 1980, 15: 702–717, pp. 711–713. See also Thomas Hodgkin, "Report of the Committee to investigate the Varieties of the Human Race," *Report of the British Association for the Advancement of Science*, 1844b, 14: 93.

30. James Cowles Prichard, "On The Extinction of Human Races," *Monthly Chronicle*, 1839 (December), vol. 4.

31. Thomas Hodgkin, "On the Importance of Studying and Preserving the Languages Spoken by Uncivilized Nations, with the view of elucidating the Physical History of Man," *London and Edinburgh Philosophical Magazine and Journal of Science*, 1835, 7: 27–36, 94–106, pp. 101–104.

32. Thomas Hodgkin, "Varieties of Human Race. Queries respecting the Human Race, to be addressed to Travellers and others. Drawn up by a Committee of the British Association for the Advancement of Science, appointed in 1839,"

Report of the British Association for the Advancement of Science, 1840, 10: 447–458; also in 1841, 11: 332–339. For a reviewer's abstract, see "On Inquiries into the Races of Man," *Report of the British Association for the Advancement of Science*, 1841, 11: 52–55.

33. Stocking (1971), p. 372.

34. Thomas Hodgkin, "On the Dog as the Associate of Man," *Report of the British Association for the Advancement of Science*, 1844c, 14 (part 2): 81; "On the Tape-Worm as prevalent in Abyssinia," p. 85, (see also *Lancet*, 1844d, 2: 56–57); "On the Stature of the Guanches, the extinct Inhabitants of the Canary Islands," pp. 81–82.

35. "A Paper on the 'Dog,'" *Punch*, 1844e (October 12), 7 (#170): 159; "A Paper on the Dog," *Illustrated London News*, 1844f (October 5), 5 (#127): 220–221.

36. Thomas Hodgkin, "On the Dog, as the Companion of Man in his Geographical Distribution," *Zoologist*, 1845a, 3: 1097–1105.

37. Thomas Hodgkin, "On the Ancient Inhabitants of the Canary Islands," *Edinburgh New Philosophical Journal*, 1845b, 39: 372–386; see also Saul Jarcho, "An Anthropological Essay by Thomas Hodgkin," *Bulletin of the New York Academy of Medicine*, 1970, 46: 889–890.

38. Johann Friedrich Blumenbach (1752–1840) received the M.D. degree in 1775 from the University of Göttingen. He founded scientific anthropology and made the first reliable survey of the characteristics and distribution of the human "races" according to the standards and understanding of the time. He attacked all political or social abuses of anthropological data, particularly the notions of racial superiority. *Dictionary of Scientific Biography*, Charles Coulston Gillispie, ed. (New York: Charles Scribner's Sons, 1970), vol. 2, pp. 203–205.

39. Thomas Hodgkin, *Biographical Sketch of James Cowles Prichard, M.D. F.R.S. &c. Late President of The Ethnological Society. Read at the Meeting of the Society on the 28. 2mo. (February) 1849* (London: William Watts, 1849), 28 pages, pp. 24–25; Richard King, "Obituary of Thomas Hodgkin, M.D.," *Transactions of the Ethnological Society of London*, 1867, new series, 5: 341–345.

40. Samuel George Morton (1799–1851) graduated from the University of Pennsylvania Medical School in 1820 and received a second M.D. degree from Edinburgh University in 1823. Morton had a collection of over 1,000 human craniums, many of American Indians. Never a field anthropologist, he depended on military and naval officers, consuls, physicians, missionaries, and naturalists for skulls and their identification. His *Crania Americana* (1839) was a landmark in anthropology. *Dictionary of Scientific Biography*, Charles Coulston Gillispie, ed. (New York: Charles Scribner's Sons, 1974), vol. 9, pp. 540–541; *Dictionary of American Medical Biography*, Howard A. Kelly and Walter L. Burrage, eds. (New York: D. Appleton and Co., 1928), pp. 874–877.

41. Thomas Hodgkin, "On the Progress of Ethnology," *Edinburgh New Philosophical Journal,* 1844g, 36: 118–136, p. 126.

42. Thomas Hodgkin, "On the Object of Post Mortem Examinations, Being an Address delivered to the Pupils of Guy's Hospital, on the Opening of the Theatre of Morbid Anatomy, Jan. 28," *London Medical Gazette,* 1828, 2: 423–431, pp. 428–429.

43. Stocking (1971), pp. 373–374.

44. Ibid., p. 376.

45. Ibid., pp. 375–377, 381–383.

CHAPTER TWELVE

1. J. B. S. Jackson, "On a Particular Derangement of the Structure of the Spleen. Communicated (with some introductory remarks and comments) by Thomas Hodgkin," *Medico-Chirurgical Transactions,* 1846, 29: 277–282.

2. Thomas Hodgkin, *Cold, Hunger, and Want of Employment; with Suggestions for their Relief* (London: William Watts, 1847a), 8 pages, pp. 4, 5.

3. Ibid., pp. 5–6.

4. Ibid., pp. 7–8.

5. Thomas Carlyle wrote in 1839 that "for the idle man there is no place in this England of ours. He that will not work, and save according to his means, let him go elsewhither; . . . let him perish according to his necessity: there is no law juster than that." Thomas Carlyle, "Chartism," in *English and Other Critical Essays* (London: Everyman Edition, n.d.), p. 177. Quoted by Gertrude Himmelfarb, *The Idea of Poverty. England in the Early Industrial Age* (New York: Alfred A. Knopf, 1984), p. 194.

6. David Owen, *English Philanthropy 1660–1960* (Cambridge, Mass.: The Belknap Press of Harvard University Press, 1964), pp. 4–5.

7. Typhus, typhoid fever, and "fever" were not distinguished in the compilation of diseases until 1869. They are caused by different microorganisms.

8. Charles Singer and E. Ashworth Underwood, *A Short History of Medicine,* 2d ed. (New York: Oxford University Press, 1962), p. 213; George Rosen, "Economic and Social Policy in the Development of Public Health. An Essay in Interpretation," *Journal of the History of Medicine and Allied Sciences,* 1953, 8: 406–430, p. 424.

9. Elizabeth Isichei, *Victorian Quakers* (London: Oxford University Press, 1970), p. 230.

10. Ibid., pp. 230–232.

11. Thomas Clarkson, *A Portraiture of Quakerism. Taken From a View of the Education and Discipline, Social Manners, Civil and Political Economy, Reli-*

gious Principles and Character, of the Society of Friends, 3 vols. (New York: Samuel Stansbury, 1806), vol. 3, p. 214.

12. Thomas Hodgkin, *A Letter to Richard Cobden, M.P. on Free Trade and Slave Labour* (London: W. Watts, 1848), 16 pages, pp. 14–16.

13. Ibid., p. 1.

14. Medical Registration Committee, "Minutes of Evidence before the Parliamentary Committee, Tuesday, June 27th, 1848, given by Thomas Hodgkin," *Lancet,* 1849, 1: 147–148, 171–172.

15. M. Jeanne Peterson, *The Medical Profession in Mid-Victorian London* (Berkeley: University of California Press, 1978), pp. 22–23, 30–34, 116–118, 123, 157.

16. Thomas Hodgkin, *Medical Reform. An Address read to The Harveian Society, at the Opening of its Seventeenth Session, October 2, 1847* (London: John Churchill, 1847b), 18 pages, p. 5.

17. "Account of an Examination at Apothecaries Hall, 1832," *Lancet,* 1832–33, 1:695–698.

18. S. W. F. Holloway, "Medical Education in England, 1830–1858: A Sociological Analysis," *History,* 1964, 49: 299–324, pp. 312–313; John D. Comrie, *History of Scottish Medicine,* 2 vols., 2nd ed., published for The Wellcome Historical Medical Museum (London: Baillière, Tindall & Cox, 1932), vol. 2, p. 575; "Report from the Select Committee of the House of Commons on Medical Education; with the Minutes of Evidence, and Appendix," *The Edinburgh Review, or, Critical Journal,* 1845, 81: 257.

19. A. P. Thomson, "The Influence of The General Medical Council on Education," *British Medical Journal,* 1958, 2: 1248–1250.

20. S. W. F. Holloway, "The Apothecaries' Act, 1815: A Reinterpretation. Part 1: The Origins of the Act," *Medical History,* 1966, 10: 107–129, p. 108.

21. *Lancet,* 1829–30, 2: 693.

22. Holloway (1966), p. 108.

23. Holloway (1964), p. 314.

24. Thomson (1958), p. 1248.

25. *London and Provincial Medical Directory (1847),* pp. xv–xvi. Quoted by Holloway (1964), p. 313; see also pp. 307–313.

26. Hodgkin (1847b), p. 3.

27. Holloway (1966), p. 125. For an editorial reaction, see *Lancet,* 1825–26, 2: 625–627. For a discussion of events and circumstances leading to passage of the Apothecaries' Act, see Holloway (1966), pp. 107–129. For aftereffects, see Holloway (1966), Part 2. The Consequences of the Act, pp. 221–236.

28. Holloway (1966), pp. 126–128.

29. F. B. Smith, *The People's Health 1830–1910* (New York: Holmes & Meier Publishers, 1979), p. 376. For a collection of excerpts from contemporary novels,

see Myron F. Brightfield, "The Medical Profession in Early Victorian England, As Depicted in the Novels of the Period (1840–1870)," *Bulletin of the History of Medicine*, 1961, 35: 238–256. For how this perception affected career choices, see Peterson (1978), pp. 196, 205–206; *Lancet*, 1858, 2: 365.

30. Hodgkin (1847b), p. 12.

31. Letter from Thomas Hodgkin to Thomas Nunneley, F.R.C.S., of Leeds, August 2, 1843. From the files of the Royal College of Physicians, London.

32. Hodgkin (1847b), pp. 13–15, 18.

33. D. B. Horn, *A Short History of the University of Edinburgh 1556–1889* (Edinburgh: The University Press, 1967), p. 113.

34. Peterson (1978), pp. 30–35.

35. Holloway (1964), p. 322; Peterson (1978), p. 65.

36. Holloway (1964), p. 299; Peterson (1978), p. 35.

37. Holloway (1964), pp. 305, 323–324.

38. For a short review of the history of quackery in Europe and America, and of some notorious quacks, see Walter P. Steiner, "The Conflict of Medicine with Quackery," *Annals of Medical History*, 1924, 6:60–70.

39. Charles Singer and S. W. F. Holloway, "Early Medical Education in England in Relation to the Pre-History of London University," *Medical History*, 1960, 4: 1–17, p. 4; Peterson (1978), p. 32; F. N. L. Poynter, "The Centenary of the General Medical Council," *British Medical Journal*, 1958, 2:1245–1248.

40. The unofficial *Medical Directory* of 1856 listed 10,220 practitioners, of whom 3.9 percent were graduates from Oxford, Cambridge, and London universities, or fellows, licentiates or extra-licentiates of the Royal College of Physicians. The remainder had diplomas from the Royal College of Surgeons of England (18.5%), the Society of Apothecaries of London (11.8%), or from both (54.6%); Scottish diplomas (7.0%), Irish diplomas (0.4%), foreign diplomas (0.4%), and in practice before the Apothecaries' Act went into effect in 1815 (3.4%). Singer and Holloway (1960), p. 4.

41. Peterson (1978), pp. 36, 90.

42. Richard H. Shryock, "Public Relations of the Medical Profession in Great Britain and the United States: 1600–1870. A Chapter in the Social History of Medicine," *Annals of Medical History*, 1930, new series, 2:308–339, pp. 314, 315, 312.

43. Ibid., p. 312.

44. Hodgkin (1847b), pp. 9–10.

CHAPTER THIRTEEN

1. Louise Creighton, *Life and Letters of Thomas Hodgkin* [1831–1913] (London: Longmans, Green, and Co., 1917), p. 18. This is the date in the Digest

of Marriages, *The Friend*, 1850, 8: 37, and in the *DNB*, vol. 9, pp. 957–958. The *Hodgkin Pedigree Book* gives 1849, and this error was repeated by Michael Rose, *Curator of the Dead. Thomas Hodgkin (1798–1866)* (London: Peter Owen, 1981), pp. 127–128.

2. Amalie M. Kass and Edward H. Kass, *Perfecting the World. The Life and Times of Dr. Thomas Hodgkin 1798–1866* (Boston: Harcourt Brace Jovanovich Publishers, 1988), pp. 432–437, 599.

3. This address is now the center of the three houses occupied by the Architectural Association. A circular blue plaque states that this was the home of Thomas Wakley from 1828 until 1849. A similar plaque honoring Thomas Hodgkin was installed by the Greater London Council on July 15, 1985. It reads: "Thomas Hodgkin 1798–1866 Physician, Reformer, and Philanthropist lived here." "Hodgkin's plaque," *Lancet*, 1985, 2: 169. See also Kass and Kass (1988), p. 438.

4. Kass and Kass (1988), p. 458.

5. A Manual of Ethnological Inquiry; being a series of questions concerning the Human Race, prepared by a Sub-committee of the British Association for the Advancement of Science, appointed in 1851 (consisting of Dr. Hodgkin and Richard Cull, Esq.), and adapted for the use of travellers and others in studying the Varieties of Man. *Report of the British Association for the Advancement of Science*, 1852, pp. 243–252, p. 244.

6. Thomas Hodgkin and Louis Alexis Chamerovzow, "To Sir John Somerset Pakington, Bart., M.P., Principal Secretary of State for the Colonial Department," *Colonial Intelligencer; or, Aborigines' Friend*, 1852, 4: 51–55, p. 54.

7. Thomas Hodgkin and Louis Alexis Chamerovzow, "The New Zealand Bill," *Colonial Intelligencer; or, Aborigines' Friend*, 1852, 4: 63–73.

8. Thomas Hodgkin, "Address in Support of the Cause from the Secretary of the Society," *Colonial Intelligencer; or, Aborigines' Friend*, 1853–54, 4: 186–188, 213–219, 366–368, p. 215.

9. Thomas Hodgkin, "To the Duke of Newcastle, Principal Secretary of State for the Colonies," *Colonial Intelligencer; or, Aborigines' Friend*, 1853, 4: 223–226, p. 224.

10. Thomas Hodgkin, "Address of the Aborigines' Protection Society to the Inhabitants of the Cape," *Colonial Intelligencer; or, Aborigines' Friend*, 1854, 4: 308–311, p. 311. "Address to Sir George Grey, Bart.," Idem., pp. 339–342, p. 342.

11. Thomas Hodgkin, "On the Communications Between the Lymphatic System and the Veins: Provisional Report from the London Committee of the British Association for the Advancement of Science, Appointed to make an Experimental Inquiry into this Subject," *Association Medical Journal*, 1854, 2: 1012–1016. See also *Report of the BAAS*, 1836, 6: 289–290; for a summary, see *London Medical Gazette*, 1836, 18: 885–886.

12. Thomas Hodgkin, "On Diabetes," *Association Medical Journal*, 1854, 2: 915–918.

13. Thomas Hodgkin, "On Certain Forms of Cachexia," *Association Medical Journal*, 1854, 2: 963–967.

14. Thomas Hodgkin, "Dr. M'Cormick's Unrequited Public Services," *Association Medical Journal*, 1854, 2: 796. For additional examples of Hodgkin's generosity and kindness to friends and colleagues in raising money or writing recommendations, see Kass and Kass (1988), pp. 446–448.

15. Letter from Thomas Hodgkin to James Buchanan, March 19, 1856. From the files of the Historical Society of Pennsylvania, Philadelphia, Pennsylvania.

16. Thomas Hodgkin, "On the Closure of Arteries at their Origin, and on Some Morbid Changes of the Heart," *Medical Times & Gazette*, 1856, new series, 12: 409–411.

17. Microfilm collection, MSS #187 (reel 10).

18. Rose (1981), pp. 122–123.

19. *The Aborigines' Friend, and Colonial Intelligencer*, 1859–1866, new series, 2: 519–522.

20. Ibid.

21. *The Friend*, 1866, 6: 81–82. From the obituary in *The Morning Star* (newspaper), April 15, 1866.

22. *Lancet*, 1866, 1: 445–446.

23. Microfilm collection, MSS #187 (reel 10).

24. Rose (1981), p. 124.

25. Many London consultants earned more than £1,500 annually, some close to £10,000. M. Jeanne Peterson, *The Medical Profession in Mid-Victorian London* (Berkeley: University of California Press, 1978), pp. 155, 207ff. Advertisements for qualified assistants offered £30 to £35 a year. *Lancet* 1847, 2: 501, 528.

26. Microfilm collection, MSS #196 (reel 19); MSS #187 (reel 10); Kass and Kass (1988), pp. 36, 102, 120, 129–131, 371, 428, 448, 509, 614.

27. Amalie M. Kass, "Friends and Philanthropists: Montefiore and Dr. Hodgkin," in *The Century of Moses Montefiore*, Sonia and V. D. Lipman, eds. (New York: Oxford University Press, 1985), p. 79; Kass and Kass (1988), p. 193.

28. Microfilm collection, MSS #187 (reel 10).

29. Thomas Hodgkin, *A Lecture Introductory to the Course on the Practice of Medicine. Delivered at St. Thomas's Hospital, at the Commencement of the Session 1842–3* (London: Richard Watts, 1842), 22 pages, p. 20.

30. "Testimonial to Dr. Hodgkin (by Justus)," *Lancet*, 1856, 2: 557.

31. "Royal Medical Benevolent College," *Lancet*, 1861, 1: 524.

32. Lucien Wolf, *Sir Moses Montefiore. A Centennial Biography with Selections from Letters and Journals* (New York: Harper & Brothers, 1885), p. 210;

Paul Goodman, *Moses Montefiore* (London: George Routledge & Sons, 1925), p. 218.

33. *Diaries of Sir Moses and Lady Montefiore. Comprising Their Life and Work as Recorded in Their Diaries From 1812 to 1883*, Louis Loewe, ed., 2 vols. (London: Griffith Farran Okeden & Welsh, 1890). Facsimile of the 1890 edition published by The Jewish Historical Society of England and The Jewish Museum (London: 1983), vol. 1, p. 55; see also vol. 2, pp. 32, 37.

34. For Montefiore's account of the 1857 visit, see Montefiore Diaries (1890), vol. 2, pp. 63–71.

35. Letter from Thomas Hodgkin to Hudson Gurney, July 28, 1857. From the microfilm collection, MSS #190 (reel 13). For observations on fund-raising and its abuses, see James Finn, *Stirring Times*, 2 vols. (London: C. Kegan Paul & Co., 1878), vol. 1, pp. 121–126.

36. F. O. 78/1383 (Political No. 1) January 1, 1858, James Finn to the Earl of Clarendon, in Albert M. Hyamson, ed., *The British Consulate in Jerusalem in Relation to the Jews of Palestine 1838–1914*, part I (1838–1861) (London: The Jewish Historical Society of England, 1939), No. 190, p. 257. Published for the Society by Edward Goldston Ltd.

37. Thomas Hodgkin, "Mechanics' Institution at Jerusalem," *The Journal of the [Royal] Society of Arts, and of the Institutions in Union* (London), 1857 (September 4), 5: 579–581. See chapter 4, note 1 (and text) for discussion of Mechanics' Institute.

38. Kass and Kass (1988), p. 453.

38. Thomas Hodgkin, "On the Isthmus of Suez, communicated by Dr. Norton Shaw," *Literary Gazette and Journal of Archaeology, Science, and Art*, 1857 (October 17), No. 2126, pp. 1005–1006; Thomas Hodgkin, "On the proposed Ship Canal through the Isthmus of Suez," *Report of the British Association for the Advancement of Science*, 1857, part 2, p. 199; *The Railway Times*, 1857 (September 19), vol. 20, No. 38, pp. 1354–1355.

40. Montefiore Diaries (1890), vol. 1, p. 31. For the British consul's report on the plans for a railroad, see James Finn to the Earl of Clarendon, June 6, 1857, F.O. 78/1294 (Political No. 23), in Hyamson, ed., No. 184, pp. 246–248. The railroad was eventually built by a French company and opened in 1892.

41. Thomas Hodgkin (comments), "On the Bayanos River, Isthmus of Panama, by Laurence Oliphant, Secy., R.G.S.," *Proceedings of the Royal Geographical Society*, 1865, 9: 280.

42. Samuel Wilks, "Hodgkin and Sir Moses Montefiore," *Guy's Hospital Gazette*, 1910, 24: 13–14.

43. For a discussion of the known portraits and photographs of Thomas Hodgkin, see Amalie M. Kass and Edward H. Kass, "The Thomas Hodgkin Portraits: A Case of Mistaken Identity," *Medical History*, 1985, 29: 259–263.

44. For Montefiore's account of the Rome visit, see Diaries (1890), vol. 2, pp. 82–99.

45. *New Catholic Encyclopedia* (New York: McGraw-Hill Book Company, 1967), vol. 9, p. 1153.

46. Bertram Wallace Korn, *The American Reaction to The Mortara Case: 1858–1859* (Cincinnati, Ohio: The American Jewish Archives, 1957); see also Morton Borden, *Jews, Turks, and Infidels* (Chapel Hill, N.C.: The University of North Carolina Press, 1984), pp. 54–56.

47. Wolf (1885), p. 158.

48. Letter from J. J. Roberts to Thomas Hodgkin, May 8, 1849. From the archives of Rhodes House, MSS. Brit. Emp. s.18, C122/57, C122/58. For criticism of the American Colonization Society for its motives and Roberts for his subservience to its white officials, see Martin Robison Delany, *The Condition, Elevation, Emigration, and Destiny of the Colored People of the United States,* published by the author, (1852) (New York: Arno Press and The New York Times, 1968 reprint), pp. 31–32, 169.

49. The letter and reply appeared in the *Colonization Herald* (newspaper), new series, No. 105, March 1859, p. 416 (col. 1 and 2). Published by the Philadelphia Colonization Society.

50. Elected in 1851, Hodgkin was the first to hold this position continuously for 11 years. As honorary secretary he handled general matters. From 1862 to 1865, he was foreign secretary and dealt with overseas matters.

51. Delany was one of three blacks admitted for the first time to Harvard Medical School in 1850. After only two months of attendance, they were asked to leave on account of the objections of some students. "Trouble among the Medical Students, of Harvard University," *The Boston Medical and Surgical Journal,* 1850–51, 43: 406; Philip Cash, "Pride, Prejudice, and Politics," *Harvard Medical Alumni Bulletin,* 1980, 54: 20–25. See also Louis Rosenfeld, "Martin Robison Delany (1812–1885): Physician, Black Separatist, Explorer, Soldier," *Bulletin of the New York Academy of Medicine,* 1989, 65: 801–818; Amalie M. Kass, "Dr. Thomas Hodgkin, Dr. Martin Delany, and the 'Return to Africa,' " *Medical History,* 1983, 27: 373–393.

52. Delany (1852), p. 45.

53. *Proceedings of the Royal Geographical Society,* 1859, 4: 186.

54. *Anti-Slavery Reporter,* 1859, new series, 7: 224–225.

55. Richard Blackett, "In Search of International Support for African Colonization: Martin R. Delany's Visit to England, 1860," *Canadian Journal of History,* 1975, 10: 307–324, p. 314.

56. Letter from Thomas Hodgkin to H. H. Garnet, August 29, 1860. From the microfilm collection, MSS #195 (reel 18); also in Kass (1983), p. 389.

57. M. R. Delany, "Official Report of The Niger Valley Exploring Party," in

M. R. Delany and Robert Campbell, *Search For a Place. Black Separatism and Africa, 1860* (Ann Arbor: University of Michigan Press, 1969 reprint), p. 122.

58. Martin Delany and Robert Campbell, "Geographical Observations on Western Africa," *Proceedings of the Royal Geographical Society*, 1860, 4: 218–222.

59. Delany (1860), pp. 129, 138; also in Kass (1983), pp. 387–388.

60. Letter from Thomas Hodgkin to R. Arthington, Jr., June 12, 1860. From the microfilm collection, MSS #195 (reel 18); also in Kass (1983), pp. 385, 387–388.

61. Montefiore Diaries (1890), vol. 2, pp. 112–114; Great Britain Public Record Office, FO 78/1549. Sir Culling Eardley to Lord John Russell, August 1, 1860.

62. Syrian Medical-Aid Association, *British and Foreign Medical Review*, 1842 (Jan.–April), 13: 579–580. For reports of its activities, see *Lancet*, 1842–43, 1: 867–870; also in *London Medical Gazette*, 1842–43, 31: 905–908; *Lancet*, 1842–43, 2: 454; 1843–44, 1: 755–759, 764–767; 1860, 2: 419, 442. For the political and missionary objectives of medical aid, see Amalie M. Kass, "The Syrian Medical Aid Association: British Philanthropy in the Near East," *Medical History*, 1987, 31: 143–159. For Hodgkin's involvement with the Syrian Medical Aid Association, see Kass and Kass (1988), pp. 363–372.

63. Great Britain Public Record Office, FO 78/1551. Sir Moses Montefiore to Lord John Russell, October 16, 1860; also in Montefiore Diaries (1890), vol. 2, pp. 117–120.

64. Great Britain Public Record Office, FO 78/1628. Lord Dufferin to Sir Henry Bulwer, February 24, 1861. See also Kass (1985), p. 89.

65. Kass and Kass (1988), p. 501.

66. *Anti-Slavery Reporter*, 1861, new series, 9: 265.

67. Thomas Hodgkin (comments), "Progress of the British North American Expedition," *Proceedings of the Royal Geographical Society*, 1857–58 (November 1857), 1st series, 2: 51–52; Thomas Hodgkin (comments), "British Columbia. Journeys in the Districts bordering on the Fraser, Thompson, and Harrison Rivers, by Lieuts Mayne, R.N., and Palmer, R. E., and Chief-Justice M. Begbie," *Proceedings of the Royal Geographical Society*, 1859–60 (December 1859), 4: 36–37.

68. Thomas Hodgkin, "A Proposal to Form a New Indian Settlement," *The Aborigines' Friend, and Colonial Intelligencer*, 1859–66 (November 1859), new series, 2: 96–98. The proposal is on pp. 92–96.

69. Thomas Hodgkin, "Address to the Duke of Newcastle," *The Aborigines' Friend, and Colonial Intelligencer*, 1859–66 (July 1859), new series, 2: 51–61, pp. 51–53ff, 56ff.

70. Letter from Thomas Hodgkin to John Ross, October 26, 1861. From the archives of the New York Yearly Meeting of the Religious Society of Friends.

71. Howard Temperley, *British Antislavery. 1833–1870* (Columbia, S.C.: University of South Carolina Press, 1972), pp. 258–260.

72. See note 21 above.

CHAPTER FOURTEEN

1. For editorials and numerous letters to the editor in a lively exchange on tobacco and smoking, pro and con, see *Lancet*, 1856, 2: 699, and issues number 1740–1753 from January 3 to April 4, 1857.

2. Thomas Hodgkin, Preface, in *Fifty-four objections to tobacco*, by Thomas Reynolds (London: 1862), 10 pages.

3. Thomas Hodgkin, "Physical, Moral, and Social Effects of Tobacco," read at Bradford, at a Meeting of the National Association for the Promotion of Social Science, 1859, *The Anti-Tobacco Journal*, 1859–60 (November 1859), 2: 1.

4. Thomas Hodgkin, "Remarks from Social Science Congress at Bradford, Yorkshire, 1859," *The Anti-Tobacco Journal*, 1866 (June), 7–8: 86.

5. R. B. Walker, "Medical Aspects of Tobacco Smoking and the Anti-Tobacco Movement in Britain in the Nineteenth Century," *Medical History*, 1980, 24: 391–402, p. 393.

6. Thomas Hodgkin (resolution proposed), "The Pharmacopoeial Weights and Measures," *British Medical Journal*, 1862, 2: 178.

7. Thomas Hodgkin, "On the Weights to be Used in Medicine," *British Medical Journal*, 1862, 2: 197–198.

8. For a review of earlier and later efforts to introduce the metric system, see Bernard Semmel, "Parliament and the Metric System," *Isis*, 1963, 54: 125–133.

9. *Diaries of Sir Moses and Lady Montefiore, Comprising Their Life and Work as Recorded in Their Diaries From 1812 to 1883*, Louis Loewe, ed., 2 vols. (London: Griffith Farran Okeden & Welsh, 1890). Facsimile of the 1890 edition published by The Jewish Historical Society of England and The Jewish Museum (London: 1983), vol. 2, pp. 141–142.

10. Thomas Hodgkin, "On Nightmare, the Action of Anaesthetics, etc.," *British Medical Journal*, 1863, 1: 501–502.

11. Amalie M. Kass and Edward H. Kass, *Perfecting the World. The Life and Times of Dr. Thomas Hodgkin 1798–1866* (Boston: Harcourt Brace Jovanovich Publishers, 1988), p. 490.

12. Montefiore Diaries (1890), vol. 2, pp. 142–143.

13. Thomas Hodgkin, *Narrative of a Journey to Morocco, in 1863 and 1864, with Geological Annotations* (London: T. Cautley Newby, 1866), p. 1; Lucien Wolf, *Sir Moses Montefiore. A Centennial Biography with Selections from Letters and Journals* (New York: Harper & Brothers, 1885), pp. 189–205. For analysis

of the foreign policy aspects and sequence of events leading to Sir Moses's trip, see David Littman, "Mission to Morocco (1863–1864)," in *The Century of Moses Montefiore*, Sonia and V. D. Lipman, eds. (New York: Oxford University Press, 1985), pp. 171–229. The Morocco trip is described in the Montefiore Diaries (1890), vol. 2, pp. 145–161.

14. The actual Jewish population of Morocco was then probably not more than 100,000. The enlarged figure may have been an attempt to impress public opinion with the importance of Moroccan Jewry and the magnitude of the injustice. Littman (1985), pp. 194, 227; Wolf (1885), p. 204.

15. Jews had to wear discriminatory clothing and walk barefoot outside the Jewish quarter. They were regularly stoned, cursed, and spat upon. Murder of Jews in Morocco was a common occurrence. Littman (1985), pp. 171–173, 197, 199.

16. Hodgkin Narrative (1866), p. 4.

17. Ibid., pp. 30–31.

18. Ibid., pp. 77–78. The visit to the capital city is described on pp. 68–87.

19. Ibid., pp. 79–80.

20. Ibid., p. 122.

21. Littman (1985), p. 195.

22. Hodgkin Narrative (1866), p. 86.

23. Thomas Hodgkin, "On some superficial Geological Appearances in North-Western Morocco, abridged from Notes taken during the late Mission of Sir Moses Montefiore to Morocco," *Proceedings of the Royal Geographical Society*, 1864–65, 1st series, 9: 24–27.

24. Hodgkin Narrative (1866), pp. 153–157.

25. The Jewish community in England about 1830 ranged between 25,000 and 30,000, of which at least two-thirds lived in London. Cecil Roth, *A History of The Jews in England*, 3rd ed. (Oxford: Clarendon Press, 1964), p. 241. Quaker membership in England and Wales in 1840 had fallen to 16,227. Elizabeth Isichei, *Victorian Quakers* (London: Oxford University Press, 1970), pp. xxv, 112. Quakers were admitted to Parliament in 1828, Jews not until 1858. For similarities between Anglo-Jewry and The Society of Friends, see Chaim Bermant, *The Cousinhood* (New York: Macmillan, 1971), pp. 423–428.

26. Moses Montefiore, "Sir Moses Montefiore's Report to the Board of Deputies of British Jews," *The Jewish Chronicle and Hebrew Observer* (newspaper), September 28, 1866, p. 4, col. 2.

27. Thomas Hodgkin (letter to the editor), "Dwellings For The Poor," *The Morning Star* (newspaper), April 4, 1866, p. 6, col. 5–6.

28. The events of this trip relating to Hodgkin are described in Montefiore Diaries (1890), vol. 2, pp. 172–173, 180, and in Chronicle and Observer (1866), p. 5, col. 1 and p. 7, col. 1.

29. Dr. Thomas Chaplin received his medical training at Guy's Hospital. He was a medical missionary assigned to the Jerusalem Hospital in December 1860 by the London Society For Promoting Christianity Amongst The Jews. W. T. Gidney, *The History of the London Society For Promoting Christianity Amongst The Jews, From 1809 to 1908* (London: London Society For Promoting Christianity Amongst The Jews, 1908), pp. 325, 377.

30. Hodgkin Narrative (1866), pp. ii–iv.

31. Ibid., pp. v–vi. The obituaries in *Lancet, British Medical Journal,* and the *Medical Times and Gazette,* all give April 5 as the day of Hodgkin's death. So does the *DNB,* vol. 9, pp. 957–958, which probably obtained the date from the obituaries. Sir Moses received "the melancholy tidings . . . during the night of the 5th of April." *The Times* of London (newspaper) printed a notice on Thursday April 12 (p. 7, col. 4) stating, "A telegram, dated 'Jerusalem, 5th April,' has been received in London, announcing the death of Dr. Hodgkin at Jaffa, after a severe attack of dysentery." This notice may be the source of the error.

32. Letter from Thomas Hodgkin to Mrs. Hodgkin, April 1, 1866. Microfilm collection, MSS #192 (reel 15). A shorter version appears in Hodgkin Narrative (1866), pp. vi–vii.

33. Chronicle and Observer (1866), p. 8, col. 2; Montefiore Diaries (1890), vol. 2, pp. 188, 190.

34. *Medical Times and Gazette,* April 14, 1866, p. 403; Montefiore Diaries (1890), vol. 2, pp. 172–173, 179, 181; see also note 31 above.

35. Moses Montefiore, *A Narrative of a Forty Days' Sojourn In The Holy Land,* 2d ed. (London: Wertheimer, Lea and Co., 1877), pp. 43–148, pp. 60, 63, 68; see also *Montefiore Diaries* (1890), vol. 2, p. 274.

36. Samuel J. Zakon, "Thomas Hodgkin, M.D. The 90th Anniversary of His Death," *Quarterly Bulletin of the Northwestern University Medical School,* 1956, 30: 362–364.

37. Hyman Morrison, "Thomas Hodgkin," *New England Journal of Medicine,* 1954, 251: 946–948.

38. P. E. Thompson Hancock, "Thomas Hodgkin," The FitzPatrick Lecture, *Journal of the Royal College of Physicians of London,* 1968, 2: 404–421.

39. Ibid., p. 418; S. Lazarus, "A Visit to the Grave of Thomas Hodgkin," *Scottish Medical Journal,* 1963, 8: 312–313; William B. Bean, "Thomas Hodgkin's Tomb," *Archives of Internal Medicine,* 1966, 117: 475–477; see also K. Aterman, "Thomas Hodgkin (1798–1866)," *American Journal of Dermatopathology,* 1986, 8: 157–167.

40. For appeals to restore the gravesite, see *Lancet,* 1978, 2: 1059, 1150; 1979, 1: 509.

CHAPTER FIFTEEN

1. Geoffrey Keynes, "The Life and Works of Sir Astley Cooper, Bart.," *St. Bartholomew's Hospital Reports*, 1922, 55: 9–36, pp. 17–18; Charters J. Symonds, "Astley Cooper," *Guy's Hospital Reports*, 1922, 72: 1–18, pp. 14–15.

2. "The Late Dr. Hodgkin," *The Aborigines' Friend, and Colonial Intelligencer*, 1859–66, new series, 2: 519–522, p. 520.

3. H. C. Cameron, *Mr. Guy's Hospital 1726–1948* (London: Longmans, Green and Co., 1954), p. 133.

4. E. H. Kass, "Thomas Hodgkin, Physician and Social Scientist," *Guy's Hospital Reports*, 1966, 115: 269–280, p. 276.

5. P. E. Thompson Hancock, "Thomas Hodgkin," The FitzPatrick Lecture, *Journal of the Royal College of Physicians of London*, 1968, 2: 404–421, pp. 419–420.

6. Michael Rose, *Curator of the Dead. Thomas Hodgkin (1798–1866)* (London: Peter Owen, 1981), p. 136.

7. Letter from Thomas Hodgkin to Mrs. Hodgkin, April 1, 1866. From the microfilm collection, MSS #192 (reel 15).

8. Rose (1981), p. 30. Quoted from the unpublished autobiography of Hodgkin's namesake nephew.

9. G.E.H. Foxon, "Thomas Hodgkin, 1798–1866. A Biographical Note," *Guy's Hospital Reports*, 1966, 115: 243–254, pp. 246, 247.

10. Kass (1966), p. 277.

11. Ben Friedman, "Thomas Hodgkin—A Maverick in his Time," *Alabama Journal of Medical Sciences*, 1975, 12: 250–251.

12. K. Aterman, "Thomas Hodgkin (1798–1866)," *American Journal of Dermatopathology*, 1986, 8: 157–167, p. 163.

13. S. Wilks and G. T. Bettany, *A Biographical History of Guy's Hospital* (London: Ward, Lock, Bowden & Co., 1892), p. 380.

14. Hyman Morrison, "Thomas Hodgkin," *New England Journal of Medicine*, 1954, 251: 946–948; C. Hardwicke, "Thomas Hodgkin 1798–1866," *Guy's Hospital Reports*, 1966, 115: 255–261, pp. 257, 260, 261; Hancock (1968), pp. 415, 419; Friedman (1975), 250–251; Aterman (1986), pp. 157, 161.

Bibliography

BOOKS AND MONOGRAPHS

Ackerknecht, Erwin H. *Medicine at the Paris Hospital 1794–1848.* Baltimore, Md.: The Johns Hopkins Press, 1967.

Allen, William. *Life of . . .* **with Selections from His Correspondence,** 3 vols. London: Charles Gilpin, 1846.

Baillie, Matthew. *The Morbid Anatomy of Some of The Most Important Parts of the Human Body,* 1st ed. London: J. Johnson and G. Nicol, 1793.

Barlow, Nora, ed. *The Autobiography of Charles Darwin 1809–1882.* New York: Harcourt, Brace and Company, 1958.

Bermant, Chaim. *The Cousinhood.* New York: Macmillan, 1971.

Bishop, W. J. "The Evolution of the General Practitioner in England." In *Science Medicine and History. Essays on the Evolution of Scientific Thought and Medical Practice* (2 vols.), E. Ashworth Underwood, ed., vol. 2. London: Geoffrey Cumberlege, Oxford University Press, 1953.

Borden, Morton. *Jews, Turks, and Infidels.* Chapel Hill, N.C.: The University of North Carolina Press, 1984.

Bradbury, S. *The Evolution of the Microscope.* Oxford: Pergamon Press, 1967.

Cameron, H. C. *Mr. Guy's Hospital 1726–1948.* London: Longmans, Green and Co., 1954.

Carswell, Robert. *An Atlas of Illustrations of Pathology Compiled (Chiefly from Original Sources) for the New Sydenham Society.* London, 1898.

Cassedy, James H. *American Medicine and Statistical Thinking, 1800–1860.* Cambridge, Mass.: Harvard University Press, 1984.

Christison, Bart, Sir Robert, The Life of, edited by his sons (2 vols.), vol. 1. Edinburgh and London: William Blackwood and Sons, 1885.

Clark, George. *A History of The Royal College of Physicians of London,* 2 vols. Oxford: Clarendon Press, 1964, 1966.

Clarke, J. F. *Autobiographical Recollections of the Medical Profession.* London: J. & A. Churchill, 1874.

Clarkson, Thomas. *A Portraiture of Quakerism, Taken From a View of the Education and Discipline, Social Manners, Civil and Political Economy, Religious Principles and Character, of the Society of Friends* (3 vols.), vols. 1 and 2. New York: Samuel Stansbury, 1806.

Comrie, John D. *History of Scottish Medicine* (2 vols.), 2nd ed. Published for The Wellcome Historical Medical Museum. London: Baillière, Tindall & Cox, 1932.

Conybeare, W. D., and Phillips, William. *Outlines of the Geology of England and Wales, with an Introductory Compendium of the General Principles of that Science, and Comparative Views of the Structure of Foreign Countries.* London: William Phillips, 1822.

Creighton, Louise. *Life and Letters of Thomas Hodgkin* [1831–1913]. London: Longmans, Green, and Co., 1917.

Cripps, Ernest C. *Plough Court. The Story of a Notable Pharmacy. 1715–1927.* London: Allen & Hanburys Limited, 1927.

Crowther, M. A. *The Workhouse System 1834–1929.* London: Batsford, 1981.

Curtin, Philip D. *The Image of Africa. British Ideas and Action, 1780–1850.* Madison: The University of Wisconsin Press, 1964.

Delany, M. R. "Official Report of The Niger Valley Exploring Party." In M. R. Delany and Robert Campbell. *Search For a Place. Black Separatism and Africa, 1860.* Ann Arbor: University of Michigan Press, 1969 (reprint).

Delany, Martin Robison. *The Condition, Elevation, Emigration, and Destiny of the Colored People of the United States,* published by the author, (1852). New York: Arno Press and The New York Times, 1968 (reprint).

Dutton, Geoffrey. *Edward John Eyre. The Hero as Murderer.* New York: Penguin Books, 1977.

Edwards, W. F. *On the Influence of Physical Agents on Life* (translated from the French by Dr. Hodgkin and Dr. Fisher). London: S. Highley, 1832.

Finn, James. *Stirring Times* (2 vols.), vol. 1. London: C. Kegan Paul & Co., 1878.

Flinn, M. W. "Medical Services Under the New Poor Law." In *The New Poor Law in the Nineteenth Century*, Derek Fraser, ed. London: Macmillan, 1976.

Gardner, Brian. *The African Dream*. London: Cassell, 1970.

Garratt, G. T. *Lord Brougham*. London: MacMillan and Co. Ltd., 1935.

Garrison, Fielding H. *An Introduction to the History of Medicine*, 4th ed. Philadelphia: W. B. Saunders Company, 1929.

George, M. Dorothy. *Hogarth to Cruikshank: Social Change in Graphic Satire*. New York: Walker and Company, 1967.

————*Catalogue of Prints and Drawings in the British Museum: Department of Political and Personal Satires*, vol. 11 (1828–1832). London: British Museum, 1954.

Gibson, William. *Rambles In Europe in 1839 with Sketches of Prominent Surgeons, Physicians, Medical Schools, Hospitals, Literary Personages, Scenery, Etc.* Philadelphia: Lea and Blanchard, 1841.

Gidney, W. T. *The History of the London Society For Promoting Christianity Amongst The Jews, From 1809 to 1908*. London: London Society For Promoting Christianity Amongst The Jews, 1908.

Gillispie, Charles Coulston. *Genesis and Geology. A Study in the Relations of Scientific Thought, Natural Theology, and Social Opinion in Great Britain, 1790–1850*. Cambridge, Mass.: Harvard University Press, 1951.

Goodman, Paul. *Moses Montefiore*. London: George Routledge & Sons, 1925.

Grant, Alexander. *The Story of the University of Edinburgh During Its First Three Hundred Years*, 2 vols. London: Longmans, Green, and Co., 1884.

Guthrie, Douglas. *The Medical School of Edinburgh*. Published for the British Medical Association Meeting in Edinburgh, 1959.

Haagensen, C. D., and Lloyd, Wyndham E. B. *A Hundred Years of Medicine*. New York: Sheridan House, 1943.

Hale-White, William. *Translation of Selected Passages from De l'Auscultation Médiate, (first edition) by R. Théophile H. Laennec*. New York: William Wood & Co., 1923.

Hill, Christopher. *The World Turned Upside Down. Radical Ideas During the English Revolution*. London: Temple Smith, 1972.

Himmelfarb, Gertrude. *The Idea of Poverty. England in the Early Industrial Age*. New York: Alfred A. Knopf, 1984.

Hodgkin, Thomas. *A Catalogue of the Preparations in the Anatomical Museum of Guy's Hospital. Arranged and Edited by Desire of the Treasurer of the*

Hospital, and of the Teachers of the Medical and Surgical School. London: S. Highley, 1829.

————. Lectures on The Morbid Anatomy of the Serous and Mucous Membranes. vol. 1, On the Serous Membranes; and, as appended subjects, Parasitical Animals, Malignant Adventitious Structures, and the Indications Afforded by Colour. London: Sherwood, Gilbert, and Piper, 1836. Also an American edition, abridged. Philadelphia: 1838.

————. Lectures on The Morbid Anatomy of the Serous and Mucous Membranes. vol. 2, part I, On the Mucous Membranes. London: Simpkin, Marshall, & Co., 1840.

————.The Means of Promoting and Preserving Health, 2nd. ed., with additions. London: Simpkin, Marshall, & Co., 1841.

————.Narrative of a Journey To Morocco, in 1863 and 1864, with Geological Annotations. London: T. Cautley Newby, 1866; New York: Arno Press and The New York Times, 1971 (reprint).

Hodgkin, Thomas (compiled by). Hodgkin Pedigree Book (1644–1906), 1907 (privately printed).

Hodgkinson, Ruth G. The Origins of the National Health Service. The Medical Services of the New Poor Law, 1834–1871. Berkeley and Los Angeles: University of California Press, 1967.

Horn, D. B. A Short History of the University of Edinburgh 1556–1889. Edinburgh: The University Press, 1967.

Hume, Alexander Hamilton. The Life of Edward John Eyre, Late Governor of Jamaica. London: Richard Bentley, 1867.

Hunter, Richard, and Macalpine, Ida. Three Hundred Years of Psychiatry 1535–1860. London: Oxford University Press, 1963.

Hyamson, Albert M., ed. The British Consulate in Jerusalem in Relation to the Jews of Palestine 1838–1914. Part I, 1838–1861. London: The Jewish Historical Society of England, 1939. Published for the Society by Edward Goldston Ltd.

Isichei, Elizabeth. Victorian Quakers. London: Oxford University Press, 1970.

Kaplan, Henry S. Hodgkin's Disease, 2nd ed. Cambridge, Mass.: Harvard University Press, 1980.

Kass, Amalie M. "Friends and Philanthropists: Montefiore and Dr. Hodgkin." In The Century of Moses Montefiore, Sonia and V. D. Lipman, eds. New York: Oxford University Press, 1985. Published for The Littman Library of Jewish Civilization in Association with The Jewish Historical Society of England.

Kass, Amalie M., and Kass, Edward H. Perfecting the World. The Life and Times *of Dr. Thomas Hodgkin 1798–1866*. Boston: Harcourt Brace Jovanovich Publishers, 1988.

Kelly, Thomas. *George Birkbeck. Pioneer of Adult Education 1776–1841*. Liverpool: University Press, 1957.

King, Lester S. *The Growth of Medical Thought*. Chicago: The University of Chicago Press, 1963.

King, Richard. *Narrative of a Journey to the Shores of the Arctic Ocean, in 1833, 1834, and 1835; Under the Command of Capt. Back, R.N.* (2 vols.), vol. 2. London: Richard Bentley, 1836.

Korn, Bertram Wallace. *The American Reaction to The Mortara Case: 1858–1859*. Cincinnati, Ohio: The American Jewish Archives, 1957.

Littman, David. "Mission to Morocco (1863–1864)." In *The Century of Moses Montefiore*, Sonia and V. D. Lipman, eds. New York: Oxford University Press, 1985.

Major, Ralph H. *Classic Descriptions of Disease. With Biographical Sketches of the Authors*, 3rd ed. Springfield, Ill.: Charles C. Thomas, 1945.

Maulitz, Russell C. *Morbid Appearances. TheAnatomy of Pathology in the Early Nineteenth Century*. New York: Cambridge University Press, 1987.

Mendelsohn, Everett. "The Emergence of Science as a Profession in Nineteenth-Century Europe." In *The Management of Scientists*, Karl Hill, ed. Boston: Beacon Press, 1964.

Montefiore, Moses. *A Narrative Of A Forty Days' Sojourn In The Holy Land, Devoted To An Investigation Of The State Of Schools, Colleges, And Charitable Institutions. Given To The Friends And Well-Wishers Of Zion, By Sir Moses Montefiore Bart., F.R.S., On His Return From His Seventh Pilgrimage To The Land Of Promise. 9 Ellul, 5635. September 9th, 1875*, 2nd ed. London: Wertheimer, Lea and Co., 1877.

Montefiore, Sir Moses and Lady. *Diaries of . . . Comprising Their Life and Work as Recorded in Their Diaries From 1812 to 1883*, Louis Loewe, ed., 2 vols. London: Griffith Farran Okeden & Welsh, 1890. Facsimile of the 1890 edition published by The Jewish Historical Society of England and The Jewish Museum (London: 1983).

Morrell, J. B. "Medicine and Science in the Eighteenth Century." In *Four Centuries. Edinburgh Life. 1583–1983*, Gordon Donaldson, ed. Edinburgh: The University Press, 1983.

Morris, James. *Heaven's Command. An Imperial Progress*. New York: A Helen and Kurt Wolff Book, Harcourt Brace Jovanovich, 1973.

Morris, R. J. *Cholera 1832. The Social Response to an Epidemic.* London: Croom Helm, 1976.

Muehry, Adolph. *Observations on the Comparative State of Medicine in France, England, and Germany, During a Journey into these Countries in the Year 1835* (translated from the German by E. G. Davis). Philadelphia: A. Waldie, 1838.

Owen, David. *English Philanthropy 1660–1960.* Cambridge, Mass.: The Belknap Press of Harvard University Press, 1964.

Parsons, Frederick G. *The History of St. Thomas's Hospital* (3 vols.), vol. 3, *From 1800 to 1900.* London: Methuen & Co. Ltd., 1936.

Pelling, Margaret. *Cholera, Fever and English Medicine 1825–1865.* London: Oxford University Press, 1978.

Peterson, M. Jeanne. *The Medical Profession in Mid-Victorian London.* Berkeley: University of California Press, 1978.

Pettigrew, Thomas Joseph. "Sir Astley Paston Cooper, Bart." In *Medical Portrait Gallery. Biographical Memoirs of the most celebrated Physicians, Surgeons, etc., etc., who have contributed to The Advancement of Medical Science* (4 vols.), vol. 1. London: Fisher, Son, & Co., 1838.

Poynter, F. N. L. "Medical Education in England Since 1600." In *The History of Medical Education,* C. D. O'Malley, ed. Berkeley: University of California Press, 1970.

Quen, Jacques M. "A History of the Anglo-American Legal Psychiatry of Violence and Responsibility." In *Violence and Responsibility. The Individual, the Family and Society,* Robert L. Sadoff, ed. New York: SP Medical & Scientific Books (distributed by Halsted Press), 1978.

Reiser, Stanley Joel. *Medicine and the Reign of Technology.* New York: Cambridge University Press, 1978.

Rich, E. E. *The History of the Hudson's Bay Company* (2 vols.), vol. 2, *1763–1870.* London: The Hudson's Bay Record Society, 1959.

Rose, Michael. *Curator of the Dead. Thomas Hodgkin (1798–1866).* London: Peter Owen, 1981.

Rosenberg, Charles E. *The Trial of the Assassin Guiteau. Psychiatry and Law in the Gilded Age.* Chicago: The University of Chicago Press, 1968.

Roth, Cecil. *A History of The Jews in England,* 3rd ed. Oxford: Clarendon Press, 1964.

Rudolf, R. de M. *Clapham and the Clapham Sect.* Clapham: published for The Clapham Antiquarian Society by Edmund Baldwin, 1927.

Shryock, Richard Harrison. *Medicine in America. Historical Essays.* Baltimore, Md.: The Johns Hopkins Press, 1966.

——. *The Development of Modern Medicine. An Interpretation of the Social and Scientific Factors Involved.* Philadelphia: University of Pennsylvania Press, 1936.

Simon, John. *English Sanitary Institutions, Reviewed in Their Course of Development, and in Some of Their Political and Social Relations.* London: Cassell & Company, Limited, 1890; New York: Johnson Reprint Corp., 1970 (reprint).

Singer, Charles, and Underwood, E. Ashworth. *A Short History of Medicine,* 2d ed. New York: Oxford University Press, 1962.

Smith, F. B. *The People's Health, 1830–1910.* New York: Holmes & Meier Publishers, 1979.

Snow, John. *On the Mode of Communication of Cholera,* 2nd ed., much enlarged. London: John Churchill, 1855. Reprinted by the Commonwealth Fund, New York, 1936.

Sprigge, S. Squire. *The Life and Times of Thomas Wakley,* Charles G. Roland, (introd.). Melbourne, Fla.: Robert E. Krieger Publishing Co., 1974. Facsimile of the 1899 edition.

Stock, Eugene. *The History of the Church Missionary Society, Its Environment, Its Men and Its Work* (3 vols.), vol. 1. London: Church Missionary Society, 1899.

Temperley, Howard. *British Antislavery 1833–1870.* Columbia, S.C.: University of South Carolina Press, 1972.

Thomas, Lewis. *The Medusa and the Snail. More Notes of a Biology Watcher.* New York: The Viking Press, 1979.

Townsend, William C. *Modern State Trials With Essays and Notes* (2 vols.), vol. 1. London: Longman, Brown, Green, and Longmans, 1850.

Turberville, A. S. *The House of Lords in the Age of Reform 1784–1837.* London: Faber and Faber, 1958.

Wilks, Samuel, and Bettany, G. T. *A Biographical History of Guy's Hospital.* London: Ward, Lock, Bowden & Co., 1892.

Williamson, James A. *A Short History of British Expansion. The Modern Empire and Commonwealth,* 4th ed. London: MacMillan and Co., Limited, 1953.

Winslow, Charles-Edward Amory. *The Conquest of Epidemic Disease. A Chapter in the History of Ideas.* Princeton, N.J.: Princeton University Press, 1944.

Woglom, William H. *Discoverers for Medicine.* New Haven, Conn.: Yale University Press, 1949.

Wohl, Anthony S. *Endangered Lives. Public Health in Victorian Britain.* London: J. M. Dent & Sons Ltd., 1983.

Wolf, Lucien. *Sir Moses Montefiore. A Centennial Biography.* New York: Harper & Brothers, 1885.

JOURNALS

Alabama Journal of Medical Sciences

American Journal of Dermatopathology

Annals of Medical History

Anti-Slavery Reporter

Anti-Tobacco Journal

Archiv der Heilkunde

Archives of Internal Medicine

Archives of Pathology

Association Medical Journal

Boston Medical and Surgical Journal

British Medical Journal

Bulletin of the History of Medicine

Bulletin of the Johns Hopkins Hospital

Bulletin of the New York Academy of Medicine

Canadian Journal of History

Cancer Research

Clio Medica

Colonial Intelligencer; or, Aborigines' Friend

Edinburgh Medical and Surgical Journal

Edinburgh New Philosophical Journal

Edinburgh Review, or, Critical Journal

Froriep's Neue Notizen aus dem Gebiete der Natur-und Heilkunde (Weimar)

Gazette des hôpitaux (Paris)

Guy's Hospital Gazette

Guy's Hospital Reports

Harvard Medical Alumni Bulletin

Historical Journal

History

Isis

Johns Hopkins Hospital Report

Journal of Laryngology and Otology

Journal of Medical Education

Journal of the History of Medicine and Allied Sciences

Journal of the Quekett Microscopical Club (London)

Journal of the Royal College of Physicians of London

Journal of the Royal Society of Medicine

Journal of the [Royal] *Society of Arts, and of the Institutions in Union* (London)

Lancet

Laryngoscope

Literary Gazette and Journal of Archaeology, Science, and Art

London and Edinburgh Philosophical Magazine and Journal of Science

London Medical Gazette

London Medical and Physical Journal

Man

Medical History

Medical Times and Gazette

Medico-Chirurgical Journal; or, *London Medical and Surgical Review*

Medico-Chirurgical Society Transactions

Monthly Chronicle

New England Journal of Medicine

New York Journal of Medicine and Surgery

New York Medical Journal

New York State Journal of Medicine

Philosophical Magazine

Philosophical Transactions of the Royal Society

Proceedings of the Royal Geographical Society

Proceedings of the Royal Society of London

Quarterly Bulletin of the Northwestern University Medical School

Quarterly Journal of Foreign Medicine and Surgery

Railway Times (London)

Report of the British Association for the Advancement of Science

Scottish Medical Journal

Social Science Review, Sanitary Review, and Journal of the Sciences

St. Bartholomew's Hospital Reports

Transactions of the Ethnological Society of London

Transactions of the Medical Society of London

Transactions of the Pathological Society of London

Zeitschrift für Heilkunde

Zoologist

NEWSPAPERS, MAGAZINES, AND MISCELLANEOUS

Biographical Catalogue of the Society of Friends

Colonization Herald (Philadelphia)

Companion to the Newspaper (London)

Dictionary of American Medical Biography (New York)

Dictionary of National Biography (London)

Dictionary of Scientific Biography (New York)

Friends' Quarterly Examiner

Illustrated London News

Jewish Chronicle and Hebrew Observer (London)

Minutes and Proceedings of the Yearly Meeting of Friends (London)

Morning Chronicle (London)

Morning Star (London)

New Catholic Encyclopedia (New York)

Punch

The Friend

The Times (London)

Index